GALILEO, BELLARMINE,
AND THE BIBLE

Galileo, Bellarmine, and the Bible

Including a Translation of
Foscarini's *Letter on the Motion of the Earth*

RICHARD J. BLACKWELL

UNIVERSITY OF NOTRE DAME PRESS

NOTRE DAME   LONDON

Library of Congress Cataloging-in-Publication Data

Blackwell, Richard J., 1929–
  Galileo, Bellarmine, and the Bible : including a translation
of Foscarini's Letter on the motion of the earth / Richard J. Blackwell.
    p.   cm.
  Includes bibliographical references and index.
  ISBN 0-268-01024-2
  1. Galilei, Galileo, 1564–1642.   2. Bellarmino, Roberto Francesco Romolo,
Saint, 1542–1621.   3. Foscarini, Paolo Antonio, ca. 1565–1616.   4. Astronomy,
Renaissance.   5. Religion and science—History—17th century.   6. Catholic
church—Doctrines—History—17th century.   7. Inquisition—Italy.
I. Foscarini, Paolo Antonio, ca. 1565–1616. Epistola . . . circa Pythagoricorum &
Copernici opinionem de mobilitate terræ et stabilitate solis. English   II. Title.
QB36.G2B574   1991
520'.94'09032—dc20
                                                                90-70858
                                                                    CIP

It is impossible for two truths to conflict. As a result we should not fear the assaults which come against us, whatever they be, as long as we still have room to speak and to be heard by people who are experts and who are not excessively affected by their own interests and feelings.

Galileo, *Letter to Castelli*

We say in general that the judge of the true meaning of Scripture and of all controversies is the Church, that is, the pontiff with a council, on which all Catholics agree and which was expressly stated by the Council of Trent, Session IV.

Bellarmine, *Controversies* I, I, 3, 3

No one ought to be so addicted to a philosophical sect, or to defend some philosophical opinion with such tenacity, that he thinks that the whole of Sacred Scripture should henceforth be understood accordingly.

Foscarini, *Defense*

"As a lily among the thistles . . . "

The Song of Songs 2:2

Contents

Preface

This book has gradually grown out of the author's curiosity over the following question: At the time of the Galileo affair, what was the intellectual ground occupied by serious Catholic thinkers who stood, as it were, on the other side of the fence from Galileo? The obvious starting point was, of course, to undertake a study of Cardinal Bellarmine, which in turn led to the views of his numerous Jesuit colleagues who happened to be among the best-informed mathematicians and astronomers of the day. Many of our findings belied our preconceptions. Large quantities of unpublished papers and letters by Bellarmine and by the other Jesuit principals in the story remain to be given the study they deserve, and perhaps they hold further unexpected insights into the Galileo affair.

Equally unstudied have been the writings of Paolo Antonio Foscarini, O. Carm. This is particularly surprising since his *Lettera* was condemned by explicit title and *in toto* in the famous 5 March 1616 Decree of the Congregation of the Index which announced the condemnation of Copernicanism. Yet there are to date no studies of this *Lettera* in English and only a very few in Italian. For the benefit of scholars we have included in Appendix VI the first modern English translation of this lengthy booklet since Thomas Salusbury's seventeenth-century English rendition which is now almost both unobtainable and unreadable because of it arcane style.

Our major debt for making this book possible is owed to the professional staff members of the various research libraries and archives who made both their research materials and advice so generously available to us. This applies first and foremost to the librarians at the Pius XII Memorial Library of Saint Louis University, and especially to Dr. Charles Ermatinger, the Director of its Vatican

Microfilm Library. Also a special word of thanks must be extended
to Rev. Francis Edwards, S.J., Archivist, and Rev. Joseph Costelloe,
S.J., Librarian, at the Archivum Romanum Societatis Iesu (ARSI) in
Rome; to Rev. Emanuele Boaga, O. Carm., Archivist at the Centro
Internazionale S. Alberto — Carmelitani, in Rome; to Dr. William
B. Ashworth, Jr., and Dr. Bruce Bradley, Librarian for the History
of Science, of the Linda Hall Library in Kansas City; and to Mrs.
Helen S. Butz, Rare Book Librarian, University Library, University
of Michigan.

We also wish to express our special appreciation to Rev. John
W. Padberg, S.J., Director, Institute of Jesuit Sources (St. Louis),
for his close critique and helpful suggestions to improve an earlier
version of chapter 6. The remaining deficiencies here and elsewhere
are due, of course, to us.

All translations used in this book were made by the author,
unless indicated otherwise in the footnotes. The *Jerusalem Bible*
was used for the English text in some of the biblical quotations.
Words placed within square brackets in direct quotations have been
added by the translator for purposes of clarification. In preparing
the translations we have attempted to achieve both accuracy and
readability, but without ever sacrificing the former to the latter.

The documents in the Appendices are the primary sources
upon which this study is based. They are not collected together
in any one other place. Many of them appear here in English for
the first time.

The completion of the writing of this book was made possible by
a sabbatical leave generously granted to us by Saint Louis University
for the fall semester of 1989.

Introduction

The Piazza della Minerva in Rome is located immediately behind the left side of Hadrian's monumental Pantheon. It derives its
name from a temple built on this site in Roman times and dedicated
to Minerva, the goddess of wisdom, of war, and of the practical arts.
The goddess must have had difficulty managing such disparate and
clashing forces, and this seems to be reflected in the subsequent
history of this Piazza.

The thirteenth-century Church of Santa Maria sopra Minerva,
which now dominates the Piazza, and which contains a statue of
Christ by Michelangelo and the burial places of Fra Angelico and
St. Catherine of Siena, has long been the main center in Rome
for the Dominican Order, which by tradition provided much of the
staff for the Inquisition. The Dominican convent building immediately to the left of, and at right angles to, the facade of Santa
Maria sopra Minerva was the headquarters of the Roman Inquisition and the site of the Galileo trial in 1633. This building faces
the derriere of Bernini's whimsical statue of an elephant carrying
an obelisk, erected in the middle of the Piazza in 1667 in a position perhaps designed as a symbolic judgment on the trial. In
1988 the elephant's head was still turned to the side, seemingly to
avoid gazing upon the spectacle of an old building on the opposite
side of the Piazza being converted into a Holiday Inn! Also in that
same year one could read on the closed side door of the Dominican Church the following grafitti in English, "It's violence, but we
like it." One wonders whether these thoughtless words of wisdom,
worthy of Madame Defarge, were addressed to Minerva or to the
Grand Inquisitor, and whether their author would change his message if he could experience the genuine violence so destructive of

1

the human spirit which the Inquisition had exerted only a few feet away across the Piazza.

Pagan gods, Christian saintliness, great art, the shadow of the Inquisition, ancient wisdom, modern science, contemporary grafitti, the Holiday Inn: somehow the juxtaposition in time of so many varied and potentially conflicting cultural forces in the Piazza della Minerva is a fitting symbol for the story we wish to tell about how science and religion encountered each other as each emerged from the sixteenth century in its recognizably modern garb.

Galileo's confrontation with the Roman Catholic Church over the biblical assessment of heliocentricism — or more simply the "Galileo affair" — has long had a special fascination. First and foremost, of course, this is because it is the paradigm case of the troubled interaction between science and religion. Another reason is the sheer dramatic power of the events involved, which continue to be attractive topics for the playwright and the novelist. Images easily multiply of the flawed tragic hero; of the struggle for intellectual freedom; of the individual pitted against the powerful institution committed to self-preservation; of plots, subplots, and counterplots worthy of a mystery writer. On another level the episode almost irresistably invites generalizations about the unstable interactions between science and religion for other ages as well. What happened was clearly a significant part of a large-scale turning-point in Western culture as the hegemony of the mediaeval religious world, shocked into facing its abuses by the Reformation, gave way gradually to the modern scientific mind-set, only dimly perceived at the time by even its most advanced proponents. Such cultural earthquakes reveal much about who we are as human beings. At still another level the Galileo affair has provided many with the occasion for ideological posturing for and against both the scientific and the religious worldviews.

The latter type of response reached its zenith towards the end of the last century with the publication of John William Draper's *History of the Conflict between Religion and Science* (1874) and Andrew Dickson White's *A History of the Warfare of Science with Theology in Christendom* (1896). The notion in these books that this warfare was inevitable and that religion, especially Roman Catholicism, was a monolithic force against truth and human betterment, had considerable influence well into the twentieth century. Fortunately more serious and careful scholarship of the past generation or two has now debunked the views of Draper and White in favor of seeing the multileveled and multivalued interactions between science and religion. Galileo scholars have been prominent in this development.

One of the results is that we now know more about what happened in the Galileo affair, and how it happened, than at any time in the past. Nevertheless an uneasiness persists; something about the episode still remains murky. The question of why it happened is still bothersome. In a recently published small booklet, Olaf Pedersen has suggested that one of the main reasons for this is that the students of the Galileo affair have for the most part been historians of science with little or no background in the history of theology and religion. His remedy is that "it may well be that the key to a more satisfactory understanding of the ultimate causes of the condemnation will be found if we so extend the perspective that the whole affair is seen not only as an episode in the history of science, but also as an important event in the history of theology."[1]

The purpose of this book is to study the Galileo affair from this perspective. But even that is too general. More specifically we will concentrate on only one of the theological issues; namely, the role played by the Bible in the Galileo affair. Thus we will place our emphasis on the views at that time of the meaning, truth status, and authority of the Scriptures in the hope of combining this with the more thoroughly studied scientific issues in a way that will help to understand why people on both sides acted the way they did. This means that we will need to raise questions like: What were the key concerns of the administrators of the Catholic Church at the beginning of the seventeenth century? What were the major theological topics and disputes of the day? What effects did the Church's major countermeasures at the time of the Reformation have on its mind-set at the start of the next century? What were the accepted views about the truth, meaning, and interpretation of the Scriptures at the time, and what were the central documents stating these views? What roles were played by the Jesuits, who were the

---

[1] Olaf Pedersen, *Galileo and the Council of Trent*, Vatican Observatory Publications: Studi Galileiani, vol. I, no. 1. (Città del Vaticano: Specola Vaticana, 1983), 1–2.

Church's scientific intellectuals and best-informed advisers? How did the Church's concerns for its power and authority and for the loyalty and obedience of its members shape the course of events?

When we come to the conclusion of this study, we will argue that of the many factors which entered into the Galileo affair, one had an especially prominent role; namely, differing views on the status of truth, i.e., truth by appeal to evidence in science vs. truth by appeal to authority in religion. At the time the newly born scientific culture and the newly reformed religious tradition had each generated a distinctive and different notion about the nature of its own truth and how it should be established. Given this, the participants within both communities acted reasonably for the most part; each set of views had its own internal logic and rationality; and the actions of their proponents are understandable accordingly. The fact that their standards of truth differed did not in itself mean that they must eventually come into conflict; but they could, and unfortunately did. And the climax of the Galileo affair in the trial of 1633 did not lessen, but magnified, the problem of relating religious and scientific claims to truth. But before we can profitably discuss these issues, we must first see what happened and why.

1

Trent and Beyond

Nicholas Copernicus's *De revolutionibus orbium coelestium* was first published in May 1543. Tradition has it that the first copy arrived in Copernicus's hands on 24 May, the day he died. Two and a half years later, in December 1545, the First Session of the Council of Trent was convened under Pope Paul III to deal with much needed reforms in the Roman Catholic Church. At that time these two events were utterly unrelated to each other. But the two lines of forces which they set in motion were destined to intersect. The collision occurred on 5 March 1616 when the Congregation of the Index, an administrative office established in the Roman Curia as a result of the Council of Trent, issued a condemnation of Copernicus's book "until corrected." How and why did these two initially independent lines of action come ultimately into conflict? To what extent was this conflict fortuitous and to what extent was it predestined? To answer these questions we need first to look closely at the Council of Trent and how it affected the views of theologians before Galileo entered the drama.

THE FOURTH SESSION OF THE COUNCIL OF TRENT

The initial occasion for convening the Council of Trent was Martin Luther's break with Rome in 1519. In many previous instances of crisis in the long history of the Church, the response had been to convene a council to settle the issues in dispute. In this spirit the Imperial Diet held at Nuremberg in 1523 called for a "free Christian Council" on German soil to deal with the questions which had split the Church. The request was repeated in 1524. The primary goal was to restore the unity of Christendom. However, an extraordinarily complex series of religious, political, diplomatic, and military disputes among various European states, with each other and with the popes of the time, postponed the opening of a council for a quarter of a century.[1] As these years passed, the potential for reunification became less and less viable. As a result when the Council of Trent finally did take place (1545–63), the focus had shifted to the goals of clarifying Catholic dogma and reforming the discipline, training, and life-style of the clergy. The eighteen years of the council were interrupted by two lengthy adjournments, first of four years (1547–51), and then of ten years (1552–62). These delays not only further decreased the likelihood of reunification but saw increasing distrust and open hostility between the Catholic and Protestant camps.

For the present purposes it is important to emphasize that matters of natural philosophy, or of what we would now call the natural sciences, in no way were of concern in the debates at the council. At best they were mentioned only casually, if at all. The primary thrust of the council can be seen in a brief list of the central topics of decision: the books of Scripture and the role of tradition in the Church, original sin, justification and divine grace, each of the seven sacraments, indulgences, the mass, the education, morals, and preaching duties of the clergy, the jurisdiction and obligation of residence for bishops. These matters clearly centered on doctrinal and disciplinary issues in the life of the Church. However, the decisions arrived at on Scripture and tradition, originally made in response to the challenges of Luther and the other reformers, would later become related to the new ideas introduced by Copernicus. It is this aspect of the Council of Trent which calls for our attention.

Before we turn to the specific conclusions of the council, a few remarks about its procedures may be helpful. The pope (first Paul III, then Julius III, and later Pius IV) convened the council and approved its decrees and canons afterwards (without any

---

[1] For a history of this period and of the council itself, see Hubert Jedin, *Geschichte des Konzils von Trient*, 4 vols. (Freiburg im Breisgau: Herder, 1957). English translation by Dom Ernest Graf, O.S.B., *A History of the Council of Trent*, 2 vols. (London: Thomas and Sons, 1961).

alterations in this case), but did not himself participate in the discussions and voting. The pope was represented by one or more legates who served, in effect, as presiding officers of the proceedings. The voting members were the cardinals, bishops, and the heads of the various religious orders in attendance, each having one vote. Numerous theologians and canon lawyers served as advisers to the voting members. A date was set in advance for a formal meeting, called a session, at which the official decisions would be made on an announced set of topics. Each session was preceded by weeks, sometimes months, of preparatory work which centered around plenary meetings of all voting members, called General Congregations, in which debate ranged widely and from which the formal documents stating the decrees and canons gradually emerged.[2] These latter documents, after the formal vote at the appropriate session, constitute the specific decisions of the council. The first three sessions at the Council of Trent dealt solely with matters of organization, procedure, and agenda. The main organizational dispute was whether to treat dogma or Church reform and discipline first. This was resolved by an agreement to deal with one set of topics from each area at each session. The Fourth Session was the first to deal with substantive matters, and the chosen topic was the status of Scripture, revelation, and tradition. This topic was undoubtedly chosen to be the first order of business because it focused on a central challenge posed by the reformers.

The Fourth Session, held on 8 April 1546, approved two decrees, the first dealing with the notion of tradition and with determining the authentic books contained in the Scriptures, and the second with the edition and interpretation of the Bible.[3] These two documents are of major importance both in the history of the Church and in the Galileo affair. One of the effects of the first decree was

---

[2] For the source material relating to the council's decisions, see *Enchiridion symbolorum, definitionum, et declarationum de rebus fidei et morum*, ed. H. Denzinger and A. Schoenmetzer, S.J., 32d ed. (Freiburg im Breisgau: Herder, 1963), and H.J. Schroeder, O.P., *Canons and Decrees of the Council of Trent: Original Text with English Translation* (St. Louis: B. Herder, 1941).

[3] See Appendix I for the full text of both decrees in translation.

to determine for the Catholic Church which of the books of the ancient religious cultures are to be taken as canonical, i.e., as writings inspired by the Holy Spirit and thus as expressing God's revelation. This, of course, was not the first attempt at listing the canonical books in the history of the Church — such attempts date back to 180 A.D. — and had previously been dealt with in a decree of the Council of Florence (4 February 1441). But the matter had become urgent because Luther had raised the issue of the content of the canon, and the Council Fathers clearly felt obliged to respond. The decision made at Trent, which in effect reaffirmed the decree of the Council of Florence, has defined the Catholic edition of the Bible ever since.

Closely related to this is the question of which edition of the Scriptures should be recommended for practical use. For centuries the Latin Vulgate edition, originally prepared by St. Jerome in the years 390–405 A.D., had been the standard Latin text in the West, and this was now declared to be "in public lectures, disputations, sermons, and expositions, held as authentic." The Council Fathers also discussed at length in the General Congregations the questions of the need to reexamine the original language Hebrew and Greek texts of the Bible and of the wisdom of using vernacular translations of the Scriptures, but chose not to speak to either of these points in the decrees. The needed revision of the Latin Vulgate edition was left by the council to the pope's later initiative. A series of three papal commissions subsequently worked on this project with the result that in 1592 there appeared the Clementine edition, which, although still not the fully corrected version envisioned at Trent, has served as the Catholic Bible into the twentieth century. It is interesting to note that in 1591 Cardinal Bellarmine recommended, and actively worked on, the final version of the Clementine edition.[4]

Of much greater historical importance, however, was the statement of the principle of tradition in the first decree. The relevant passage reads as follows:

---

[4] For the history of these developments, see Xavier-Marie Le Bachelet, *Bellarmine et le Bible Sixto-Clémentine: Étude et documents inédits* (Paris: Beauchesne, 1911).

The Council also clearly maintains that these truths and rules are contained in the written books *and* in the unwritten traditions which, received by the Apostles from the mouth of Christ Himself or from the Apostles themselves, the Holy Spirit dictating, have come down to us, transmitted as it were from hand to hand. Following then the examples of the orthodox Fathers, it receives and venerates with a feeling of equal piety and reverence both all the books of the Old and New Testaments, since one God is the author of both, and also the traditions themselves, whether they relate to faith or to morals, as having been dictated either orally by Christ or by the Holy Spirit, and preserved in the Catholic Church in unbroken succession.[5]

A number of points need to be carefully noted in this famous text. First its main thrust asserts the existence of "unwritten traditions." Second these traditions, i.e., things "transmitted as it were from hand to hand," are asserted to be either words spoken by Christ himself or by the Apostles themselves under the inspiration of the Holy Spirit. As such they are taken to be divinely revealed truths, and to have been passed on from generation to generation within the Church in an "unbroken succession" up to the present day. Third, since God is the author of both the written revelation (i.e., Scripture) and the unwritten Apostolic traditions, each is to be received with "equal piety and reverence" (*pari pietatis affectu ac reverentia*), and not merely with "similar" respect, a word used in earlier drafts but replaced by "equal" (*pari*) in one of the preparatory General Congregations. As we said above, the main point made by the council in this declaration on tradition was to assert the existence of a set of unwritten Apostolic traditions. This was intended to counter the view of Luther that revelation, and thereby salvation, comes through Scripture alone (*sola Scriptura*). This passage is thus seen to have its full significance only when understood in this Counter-Reformation context.

Furthermore it should be carefully noted that, in the passage of the first decree quoted above, we have emphasized the word "and." That single word covers a complex theological dispute which erupted at the council, and which had impact in the Galileo affair. The problem debated by the bishops was the following: If we grant

---

[5] From Appendix I, emphasis added.

that divine revelation comes to us under two forms, the written Scriptures and the unwritten traditions, should we say (1) that only part of the revelation is contained in each, or (2) that the whole of revelation is contained in each?[6] It is certain that the first alternative was considered in detail in the General Congregations since the earlier versions of the decree contain the terms "partly . . . partly . . . " (*partim . . . partim . . .*). This would mean that tradition contains some revealed truths which are not contained in the Scriptures (and vice versa). But this met with strong opposition in the General Congregations by advocates of the second alternative. If the whole of revelation is contained in both Scripture and tradition, then neither contains a revealed truth not found in the other. This is closer to Luther's "Scripture alone" principle, although it is fundamentally quite different from it since it does not reject tradition as a carrier of revelation, the main point of dispute in this area between the reformers and the council.

Faced with this dispute about the double form of revelation, the council simply sidestepped the issue by replacing "partly . . . partly . . . " with "and" in the final version of the decree. In so doing, they chose not to speak to the question. Their purposes, i.e., rejecting Luther's "Scripture alone" principle, were adequately served by stating that *both* Scripture and tradition express God's revelation without specifying what content they may or may not share. This unresolved issue has been debated by Catholic theologians ever since, the most recent instance being in the decade immediately following Pope Pius XII's proclamation in 1950 of the bodily Assumption of the Blessed Virgin into heaven as a dogma of the Catholic faith.[7]

---

    [6] Two other alternatives — apparently not explicitly considered at the council — would be that the whole of revelation is contained in Scripture but only a part in tradition, and vice-versa.

    [7] This proclamation was published in Pius XII's Apostolic Constitution *Munificentissimus Deus* (1 November 1950). For discussion of the Scripture plus tradition doctrine and of the "partly . . . partly . . . " controversy since the Council of Trent, see Yves Congar, O.P., *La tradition et la vie de l'église* (Paris: Libraire Artheme Fayard, 1963); English translation by A.N. Woodrow, *The Meaning of Tradition* (New York: Hawthorn Books, 1964). See also Gabriel Moran, F.S.C., *Scripture and Tradition: A Survey of Tradition* (New York: Herder and Herder, 1963), and Josef Gieselmann, "Das Konzil von Trient über das Verhältnis der Heiligen Schrift und

In the latter half of the sixteenth century most of the theologians, including Bellarmine,[8] understood the Fourth Session of Trent in the "partly . . . partly . . . " interpretation. In fact this was what gave rise to the "two sources" doctrine in the history of theology. But if this reading is granted, then one places an increased importance on the Fathers of the Church (e.g., Basil, Gregory of Nyssa, Gregory of Nazianzus, Jerome, Ambrose, Chrysostom, Augustine, Cyril of Alexandria). For they constituted the chief links in the unbroken chain of succession from which one acquires some distinctive divinely revealed truths not otherwise known in the Scriptures. This helps to understand the prominence in the Galileo affair of the great respect for the common agreement of the Fathers, the significance of which may otherwise be missed. This was not merely a general respect for revered ancestors; it was rather a respect for what was understood to be the conduit for a unique body of truth revealed by God, which was to be held in a reverence equal, according to Trent, to that of Scripture itself. Whether the theologians contemporary with Galileo were correct in their understanding of the Fourth Session is not relevant at present. The fact is that that is what many, if not all, of them thought. The important consequent was that the "unanimous agreement of the Fathers on matters pertaining to faith and morals" was used by them as a touchstone to determine the content of the Apostolic tradition of revelation from God.

As far as the Galileo affair is concerned, a still more significant decision of the council is to be found in the second paragraph of the second decree. The relevant passage reads as follows:

> Furthermore, to control petulant spirits, the Council decrees that, in matters of faith and morals pertaining to the edification of Christian doctrine, no one, relying on his own judgment and distorting the Sacred Scriptures according to his own conceptions, shall dare to

---

der nicht geschrieben Traditionen," in *Die mündliche Überlieferung*, ed. Michael Schmaus (Munich: Hueber, 1957), French translation in *Istina* 5 (1958): 197–214.

    [8] Robert Cardinal Bellarmino, *Disputationes de controversiis christianae fidei adversus hujus temporis haereticos* (1586–93) I, I, 4, 12 [hereafter referred to as *De controversiis*], in vols. 1–4 of *Opera omnia* (Neapoli: Apud Josephum Giulano, 1856–62).

interpret them contrary to that sense which Holy Mother Church, to whom it belongs to judge of their true sense and meaning, has held and does hold, or even contrary to the unanimous agreement of the Fathers, even though such interpretations should never at any time be published. Those who do otherwise shall be identified by the ordinaries and punished in accordance with the penalties prescribed by the law.[9]

Again, to be properly understood, this passage must be read in the context of the Reformation. It is primarily a rejection of Luther's doctrine of private interpretation, i.e., that the *locus* of determining the meaning of Scripture is in the individual person. Instead it is decreed that the Church is to serve as the judge of their "true sense and interpretation." This passage is not about dogma but about authority. Note also that the "unanimous agreement of the Fathers" is mentioned explicitly, and is consistent with the principle of tradition affirmed in the first decree. As in the first decree, the phrase "in matters of faith and of morals" is used, but no specific criteria are provided in either passage as to *how* it is to be determined what is and what is not a matter of faith and morals. As we shall see, disputes in this area were to become a major factor in the Galileo affair. Finally it should be noted that this passage speaks only of *who* is to interpret Scripture, i.e., the Church, but not about *how* the interpretation is to be formulated. In short, principles of exegesis are simply not mentioned in the decree, although the Council Fathers were certainly aware of the elaborate principles and methods of biblical exegesis which had long ago been developed and employed in the history of the Church. As the years passed after the council, some theologians of the late sixteenth century read this passage to assert the primacy of literal interpretation. This simply is neither affirmed nor denied in the decree, which was concerned rather with what we may call the principle of interpretive authority.

It should also be carefully noted in passing that this paragraph contains the widely used phrase *"in rebus fidei et morum,"* which is usually but somewhat misleadingly translated as "in matters of faith and morals." *"Mores"* is not limited to morality. It also includes such other "practical" matters as the determination of the canon, edition,

---

[9] From Appendix I.

and translations of Scripture, the legitimacy of councils and papal elections, the canonization of saints, and the determination of the sacrament of ordination.

The second paragraph of the second decree of the Fourth Session, along with its later theological ramifications and interpretations, provided the major religious framework for Galileo's conflict with the Church. Some of his theological enemies must have seen the phrase *"to control petulant spirits"* as a prescient reference to Galileo.

There is also another theme from the Council of Trent which enters later into the Galileo affair. The third paragraph of the second decree of the Fourth Session states that "any books whatever on sacred matters" are not to be published without ecclesiastical approval. This reflected a more or less unstructured and long-standing historical practice in the Church of proscribing books judged to be dangerous to faith or morals. As a part of the Counter-Reformation this practice was formalized in the Eighteenth Session (25 February 1562) and the Twenty-fifth Session (3–4 December 1563) with the recommendation of the creation of what came to be called the *Index librorum prohibitorum*, a list of books which Catholics were forbidden to read without special permission. The council established ten rules to be followed in evaluating books,[10] but left the formulation of an actual list of proscribed books to the later action of the pope. This led in time to the establishment of the Congregation of the Index (which was so prominent in the Galileo affair) and to a series of revised versions of the *Index* over the years. The *Index* was abolished in 1966 in the aftermath of the Second Vatican Council.

As mentioned earlier, the decrees accepted by the council required later confirmation by the pope before they became the official teachings of the Church. This was accomplished by various documents, including the Papal Bull *Iniunctum nobis* (13 November 1564) which contained the Tridentine profession of faith in the form of an oath, which subsequently played a role in the Galileo affair. The first paragraph of this oath was the familiar Nicene Creed, which is still recited today as part of the Catholic Mass. The second

---

[10] For these rules, see *Enchiridion symbolorum*, #1851–60. For an English translation, see Schroeder, *Canons and Decrees*, 273–278.

paragraph, which obviously is focused on the Fourth Session of the Council, reads as follows:

> I most firmly accept and embrace the Apostolic and ecclesiastical traditions and the other observances and constitutions of the Church. I also accept Sacred Scripture in the sense in which it has been held, and is held, by Holy Mother Church, to whom it belongs to judge the true sense and interpretation of the Sacred Scripture, nor will I accept or interpret it in any way other than in accordance with the unanimous agreement of the Fathers.[11]

The condemnation of Copernicanism in 1616 was based on the decision that the heliocentric model of the universe was contrary to the Scriptures when read in precisely this way. This indeed left little room to maneuver in the debates about this issue, both before and especially after the condemnation. The continued wide use of this oath, for example, in the installation of Church officials, kept these standards of biblical interpretation in clear focus.[12]

THE THEOLOGICAL REPERCUSSIONS OF THE FOURTH SESSION

Fifty years separated the end of the Council of Trent and the beginning of Galileo's confrontation with the Church. During that period the decisions of the council were gradually but firmly put into place. The disciplinary reforms were initiated primarily by the popes of the time, especially Pius V (1566–72), Gregory XIII (1572–85), Sixtus V (1585–90), and Clement VIII (1592–1605), resulting in a considerable improvement in daily life in the Church. To mention only the most prominent example, before Trent there were no established general educational or spiritual formation requirements for new members of the priesthood. A candidate simply presented himself to a bishop, incredibly enough, with whatever qualifications

---

[11] *Enchiridion symbolorum,* #1863.

[12] It is reported by Giovanni Battista Riccioli, S.J. (*Almagestum novum* [Bononiae: Typis Haeredis Victorii Benatii, 1651], Part II, p. 479) that it was the regular custom at the Jesuit colleges to open each school year with all the students and faculty of Theology and Arts publicly reciting the profession of faith prescribed by the Council of Trent, taking the oath on the Bible.

he might or might not have. After Trent a system of seminaries (literally "nurseries") came into existence in many dioceses for the training of future priests. The recently established Jesuit order had already founded numerous new colleges at a more advanced level throughout Europe, a development encouraged by the reforms at the council.

On the side of dogma the consequences of Trent were less visible at first but of still greater, albeit more subtle, impact. This can be seen clearly in the writings of Catholic theologians during and shortly after the council. By the end of the sixteenth century a refocused way of thinking had been generated in theology, particularly around topics connected with the foundations of Catholic belief. Since the details of this development form the immediate theological environment for the Galileo affair, here and in the next chapter we will look with some care at the specific views of several prominent Catholic theologians during and immediately after Trent on topics dealt with in the Fourth Session. Hopefully such a survey will not only identify the specific ways that the relevant decrees of the council were interpreted but also will somewhat capture the theological spirit of the time.[13]

The earliest of the reactions came from the Dominican Melchior Cano (1509–60), who is second in importance only to Bellarmine a generation later in the formulation of post-Tridentine theology. His De locis theologicis, published posthumously in 1563 without the last two books intended by its author, became a landmark of logically ordered and clearly written theological doctrine and the founding document of what has come to be called fundamental theology, i.e., the study of the revelatory and philosophical sources of theology modeled as a science. The De locis was widely known and still used as a standard text in theology in Galileo's day. Cano served as a theological adviser at the council in 1551–52, so he was thoroughly acquainted with the work of the early years. Although he quotes the council decisions somewhat infrequently, perhaps because the formal documents were not yet completely confirmed

---

[13] For a very helpful review of Catholic biblical exegesis in the period 1563–1664, see Rinaldo Fabris, *Galileo Galelei e gli orientamenti esegetici del suo tempo* (Vatican City: Pontifical Academy of Sciences, Scripta varia 62, 1986), esp. 23–42.

during his lifetime, it is evident that his views strongly reflect the thinking at Trent. According to Benito Pereyra, S.J., "Of all the theologians who participated in the Council of Trent, Melchior Cano was the most illustrious and the most renowned. No one in our day has better explained the mysteries of the Sacred Scriptures."[14]

The assertion of the principle of tradition at the Fourth Session led theologians to consider the following questions to specify its meaning more concretely. What criteria should be used to distinguish what is to be counted as a matter of faith from other things which are not included? What standards should be used to identify the content of tradition? Are there different types of religious belief, and varying degrees of religious certitude?

Cano attempts to answer these questions quite directly.[15] As many theologians had maintained earlier, he argues that the Church, i.e, the assembly of believers, is much older than the Scriptures. Thus faith and religion not only can, but did, at one time exist without the Scriptures. This refers to the earliest biblical times and beyond when God's interactions with the Jewish people revealed the first outlines of the religious message, which was then handed down in such unwritten form as memorials, religious rituals, and word of mouth. Some, but not all, of these traditions later became gradually committed to writings in which further inspired revelations also appeared. The same pattern was repeated by Christ, who left no writings of his own, but who clearly revealed many more things to his Apostles than they in turn committed to writing later in the books of the New Testament. Thus tradition precedes Scripture, and each contains only a part of divine revelation.[16] Cano even speculates that the greater part is in tradition.[17] Another consequence is that some revealed truths are not contained in the Scriptures at all, not even obscurely.

If all this be granted, then the question of what criteria are to be used to identify matters of faith and morals requires a complex

---

[14] B. Pereyra, *Commentariorum in Danielem prophetam libri sexdicem* (Romae: Apud Georgium Ferrarium, 1587), XII, 7.

[15] Melchior Cano, O.P., *De locis theologicis*, in *Opera*, vol. I (Roma: Ex typographia Forzani et Soc., 1890), Liber III, Caput 3.

[16] Ibid., III, 3, 7.

[17] Ibid., III, 3, 6.

answer. First Cano argues that in cases where the meaning of Scripture is clear and plain (either from the context or from some other place in Scripture or from the meaning of the words themselves), then Scripture itself serves as the standard of religious truth.[18] For all other cases he lays down the following elaborate set of eight rules:

1. If the meaning of Scripture is obscure, then the true meaning of Scripture is the meaning of the Church. . . .

2. The word "Church" refers not only to the assembly of all the faithful but also to the pastors and doctors of the Church, especially when meeting in a council. . . .

3. If the Apostolic See defines a meaning in Scripture, that must be considered to be a Catholic truth. . . .

4. An understanding of Scripture which is commonly accepted and agreed to by all of the saints is a truth of the Catholic faith. . . .

5. If it is a common custom of the Church to accept a particular interpretation of Scripture from the tradition of the apostles, then that must be held as a truth of the faith. . . .

6. If something has been held to be a dogma of faith either by the Church or by a council approved by the authority of the pope, or has been prescribed to the faithful by the pope himself, or has been constantly and consistently held to be certain by all the saints, then we must accept that to be a Catholic truth, and the contrary to be heretical, even though it is not contained in the Sacred Scriptures either openly or obscurely. . . .

7. If either the Church or a council or the Apostolic See or even the saints, speaking in one mind and with the same voice, derive a theological conclusion and also prescribe it to the faithful, then this is to be considered to be as much of a Catholic truth as if it had been directly revealed by Christ; and he who rejects it is as much of a heretic as if he had opposed the Sacred Scriptures or the Apostolic traditions. By a "theological conclusion" here I mean specifically what is deduced by a certain and firm inference from the principles of this science. . . .

---

[18] Ibid., XII, 5, 3.

8. If all scholastic theologians have established the same firm and fixed conclusion with one voice, and if they have constantly and perpetually taught it as a certain theological decree to be embraced by the faithful, then the faithful certainly should embrace it as a Catholic truth. . . . [19]

We have quoted the text of these rules in full (each is also accompanied by a lengthy defense) both to illustrate the complexity of the issue and to preserve the precise theological terminology intended by Cano. It is clear from the context that the term "saints" refers to the Fathers of the Church. Note that the first five rules refer to the interpretation of Scripture. Rules six and seven are concerned primarily with those parts of tradition which are not also included in Scripture. In these cases the weight of truth is equal to that of Scripture itself, and one of the suggested criteria to identify them is the unanimous agreement of the Fathers of the Church. This appeal to the Fathers thus carries a special theological force. The eighth rule, clearly even more debatable, is given a weaker wording at the bottom of the list.

One of the central disputes in the Galileo affair was whether the motion of the earth and the stability of the sun are matters of Catholic faith and morals. After the decrees at Trent on Scripture and tradition, such a question had become considerably more complicated. Given Cano's criteria, one can see why this issue could be, and was, debated at the levels of both Scripture and tradition, and the latter primarily in terms of the "unanimous agreement of the Fathers" criterion.

Since this last point was destined to play such a prominent role later, it will be helpful to quote Cano's views on the types and degrees of the authority of the Fathers when such an appeal is made in theological argumentation.

1. When the authority of the saints, be they few or many, pertains to the faculties contained within the natural light of reason, it does not provide certain arguments but only arguments as strong as reason itself when in agreement with nature. . . .

---

[19] Ibid., XII, 5, 5–14.

2. The authority of only one or two of the saints, even in matters pertaining to Sacred Scripture and the doctrines of the faith, can provide a probable argument but not a strong one. . . .

3. The authority of many saints is not sufficient to provide strong arguments for the theologian if a few other saints loudly disagree. . . .

4. In the case of matters which pertain very little to the faith, the authority of even all the saints creates a probable belief but not a certain one. . . .

5. In regard to the exposition of the Sacred Scriptures, the common interpretation of all the old saints provides the theologian with a most certain argument for the corroboration of theological assertions; for indeed the meaning of the Holy Spirit is the same as the meaning of all of the saints. . . .

6. All the saints taken together cannot err on dogmas of the faith. . . . [20]

Do the motion of the earth and the stability of the sun fall under points (5) and (6) above, as Bellarmine was to suggest? Or under (1), as Galileo will argue? It is interesting to note that in the defense of his *Lettera* arguing for the reconciliation of Copernicanism with the Scriptures (which we will examine in detail in chapter 4), Foscarini quotes *verbatim* the whole of point (1) along with Cano's two additional paragraphs of explication.[21]

Cano's criteria and distinctions were, of course, much more specific, and much less authoritative, than the decrees of the Fourth Session of the Council of Trent. But they do reveal very much about the concrete theological world after Trent in which the Galileo case was argued.

Virtually all of Cano's distinctions would certainly have been rejected by the Protestant reformers because they did not accept the principle of tradition which was the basis of Cano's analysis. This is best seen in Martin Chemnitz's four volume *Examen Concilii Tridentini* (1565–73), which is the most extensive and pointed Protestant assessment of the council. Without tradition the criteria

---

[20] Ibid., VII, 3.
[21] See Appendix VIIB, paragraph 3.

for settling issues of religious belief are quite different, as Chemnitz
points out.

> When therefore we shall have shown also concerning the doctrine of
> the apostles, as we have already proved concerning the doctrine of
> Christ, that as much as the Holy Spirit judged necessary and sufficient
> for us for dogmas and morals was consigned to writing . . . , it will be
> clear that the sacred Scripture is the canon, norm, rule, foundation,
> and pillar of our whole faith, so that whatever is to be accepted under
> this title and name that it is the doctrine of Christ and of the apostles
> must be proved and confirmed from the Scripture. For in religious
> controversies all things must be tested and examined according to
> this norm in such a way that the saying of Jerome remains in force:
> "Whatever does not have authority in Holy Scripture can be rejected
> as easily as it can be approved." This is the chief point of controversy
> between us and the papalists.[22]

In addition to the field of systematic theology, which was dominated by Cano, the impact of the decrees of the Fourth Session of
Trent can also be seen in the work of the Catholic biblical commentators of the latter half of the sixteenth century. For one example let
us look to the views of the Spanish Jesuit Benito Pereyra (Benedictus
Pererius) (1535–1610) who at the end of the century was the most
prominent biblical exegete in the Catholic world, due in large part
to his enormous four volume commentary on Genesis.[23] His work is
especially interesting because he was more sensitive than the other
exegetes of his day to the issues of the relations between science
and the Scriptures.

Near the beginning of his commentary, Pereyra recognizes that
Genesis has received over the centuries an enormous number of
conflicting interpretations, many of which he intends to examine. To
assist the reader in judging which of these are true and which are
false, and among the non-false, which are more or less probable, he
offers a set of interpretive principles for the reading of Genesis. The
first is that the writings of Moses are to be taken in their proper literal

---

[22] Martin Chemnitz, *Examination of the Council of Trent*, trans. Fred Kramer
(St. Louis: Concordia, 1971), 101.

[23] Benedictus Pererius Valentini (Pereyra), *Commentariorum et disputationum in Genesim tomi quatuor* (Romae: Apud Georgium Ferrarium,
1591–95).

or historical sense, i.e., in terms of the common, everyday meaning of the words used. For if a figurative or spiritual reading is taken as primary, then the meaning of the text is as varied as the human imagination can make it, and we are left with no firm and stable views from Genesis about the creation of the world. Furthermore the Catholic Church has included in its articles of faith certain teachings from Moses, e.g., the fall of Adam and Eve and the consequent need for salvation, which depend on a literal reading of the texts. This increasing emphasis on literalism was characteristic of the Counter-Reformation response to Trent.

Furthermore Pereyra does not view creation as simply an exertion of the will of God, but rather as proceeding also from the wisdom of God. As a result the created world has its own internal natural laws, which the exegete should consider. One consequence of this is that in cases where the natural sciences have established conclusions by evident fact or proof,[24] one should follow Augustine's advice to interpret the Bible accordingly. For the unity of truth requires consistency between the truths of natural science and the word of God in the Scriptures. A danger to be avoided is to be so enamored by one's own reading of the Bible that one pridefully rejects other readings which may later be proven by the sciences, and thus create a scandal for the interests of religion, another theme from Augustine. Since these views of Pereyra play a direct role later in our story, it is well to quote his four rules explicitly.

> First Rule: The teaching of Moses about the creation of the world is clearly historical. . . .
> Second Rule: In discussing and explaining this teaching of Moses, one should not appeal without cause to miracles and to the absolute power of God. . . . For in the creation of the world and the first arrangement of all things, one should not consider what God absolutely and simply could do, but rather that he made the world

---

[24] It is interesting to note that Pereyra's examples of this (Ibid., I, 13) are the roundness and the mobility of the earth, the existence of the antipodes, that the stars do not move through the heavens like fish through water or birds through the air (the contrary of this was maintained by Bellarmine throughout his life), and that in no places are the waters of the seas deeper than the highest mountains on the earth.

according to his wisdom and that he made things in accordance with their own natural powers, dispositions, and harmony. . . .

Third Rule: Be careful that you do not immediately fall in love with and embrace your own opinion, and not only hold it fast and defend it tenaciously, but also contend that it is the correct meaning of Scripture, with the result that you would claim that any different and opposed view is contrary to the Scripture. They abuse Scripture who wish to force and confine it within the narrowness of their own opinions and imagination, for Scripture is clearly very broad by its very nature and is open to various readings and interpretations. . . .

Fourth Rule: This also must be carefully observed and completely avoided: in dealing with the teachings of Moses, do not think or say anything affirmatively and assertively which is contrary to the manifest evidence and arguments of philosophy or the other disciplines. For since every truth agrees with every other truth, the truth of Sacred Scripture cannot be contrary to the true arguments and evidence of the human sciences.[25]

It should be noted that Galileo was directly influenced by these four rules. There is clear evidence that when he wrote his *Letter to the Grand Duchess Christina* in 1615, Galileo explicitly consulted Pereyra's commentary.[26] In so doing, he was able to enlist a prominent Counter-Reformation authority in support of his own quite similar views on science and religion. In fact Galileo may well have derived some of his key views on this topic from his reading of Pereyra's commentary.

---

[25] Ibid., I, 10–13.

[26] This evidence is that (1) Galileo quotes Pereyra's rule 4 *verbatim* in his *Letter to the Grand Duchess Christina*, and (2) in three places he uses in that work the exact same quotations from Augustine (*De Genesi ad litteram* I, 18, and I, 21, and the *Seventh Letter to Marcellinus*) used by Pereyra to support his third and fourth rules. This connection was pointed out to me in private conversations with Ugo Baldini, who also made the reasonable suggestion that it probably was Castelli who first directed Galileo's attention to Pereyra's *Commentary on Genesis* as Galileo prepared to write his *Letter to the Grand Duchess Christina*. See also Fabris, *Galileo Galilei*, 29–33.

COPERNICANISM AND
SIXTEENTH-CENTURY THEOLOGY

In the second half of the sixteenth-century religion and the new astronomy lived together with relatively little interaction. Copernicanism became accepted only very slowly and gradually.[27] By 1600 it still had rather few advocates, even among astronomers, and so was not threatening yet to the theologians. Luther, Calvin, and to a greater extent Melanchthon made only passing remarks about Copernicanism which indicate a general concern about reconciling it with various passages of Scripture.[28] The command that the sun stand still in Joshua 10:12, which was to become so famous later, seems to have been first mentioned in this context by Luther as early as 1539.[29]

On a more significant level the Protestant theologian Andreas Osiander (1498–1552), who by chance served as the final editor of the *De revolutionibus*, on his own initiative added an anonymous preface to the book which claimed that Copernicus's work should be taken only as a convenience for mathematical computations and not as a description of the physical world. His motivation was to avoid potential clashes of Copernicanism with Aristotelianism and with the accepted literal readings of Scripture. This instrumentalist interpretation of the new astronomy was adopted later by many for the same purposes. Also Copernicus's earliest disciple, Georg Joachim Rheticus (1514–74), wrote a treatise, long lost, dealing with the reconciliation of the motion of the earth with the Scriptures. This treatise has recently come to light,[30] but it had little or no impact in its own day. At any rate these very early reactions give evidence of concerns from the very beginning, in Protestant as well as Catholic circles, of potential clashes between Copernicanism and the Bible.

---

[27] See Dorothy Stimson, *The Gradual Acceptance of the Copernican Theory of the Universe* (New York: Baker & Taylor, 1917); Francis R. Johnson, *Astronomical Thought in Renaissance England* (Baltimore: Johns Hopkins Press, 1937); Thomas S. Kuhn, *The Copernican Revolution* (Cambridge, Mass.: Harvard University Press, 1957), chap. 6.

[28] Kuhn, *Copernican Revolution*, 191–192.

[29] Martin Luther, *Tischreden* (Weimar: H. Böhlaus, 1912–21), IV, no. 4638.

[30] See R. Hooykaas, "Rheticus' Lost Treatise on Holy Scripture and the Motion of the Earth," *Journal for the History of Astronomy* 15 (1984): 77–80.

The reactions on the Catholic side were even more minimal at first. As we have already pointed out, no mention of the issue was made at the Council of Trent. Recently, however, there has been published a short treatise[31] written in about 1544–47 by the Dominican astronomer and theologian Giovanni Maria Tolosani (1470/71–1549) which seems to be the first Catholic response to the *De revolutionibus*. Tolosani opposes Copernicanism primarily on the grounds that it violates the requirements for a *"scientia media"* in the Aristotelian hierarchy of the sciences. The essay, however, was unpublished, and had little or no influence in the sixteenth century.[32]

It was only towards the end of the century that the Catholic response begins to emerge. A good example is the work of the most prominent Jesuit astronomer of the day, Christopher Clavius (Christoph Clau) (1537?–1612). His most lasting contribution is our present-day calendar, which was adopted amid controversy in 1582 by Pope Gregory XIII.[33] This calendar reform began at the Fifth Lateran Council (1512–17). The project was recommended to Copernicus, who cites it in his Dedication in the *De revolutionibus* as a prime motive for his reexamination of the foundations of astronomy. In reforming the calendar Clavius used the Prutenic Tables which had been based on Copernicus's work. Yet ironically up

---

[31] Tolosani's brief critique of Book I of Copernicus's *De revolutionibus* was part of the analysis of a much larger set of topics investigated by many scholars as preparatory material for the debates at the Council of Trent. For Tolosani's text, see Eugenio Garin, "Alle origini della polemica anticopernicana," in *Colloquia Copernicana* (Wrocław: Ossolineum, 1975), vol. 2, Studia Copernicana 6, pp. 31–42. See also Edward Rosen, "Was Copernicus's *Revolutions* Approved of by the Pope?" *Journal of the History of Ideas* 36 (1975): 531–542; and Robert S. Westman, "The Copernicans and the Churches," in *God and Nature*, ed. David C. Lindberg and Ronald L. Numbers (Berkeley: University of California Press, 1986), 87–89.

[32] It should be pointed out, however, that we know from a marginal note in the manuscript that it was read by Tommaso Caccini, O.P., who denounced the Copernicans from the pulpit in Florence on 20 December 1614 and who testified secretly against Galileo before the Holy Office in Rome on 20 March 1615, which will be discussed in chapter 3. See Westman, "Copernicans and the Churches," 99.

[33] For Clavius's response to the critics of the new calendar, see his *Novi calendarii romani apologia* . . . (1595) in *Opera mathematica* (Moguntinae, 1611–12), vol. V.

to the last year of his life Clavius never wavered in his commitment to the Ptolemaic worldview.

Clavius's work in astronomy is contained primarily in his *In sphaeram Ioannis de Sacro Bosco commentarius*,[34] first published in 1570. This book went through numerous editions during Clavius's lifetime and many further re-publications on both sides of the Alps up past the middle of the next century, indicating its popular use as a textbook. In it he refers to the Copernican worldview rather infrequently (it does not seem to be a major concern yet), and when he does he disagrees with it, primarily on astronomical and physical grounds but also for Scriptural reasons. He summarizes his analysis near the end of the book as follows:

> If the position of Copernicus involved nothing false or absurd, it would be doubtful whether one should adhere to the opinion of Ptolemy or Copernicus in regard to saving the phenomena better. But many errors and absurdities are contained in the Copernican position, for example, that the earth is not in the center of the universe; that it is moved by a triple motion, the reason for which is hardly understandable since according to the philosophers each simple body has only one motion; that the sun stands in the center of the world and has no motion at all. All of this is contrary to the common teaching of philosophers and astronomers and seems to contradict what is taught in many places in the Sacred Scriptures, as we have extensively discussed in Chapter 1. Therefore it seems that Ptolemy's opinion should be preferred over Copernicus's invention.[35]

The lack of doubt expressed here is further supported by the claim that "also in agreement with this opinion [Ptolemaic geocentrism] are the Sacred Scriptures which state in many places that the earth is immobile, and that the sun and the other stars move."[36] He then goes on to quote Psalms 19:5–6, and 104:5 and Ecclesiastes 1:4–6 for support, a role these passages would often assume in the near future. Clavius's point of view reflected the common opinion in the educated Catholic world just as the Galileo affair began to

---

[34] In *Opera mathematica*, vol. III.

[35] Ibid., III, 301.

[36] Ibid., III, 106.

develop. However after reading Galileo's *Sidereus nuncius* (1610), Calvius himself appears to have found room for doubt. In his last revision of the *In sphaeram* in 1611, after reviewing the new telescopic observations of his friend Galileo and having personally confirmed them, Clavius candidly adds, "Since these things are so, astronomers should consider how the celestial orbs are constituted so that these phenomena can be saved."[37] When good advice like this is ignored, something else usually is taken to be more important.

An extraordinary exception to the prevailing point of view was the Spanish Augustinian theologian Diego de Zuñiga (Didacus à Stunica) (1536–98). In writing his *Commentary on Job* (1584) he came in time to the passage at 9:6, "He who moves the earth from its place, and its pillars are shaken," which seems to say that the earth moves.[38] After saying that this passage is clarified by the heliocentric system, Zuñiga goes on to make two general claims: (1) Copernicanism is clearly better than Ptolemaic geocentrism on scientific grounds, and (2) much more boldly, passages in Scripture which seem to say that the earth is motionless are easily reconciled with Copernicanism. The argument for this latter point is that the most explicit text in Scripture for a motionless earth is Ecclesiastes 1:4, "Generations will come, and generations will pass away, but the earth remains forever." Zuñiga interprets this to mean that the succession of many human generations on the earth leaves the earth itself unchanged as such, but not that it is motionless. By implication other less direct passages of Scripture are to be interpreted analogously as conforming to heliocentricism.

Zuñiga's attempt to reconcile Copernicanism and the Scriptures was soon under fire. Commenting on the same passage in Job at the turn of the century, the Spanish Jesuit Joannis de Pineda (1558–1637) concluded:

> We will not say anything further now concerning this opinion [Copernicanism] except that it is plainly false (others indeed say that it is foolish, frivolous, reckless, and dangerous to the faith, and that Copernicus and Caelio Calcagnini have revived it from the dead remains of

---

[37] Ibid., III, 75.

[38] For a full English translation of Zuñiga's commentary on this passage, see Appendix II.

those ancient philosophers more as a figment of their own imaginations than as something good and useful for philosophy).[39]

In his *Commentary on Job* Zuñiga in effect had introduced his own new interpretation of Scripture in the light of Copernicanism instead of using the usual interpretation of the Church in accordance with the universal agreement of the Fathers. Was this a violation of the principle of interpretive authority in the second decree of the Fourth Session of Trent? Apparently the Holy Office thought so, because on 5 March 1616 it condemned Zuñiga's *Commentary on Job* until this offending passage was corrected. Did the offense arise because of the *content* of the reinterpretation or because of *who* offered it, an individual of low rank in the clergy rather than a bishop or a council representing the Church as a whole?

At any rate the very fact that Zuñiga's ideas were condemned shows how still uncommon and threatening they must have been thirty-two years after they were first published, as compared to the contrary view stated by Clavius. Although in his last days Clavius began to have his doubts, few others did. Shortly after the turn of the century astronomy and theology had come to share some degree of peaceful coexistence. But it was a false peace, based more on lack of communication than on mutual understanding and territorial respect. The shadow of Trent was growing darker.

---

[39] As quoted by Hartmann Grisar, S.J., *Galileistudien* (Regensburg: Friedrich Pustet, 1882), 264.

2

Bellarmine's Views
Before the Galileo Affair

As we have seen, during the half century after Trent the decisions of the council were gradually integrated into the Catholic mind-set. No one was more active and more prominent in this process than Robert Cardinal Bellarmine (1542–1621). By the turn of the century he had taken his place as the preeminent Catholic theologian of the day. His general reputation for erudition also made him the logical choice when Pope Paul V sought his best representative to meet with Galileo in 1616 over the issue of Copernicanism. Thus Bellarmine became the most direct link between the Council of Trent and the Galileo affair, and is an ideal source to study to understand how the theological issues took shape.

Cardinal Bellarmine was already seventy-three years old at the time of his crucial audience with Galileo. His views at that meeting regarding the relevant theological and ecclesiastical issues had been formed long before. As a scarred veteran of the theological wars of the Counter-Reformation, he had won at least the respect of his bitterest Protestant opponents for his enormous historical erudition in the theology of both sides and for his unflagging polemical energies. He spent most of the last two decades of the sixteenth century honing his conceptual weapons for these battles. His primary arsenal was the monumental, three volume *Disputationes de controversiis christianae fidei adversus hujus temporis haereticos* (1586–93), which went through numerous editions and

reprintings.[1] The strong tone of polemicism against the reformers that this title suggests was a major ingredient in an environment which was to carry over into the scientific disputes concerning
Copernicanism twenty-five years later. The latter cannot be understood properly without an appreciation for this sense of defen-
siveness so characteristic of the Counter-Reformation. Because his
theological convictions had been so thoroughly spelled out earlier
in his writings to meet another set of challenges, Bellarmine's views
on the biblical and religious issues which were to be relevant later
in the Galileo affair can be examined in almost pristine isolation
from any scientific coloring. This provides a near ideal opportunity
to study the theological scenery in the background before Galileo
stepped onto the stage.

Bellarmine himself was not a stranger to theological condemnation. In August 1590 Pope Sixtus V decided to place the first volume
of the *Controversies* on the *Index* because Bellarmine had argued
that the pope is not the temporal ruler of the whole world and
that temporal rulers do not derive their authority to rule from God
through the pope but through the consent of the people governed.[2]
However Sixtus died before the revised *Index* was published, and
the next pope, Urban VII, who reigned for only twelve days before
his own death, removed Bellarmine's book from the list during that
brief period.[3] The times were precarious.

THE TRUTH AND THE MEANING OF THE SCRIPTURES

When Bellarmine wrote the *Controversies*, it is quite likely
that he had copies of the documents of the Council of Trent spread
out in front of him. It is easy to correlate the major divisions and
subdivisions of his book with various specific sessions of the council.
The first substantial business at the council was taken up at the

---

[1] The edition used in the present study is contained in Roberto Cardinal
Bellarmino, S.J., *Opera omnia*, 6 volumes in 8. (Neapoli: Apud Josephum Giulano,
1856–62), vols. 1–4.

[2] The offending passages are located at *De controversiis* I, III, 5: "De tem-
porali dominio et potestate ejusdem pontificis."

[3] For the history of this episode, see Xavier-Marie Le Bachelet, S.J., "Bellarmin à l'Index," *Études* 108 (1907): 227–246.

Fourth Session. This corresponds with the first general controversy in Bellarmine's treatise, which is entitled "On the Word of God," and which is subdivided into four chapters which are reflections of the decrees of the Fourth Session: on the canonical books, on their editions, on interpreting the word of God, and on the doctrine of tradition.

Most of Bellarmine's ideas in this book were not original, of course; any claim to originality would indeed have defeated his whole purpose. But his tone and emphasis are unique, and his style is clear and direct. On the foundations of religious faith, he writes:

> —— Scripture is the immediately revealed word of God, and was written as dictated by God. . . . Thus we say that the sacred writers had immediate revelation and wrote the words of God himself either because new things previously unknown were revealed to them by God . . . or because God immediately inspired and moved them to write things which they had seen or heard, and guided them lest they err in any way. . . .
>
> —— There can be no error in Scripture, whether it deals with faith or with morals, or whether it states something general and common to the whole Church or something particular and pertaining to only one person. For it is a certain matter of faith both that no one is saved without the grace of the Holy Spirit and that Peter, Paul, Stephen, and many others truly had the Holy Spirit and are saved. The same Scripture truly declares both of these things. . . .
>
> —— In the Scriptures not only the opinions expressed but each and every word pertains to the faith. For we believe that not one word in Scripture is useless or not used correctly.[4]

The first quotation makes the familiar foundational claim that God is the direct author of the Scriptures. Both Bellarmine and his Protestant adversaries agreed on this, of course. The non-believer who would deny it would also thereby reject all specific religious doctrines built upon it. But if this is granted, then it follows for Bellarmine that *everything* in the Scriptures is true, for God cannot deceive anyone. For Bellarmine this truth guarantee applies not only to matters of faith and morals (i.e., what we need to know for salvation) but also to both general and even specific claims made in the Scriptures. For example, the book of Tobit speaks of Tobias's dog;[5]

---

[4] *De controversiis* II, II, 12.

hence there actually did exist such a dog. The third quotation goes
even further. Not only is the information provided by the Scriptures
a matter pertaining to religious faith, but so also are the very words,
without exception. These three quotations, taken in order from the
same page, reveal a very strictly literal, indeed verbalistic, understanding of biblical truth. As an alternative one might suggest the
more moderate view that many, perhaps most, of the sentences of
Scripture deal with historical or lyrical matters having little or nothing to do with religious salvation; and that therefore the strong truth
status mentioned above should not be claimed for these cases also.
Bellarmine's response is,

> In Scripture there are many things which of themselves do not pertain
> to the faith, that is, which were not written because it is necessary
> [for salvation] to believe them. But it is necessary to believe them
> because they were written, as is evident in all the histories of the
> Old Testament, in the many histories in the Gospel and in the Acts
> of the Apostles, in the greetings of Paul in his Epistles, and in other
> such things.[6]

Bellarmine's logic is relentless. If God is the author of Scripture, everything in the Bible is true, whether it is essential to salvation or merely a piece of accidental historical information. And his
reason for this is of crucial importance. "It is necessary to believe
them *because they were written*." Whatever the piece of information
is, and whatever God's purpose may have been in including it, the
very fact that something is written in Scripture determines that it is
true. This truth condition, which is certainly not limited to only Bellarmine's presentation, was clearly destined to clash with Galileo's
scientific standard of truth.

Although the above framework for scriptural truth remains
firmly in place for Bellarmine, he realizes, of course, that matters
of religious truth are by no means as simple and as fundamentalist
as this seems to indicate. The reason is the obscurity, indeed the
extreme obscurity, of the Scriptures, which arises from two sources:
religious truth deals with the highest mysteries of the divine reality

---

[5] This is Galileo's example from his unpublished notes on Bellarmine's Letter
to Foscarini (12 April 1615). See Appendix IX, paragraph 4.

[6] *De controversiis* I, I, 4, 12.

and salvation history, and is presented in highly complex language structures. This opens the door to the difficult terrain of biblical exegesis, for Bellarmine is quite aware that questions of meaning precede questions of truth. In his most direct examination of these issues in the *Controversies*,[7] he discusses two questions: (1) what *levels of meaning* must be distinguished in the Scriptures, and (2) *who* is to determine the correct meaning of the text. Because of his immersion in the Counter-Reformation, Bellarmine was much more concerned with the second question, which carried over in a vital way into the Galileo affair.

Bellarmine's answer to the first question is an especially clear statement of a centuries-old tradition in Catholicism about the meanings of the Scriptures. Every sentence[8] in the Bible has a *literal* or *historical* meaning, i.e., "the meaning which the words immediately present" (e.g., Abraham had two wives and two children.) In addition to this, some, but not all, sentences in the Bible also have a *spiritual* or *mystical* meaning, i.e., a meaning which "refers to something else other than that which the words immediately signify" (e.g., Abraham's two wives and two sons signify allegorically that God is the author of two testaments and the father of two peoples). Each of these in turn has several subdivisions.

Literal meaning is either *simple*, "which consists of the proper meaning of words," or *figurative*, "in which words are transferred from their natural signification to another." To use Bellarmine's example again, "I have other sheep which are not of this fold" refers to farm animals outside the flock when taken simply, and to the inclusion of non-Jews in the Church when taken figuratively. To use another example taken from Foscarini's *Letter*,[9] "the right arm of God," taken simply, refers to a limb of God's body; taken figuratively, it refers to God's power. In both of these cases the intended literal

---

[7] *De controversiis* I, I, 3, 3. See Appendix III for a translation of the full text.

[8] Bellarmine was aware in general of the contextuality of meaning (i.e., that the meaning of a sentence is partially due to the larger narrative context in which it is situated) as evidenced by his occasional discussion of the context when dealing with the meaning of a particular sentence. But he does not build this into his account of meaning in a systematic way. His tendency is to view each sentence, sometimes an individual word, as an independent unit of meaning.

[9] Appendix VI.

meaning is the figurative one. There are in turn as many different types of figurative meaning as there are types of literary figure.

Spiritual meaning has three species. It is called *allegorical* when it "signifies something which pertains to Christ or the Church" (e.g., the manna in the desert is a presignification of the consecrated bread of the eucharist). It is *tropological* when it "signifies something which pertains to morals" (Bellarmine's example: "Do not muzzle an ox treading corn" signifies that preachers should not be barred from accepting food from the people). It is *anagogical* when it "signifies eternal life" (e.g., the promised land refers to life with God after death).

Pulling all of this together, the different types of meaning in Scripture are to be distinguished from each other, according to Bellarmine, as follows:

MEANINGS OF SACRED SCRIPTURE:

I. *Literal or Historical* (Meaning which the words immediately present)
   a. *Simple* (Proper meaning of words)
   b. *Figurative* (Words are transferred from their natural signification to another)
II. *Spiritual or Mystical* (Refers to something else other than that which the words immediately signify)
   a. *Allegorical* (Signifies something pertaining to Christ or the Church)
   b. *Tropological* (Signifies something pertaining to morals)
   c. *Anagogical* (Signifies eternal life)

Granting all this, the next point is that spiritual meaning is based upon, and thereby presupposes, literal meaning, which thus is the primary meaning of Scripture. Further Bellarmine advises us that effective arguments should deal only with literal meanings for there, he maintains, the correct meaning of the Holy Spirit as author of the Bible can be determined. On the other hand the same passage may have several spiritual meanings attributed to it, and we cannot be sure which, if any, is the intended meaning. This is an interesting restriction on theological argumentation. But fortunately for our concerns, we can put all of the spiritual meanings to one side since they do not enter into the later debates about the relationships between Copernicanism and the Scriptures. Galileo was certainly not foolish enough to enter the murky (and for him unnecessary) domain of determining the spiritual meanings of Scripture. The closest he came perhaps were his occasional comparisons between the sun radiating light and God in his glory, both in the center of the universe, with the sun rotating on its axis and moving the world as God governs all.[10] But this is more properly seen as an illustration of Galileo's Neo-Platonism, providing him with a figurative reading of certain biblical passages and not an exercise in spiritual interpretation as defined above.

On the reasonable assumption that Bellarmine would have had all these distinctions of scriptural meaning in mind when he entered upon the Galileo affair, it follows that he saw the textual issues in that case as falling into the area of literal meaning. And it is quite clear that all the other participants in the debate also saw the issues as defined in this way. Still, there was plenty of room for dispute, since it is often not clear whether the literal meaning of a passage is to be taken simply or figuratively. As far back as 1586 Bellarmine had argued that serious exegetical errors can arise either by reading figuratively what should be taken as simply literal or by reading as simply literal what should be taken as figurative. His early example is quite instructive. The words of consecration, "This is my body," spoken in Matthew 26:26, were taken by the followers of Zwingli to be figurative, while they are simply literal for Bellarmine. This led to a bitter dispute. And this very same dispute over the eucharist, a central theological concern, may well have been still prominent in Bellarmine's mind thirty years later as terrain to be protected at all cost when the Copernican issue finally surfaced.[11]

Be that as it may, the exegetical framework behind the Galileo affair is now partially clarified. The Scriptures often talk of the earth

---

[10] For example, see the last few pages of Galileo's Letter to Dini (23 March 1615) in Appendix V, C.

[11] In his recent and highly controversial *Galileo eretico* (Torino: Giulio Einaudi, 1983) (English translation by R. Rosenthal, *Galileo Heretic* [Princeton, N.J.: Princeton University Press, 1987]), Pietro Redondi has argued that charges of heresy over the eucharist were the primary but concealed complaints against Galileo at the Holy Office and throughout his trial.

as being at rest and in the center of the world, and of the sun as being in motion and away from the center. Is the literal meaning of such passages the simple, proper, natural sense of the words, or is it figurative and to be taken in some non-simple sense? More specifically, does Copernicanism as formulated and supported in 1616 require a change from the traditional simple sense of these passages, which is how they were universally understood by the ancient Fathers of the Church, to a new figurative sense as the true literal meaning intended by the Holy Spirit? That was the exegetical problem as seen by Bellarmine.

However, there is good reason to believe that this was not the main issue in Bellarmine's mind. In the long passage from the *Controversies* which we have been discussing,[12] issues relating to the meaning of Scripture are subordinated to the question of *who* is to judge what the true meaning is. In classic Counter-Reformation fashion Bellermine argues vigorously that it is not the individual person but the institutional Church who is to play that role. His reference is to the condemnation of individual interpretation at the Council of Trent: "the judge of the true meaning of Scripture and of all controversies is the Church, that is, the pontiff with a council, on which all Catholics agree and which is expressly stated by the Council of Trent, Session IV."[13] This is an appeal to what we have called the principle of interpretive authority in the second paragraph of the second decree of that Session.[14] Note that this paragraph from the council documents speaks specifically of "matters of faith and morals," while Bellarmine has expanded this to include "the true meaning of the Scripture and of all controversies," as Galileo will carefully point out later.

There is decisive evidence to indicate that for Bellarmine the protection of the Church's interpretive authority was a separate and more basic issue than the specific question of whether the motion of the sun and the stability of the earth should be taken as simply literal or as figurative. It is essential to appreciate this if one is to understand how the theological issues took shape. The individual judge

---

[12] *De controversiis* I, I, 3, 3, in Appendix III.
[13] Ibid.
[14] Appendix I.

of Scripture (e.g., Galileo or Foscarini) faced a double jeopardy; one relating to the content of the interpretation, the other to assuming the role of being an interpreter. No matter what the merits of the former, the individual was always in jeopardy on the latter, according to Bellarmine's analysis, if he undertook an actual reinterpretation of the Church's traditional reading of a particular problematic text. Galileo's enemies knew this and used it against him.

While discussing Bellarmine's response to the Council of Trent as background to the Galileo affair, it will be helpful to add a few words about his views on the principle of tradition in the first decree of the Fourth Session. He usually refers to tradition as the "unwritten word of God." It carries the same ultimate authorship, truth value, and respect as the written Scriptures (a major bone of contention between Bellarmine and the reformers), and the whole of revelation for Bellarmine is contained partly in Scripture and partly in tradition.[15] One of his main concerns is to provide criteria to identify the true and genuine Apostolic traditions of the Church. To this end he presents the following five rules, which also display his sense of the doctrine of tradition.

> 1. When the universal Church embraces something as a dogma of faith which is not contained in the Sacred Scriptures, then it is necessary to say that it is derived from the tradition of the Apostles. . . .
> 2. When the universal Church preserves something which only God could have determined but which nevertheless is not to be found in writing, then it is necessary to say that this is a tradition from Christ himself and the Apostles. . . .
> 3. That which has been preserved in the universal Church and in all previous times is rightly believed to have been instituted by the Apostles even if it is something which could have been instituted by the Church. . . .

---

15 "Totalis enim regula fidei est verbum Dei, sive revelatio Dei Ecclesiae facta, quae dividitur in duas regulas partiales, Scripturam et Traditionem." *De controversiis* I, I, 4, 12. Like most of his contemporaries in Catholic theology, Bellarmine accepted the "partly . . . partly . . ." interpretation of revelation, as examined in chapter 1.

4. When all the Doctors of the Church, either gathered together in a general council or writing separately in their books, teach with common agreement that something is derived from the Apostolic tradition, then it must be granted that that is an Apostolic tradition. . . .

5. Something must be believed without doubt to be derived from the Apostolic tradition if it is taken as such by those churches which have a unified and continuous succession from the Apostles. . . . [16]

It is virtually certain that Bellarmine would not have considered geocentrism to be a matter of tradition in any of these senses. Just about the only area open even to raising this point would be the second phrase in rule 4 which talks about the "Doctors of the Church . . . writing separately in their books." Regarding this Bellarmine makes the following interesting comment.

An example of the second is hardly to be found if it means that absolutely all the Fathers who wrote expressly said something; but it seems to suffice if some of the Fathers of great name expressly asserted something and the others did not contradict it when they turned their attention to it; for then it could be said without chance to be the opinion of all; for when one of the Fathers has erred on a serious matter, many others are always found who contradict him.[17]

These remarks are noteworthy for two reasons. First, they help to define the phrase "the common or universal consent of the Fathers," which was so widely used in the disputes over Copernicanism. It does not mean, at least for Bellarmine, that each and every writer recognized as a Father of the Church has expressly said the same thing. Rather it has the weaker sense that some Fathers (but not just one) of great reputation have said something which was not rejected by the others who considered the matter. Second, Galileo may have been familiar with this passage. At least he was quite aware of its central idea which he turns to his own advantage on several occasions in one of his favorite arguments: the Fathers never really turned their attention to geocentricism or

---

[16] *De controversiis* I, I, 4, 9.
[17] Ibid.

heliocentricism, for they never had occasion to; consequently an appeal to the "common agreement" of the Fathers is irrelevant.

Be that as it may, we can now draw the following conclusions about the relationship of Copernicanism to the theological environment as created by Bellarmine immediately prior to the Galileo affair. First, heliocentricism would raise problems regarding Scripture but not tradition, i.e., no one in the dispute claimed that geocentricism was based in the *unwritten* divine revelation. Second, these problems would relate to the literal but not the spiritual meaning of the Scripture, more specifically, to the figurative vs. simple literal interpretation of some biblical passages. And third, they would threaten the principle of the interpretive authority of the institutional Church as stated in the Fourth Session of the Council of Trent.

There are no reasons to believe that Bellarmine had changed his mind in any significant way about his views concerning the meanings of Scripture, and the authority to interpret it, when he confronted Copernicanism in 1615–16. Moreover these same views can be found in a book published in 1612 by the German Jesuit Niccolò Serario (Nicolaus Serarius) (1555–1609).[18] Referring to Bellarmine extensively, Serario distinguishes between the literal or historical meaning of the Bible (which may be either proper or figurative) and its spiritual senses (which may be either allegorical, tropological, or anagogical).[19] Furthermore he also raises the specific question of who is to judge the true sense of Scripture, and answers, with Bellarmine, that the Fathers of the Church and the Council of Trent, Session IV, have reserved this authority to the Catholic Church.[20] Serario's biblical commentaries were significant not only because they were published immediately prior to the disputes over the orthodoxy of Copernicanism in 1615–16, but also because Serario's comments on Joshua 10:12 were directly referred to by Tommaso Caccini in his deposition against heliocentricism to the Holy Office (20 March 1615),[21] as we shall see in chapter 5. By quoting Serario

---

[18] N. Serarius, *Prolegomena biblica et commentaria in omnes epistulas canonicas* (Maguntiae, 1612).

[19] Ibid., Caput XXI, 138–156.

[20] Ibid., Caput XXI, Questiuncula ultima, 156.

[21] See S. M. Pagano, ed., *I documenti del processo di Galileo Galilei*, Scripta varia 53 (Vatican City: Pontifical Academy of Sciences, 1984), 81.

in this context, Caccini was able indirectly to enlist the authority of Bellarmine's *Controversies* against Copernicanism.

BELLARMINE'S BIBLICAL COSMOLOGY

Recently published documents show that very early in his career Bellarmine formulated a biblical cosmology which was quite non-Aristotelian in character.[22] Other evidence proves that he was convinced of the truth of this cosmology, in basically the same form, up to the end of his life.[23] He based these views almost exclusively on his reading of the Scriptures and the early Church Fathers. It would be reasonable to maintain that throughout his life he personally believed this cosmology, at least in its major outlines, to be a certain truth revealed by God in accordance with the simply literal sense of Scripture.

The occasion for formulating this cosmology arose from his role as a professor of theology at Louvain from 1570 to 1576. The constitutions of the Jesuits prescribed the teaching of Thomas Aquinas in theology. Accordingly from October 1570 to Easter of 1572 Bellarmine lectured on the first seventy-two Questions of the First Part of Aquinas's *Summa Theologica*.[24] The last ten of these Questions deal with the six days of creation, and thus the topic of cosmology presented itself.

---

[22] Ugo Baldini and George V. Coyne, S.J., *The Louvain Lectures (Lectiones Lovanienses) of Bellarmine and the Autograph Copy of his 1616 Declaration to Galileo*, Vatican Observatory Publications, Studi Galileiani: vol. I, no. 2. (Vatican City: Specola Vaticana, 1984).

[23] The main piece of evidence is Bellarmine's Letter to Cesi (25 August 1618), translated in full at the end of this section of this chapter. This letter was first published, in its original Italian version with a Latin translation, by Christopher Scheiner, S.J., in his *Rosa ursina sive sol* (Bracciani: A. Phaeum, 1626–30), 783–784. Other evidence is presented in Baldini and Coyne, *Louvain Lectures*, 42. See also Ugo Baldini, "L'astronomia del Cardinale Bellarmino," in *Novità celesti e crisi del sapere*, A cura di P. Galluzzi (Firènze: Giunti Barbèra, 1984), 293–305.

[24] For unknown reasons Bellarmine decided never to publish these lectures, which ultimately comprised four volumes. In his will he bequeathed the manuscripts to the Collegio Romano. The autographs of these lectures are now in the Archivum Romanum Societatis Iesu (ARSI) at the Jesuit Curia in Rome.

Leaving aside many details and some important interpretive alternatives,[25] Bellarmine's cosmology took the following general form. The earth is spherical, at rest, and in the center of the universe. Going out from this center, the heavens as a whole are divided into three parts, described as follows: "it is correct to allow at least three heavens, the airy one, the starry one, and the empiraeum; the first is completely transparent, the second is partially transparent and partially capable of reflecting light, the third reflects light all over."[26] The first heaven is the familiar atmosphere of air around the earth, the home of birds and clouds, of winds and rain. The second is the realm of the heavenly bodies, the sun and moon, the planets and stars. The third heaven, having the sole physical property of reflecting light and envisioned as spatially outside the realm of the stars, is the abode of the blessed. Since the damned must be as far away as possible from the blessed, hell is located in the center of the earth. Bellarmine quotes Basil and Chrysostom with approval to the effect that "we know that the firmament exists: what it is and how it is we will know when we have gone up there."[27]

The second heaven of the celestial bodies is understood by Bellarmine in a quite non-Aristotelian fashion. It is not hard, nor impenetrable, nor immutable, and is not composed of a special matter, the quintessence, subdivided into concentric revolving spheres. Rather it is a sea of soft, easily penetrable matter, probably composed of fire, which as a whole is stationary, i.e., it does not revolve around the center of the universe. Furthermore this realm is not only mutable or corruptible but will actually undergo profound changes at some time in the future, although it is not known now whether this dissolution of the heavens, i.e., the end of the world, will be substantial or accidental in character. Bellarmine's reasons for this were, of course, scriptural, so it is purely a historical accident that he had already taken such an anti-Aristotelian stance only a few months before the observation of the nova in November 1572, which was

---

25 See Baldini and Coyne, *Louvain Lectures*, for a discussion and evaluation of these points.

26 Ibid., 16.

27 Ibid., 14.

the beginning of the decline of the Aristotelian notion of the immutability of the heavens.

Granted that the second heaven is a stationary sea of thin matter, "we must then of necessity say that the stars are not transported
with the movements of the sky, but they move of themselves like
the birds of the air and the fish of the water."[28] Each heavenly
body thus is moved by its own, otherwise unspecified, internal power
(not by the thin medium, nor by anything like the traditional solid
spheres, nor by the angelic intelligences of the scholastics). The
natural and true motion of each body is its observed daily motion
toward the west. The varying velocities of these motions give the
false impression that the moon and the planets also have a second
slower retrograde motion toward the east, but this is really due to
the fact that their westward motions are slower than the sun's. The
north-south annual motion of the sun is due to its true path being a spiral. The fixed stars are not really fixed but move separately
from each other. Those over the equator move faster than those
closer to the poles, and their absolute velocities decrease toward
the poles in such a precise way that all the independently moving
stars always undergo exactly the same angular displacement (which is
virtually miraculous).

In this cosmology the account of the motions of all the heavenly
bodies, but especially that of the fixed stars, is a major weakness, as
Bellarmine was quite aware. The primary counterview was Aristotle's
double motion theory of spheres. In 1572 Bellarmine replied to this
as follows.

> In response to this argument first of all I say it is not the task of the
> theologian to analyze this order of phenomena especially when the
> controversies over the explanations are still lively among astronomers.
> In fact some attribute these phenomena to the movement of the
> earth, all of the heavenly bodies being still; others have recourse to
> the hypothesis of epicycles and eccentrics; others to the autonomous
> motion of the heavenly bodies. Thus it is possible for us to select
> among them the one which best corresponds to the Sacred Scriptures.
> If then one ascertained with evidence that the motions of the heavenly
> bodies are not autonomous, but they follow those of the heavens, one

---

28 Ibid., 19–20.

would have to consider a way of interpreting the Scriptures which would put them in agreement with the ascertained truth: for it is certain that the true meaning of Scripture cannot be in contrast with any other truth, philosophical or astronomical. Secondly I say that it appears to me, also based on the Scripture, that the heavenly bodies do not possess other than their own motion, that is, the one from east to west, and that the other is not real but only apparent. Such an apparent motion comes from the fact that velocity differs from one heavenly body to another.[29]

These problems were still not resolved in Bellarmine's mind as late as 1618 when he wrote to Prince Cesi about his cosmological views. Since this letter is not readily available, and since it also shows clearly that Bellarmine personally still believed in the truth of his early biblical cosmology, we will give here a translation of the whole letter.

I read your letter to me with great relish. It is indeed erudite, and novel, and contains many things which conform to opinions which I hold to be true. Only one thing is not completely to my taste, that is, when you deny that the shape of the heavens is round, quoting St. Chrysostom and others. I on the contrary hold to the Scriptures at Ecclesiasticus 24, where it is said, "Alone I encircled the vault of the sky." And we see that the sun, moon, and stars rotate around the globe of the earth. And Solomon said in Ecclesiastes, "The sun circles through the meridian. . . . " Finally there is no doubt that the circular shape is more perfect, and we know that the works of God are perfect. But what I desire from you is not to know that the Sacred Scripture and the Holy Fathers have said that the heavens stand firm and the stars are moved, and that the heavens are not hard and impenetrable like iron, but are soft and easily penetrable like air. All this I already know. Rather I wish to learn from you how the motions of the sun, and especially of the fixed stars which are always together, are explained, and how they complete their larger or smaller circles in proportion to how far or how close they are to the pole. For this is the reason why the philosophers and astrologers assign seven heavens to the seven planets and only one heaven to all the fixed stars. I especially desire to know how diverse motions in one and the same star are to be explained, if there is only one

---

[29] Ibid., 20.

heaven which is immobile. When I was young, I tried to account for the motion of the planets from west to east, which is contrary to their motion from east to west, by saying that their motion from east to west did not occur in all cases in twenty-four hours. Rather the motion of the sun took twenty-four hours, but the motion of the moon occurred in twenty-four and one-quarter hours. Hence it seemed that the moon with its proper motion moved backwards somewhat, and thus gradually receded and later approached the sun again. I attempted to explain the motion of the planets from south to north by saying that the motion of the planets is not a perfect circle but a spiral, and thus continually progresses from south to north and later returns the same way. But this invention of mine was not satisfactory for any of the planets, nor for the firmament of the stars. For since the latter have the longest motions when they are on the meridian circle and the shortest motions when they are towards the pole, this seems clearly to demonstrate that they are moved by the heavens, and therefore they make the longest circles in the middle and the shortest in the extremities. I wish to learn these and similar things from you so that perhaps, when applied to my personal considerations, they could explain the motions of the stars in this way, and also would explain the opinion of the Holy Fathers who assert that the heavens are immobile and that the stars move. But I do not wish to occupy you with these speculations if you are busy with other more important occupations. My Lord, let us take care to live in the holy fear of God, so that when we have arrived in heaven, we will understand everything in an instant. May God preserve your health, and govern over me. I am returning your letter in case you perchance did not retain a copy for yourself; otherwise it will be lost among my endless notebooks.[30]

It should be carefully noted that Bellarmine's view in 1572 was that since the astronomers who deal directly with these matters are not in agreement about the motions of the heavens, then one can and should adopt the view which best fits the Scriptures. If a different view were to be established by astronomers later, then one should consider reinterpreting Scripture accordingly, for two truths cannot conflict. This is precisely what Bellarmine will say in 1615 in

---

[30] Bellarmine's Letter to Cesi (25 August 1618). Printed in Scheiner, *Rosa ursina sive sol,* 783–784.

his famous letter to Foscarini.[31] In 1618 he must have still thought that the astronomers had yet to reach agreement.

Our review of Bellarmine's cosmological opinions shows that throughout his career he was personally convinced of the truth of a non-Aristotelian, biblical model of the universe. And he personally maintained these non-Aristotelian views despite numerous rules and regulations among the Jesuits to teach only Thomism in theology and Aristotelianism in philosophy, as we will explain in detail in chapter 6. As a result it is quite erroneous to argue, as some have,[32] that Bellarmine's personal commitment to Aristotelianism led him to oppose Copernicanism. If his personal beliefs entered into it at all, it would have been his literalistic biblical cosmology which was threatened by Copernicanism, and this throws a distinctively different light on what happened.

BELLARMINE'S ROLE IN THE BRUNO TRIAL

The trial and execution of Giordano Bruno (1548–1600) became a *cause celebre* during the Risorgimento in late nineteenth-century Italy. At that time the Italian scholar Domenico Berti argued that the Church's main complaint against Bruno was his advocacy of Copernicanism.[33] Berti's thesis, which was widely influential for many years, claimed in effect that Bruno's struggles with the Inquisition were a precursor of, and a prototype for, Galileo's confrontation with the Church which began sixteen years later.

---

[31] See Appendix VIII.

[32] For example, in assigning primary responsibility to Bellarmine alone for the Church's condemnation of Copernicanism in 1616, Giorgio de Santillana says, "Bellarmine was semiconsiously frightened by a problem he had never faced: What if the Aristotelian substructure were to prove unreliable? The problem went beyond his training and his mental capacities. He decided it was no problem at all and fell back on the police for an estimate of the situation" (*The Crime of Galileo* [New York: Time Incorporated, 1962], 152). This is nonsense. Bellarmine not only was capable of dealing with this problem, but did so, and consciously rejected Aristotelian cosmology, all as early as 1572.

[33] Domenico Berti, *Copernico e le vicende del sistema copernicano in Italia nella seconda meta del secolo XVI e nella prima del XVII* (Roma: G.B. Paravia, 1876), and *Giordano Bruno da Nola: Sua vita e sua dottrina* (Torino: G.B. Paravia, 1889.)

If this interpretation is correct, then a particularly sinister light is cast upon the character of Cardinal Bellarmine, for he served both as a Cardinal Inquisitor of the Holy Office in the role of a judge at the Bruno trial and as the pope's representative designated to meet with Galileo in February 1616 to inform him of the condemnation of Copernicanism and to solicit Galileo's acceptance of that judgment. Berti saw Bellarmine as an enemy of reason and of science in these two proceedings. An even more sinister reading would be that the ambiguity in the official document reporting on the meeting with Galileo was deliberate, and was intended to ensnare Galileo if he were to advocate Copernicanism later.

This, however, is all quite speculative, for Berti's thesis is now generally rejected by scholars as simply not justified by the available documents. The presently accepted view is that the Inquisition's complaints against Bruno were primarily religious and theological in character[34] and had little or nothing to do with the idiosyncratic version of Copernicanism which he maintained.[35]

Quite recently a sort of inverse of Berti's thesis has been advanced by Lawrence S. Lerner and Edward A. Gosselin.[36] They have suggested that a main issue behind Galileo's trial was the mistaken perception at that time that he advocated a continuation of the hermetic and magical doctrines for which Bruno had already been condemned. Thus the Bruno trial was a precursor of the Galileo trial in a quite different sense. But the available documents do not adequately support this interpretation either.

The question of Bellarmine's comparative role in the two cases remains rather ill-defined, primarily because very little is known about the specific details of Bruno's trial in Rome. There apparently is no discussion of Bruno's trial in either Bellarmine's published or private papers. This is to be expected in light of the strict rules of

---

[34] For example, see Frances A. Yates, *Giordano Bruno and the Hermetic Tradition* (Chicago: University of Chicago Press, 1964), 354–355.

[35] For a summary discussion and evaluation of various contemporary interpretations of Bruno's heliocentricism, see Ernan McMullin, "Bruno and Copernicus," *Isis* 78 (1987): 55–74.

[36] Lawrence S. Lerner and Edward A. Gosselin, "Galileo and the Specter of Bruno," *Scientific American* 255, no. 5 (November 1986): 126–133.

secrecy imposed upon the participants by the Holy Office. Further-more the official record of Bruno's trial in Rome was either lost or destroyed early in the nineteenth century when the documents were transferred to Paris by order of Napoleon. However the interroga-tions of Bruno by the Venetian Inquisition have been published,[37] as well as a more recently discovered summary of part of the Roman proceedings.[38]

What is known about Bellarmine's role is the following:[39] He appears to have been involved in no way at all in the investigations of Bruno in Venice in 1592, in his extradition to Rome in 1593, and in his subsequent imprisonment in Rome. Before he was appointed a cardinal in March 1599, Bellarmine had been named a consultor of the Holy Office. In that capacity he was asked, together with the Commissary General Alberto Fragagliolo, O.P., to review Bruno's publications and the reports on his earlier interrogations in Venice for unorthodox doctrines. This resulted in January 1599 in a list of eight propositions, which to this day remain unidentified,[40] which Bruno was asked to recant as heretical. Bruno's continued refusal to reject these claims was the direct cause of his condemnation and execution a year later. After his promotion to cardinal, Bellarmine was immediately appointed by Pope Clement VIII to be a member of the Holy Office, and thereby he became one of the judges at the trial. The final session of the trial was held on 20 January 1600; Bel-larmine concurred in the vote of condemnation; the pope accepted

---

[37] Published in Domenico Berti, *Vita di Giordano Bruno da Nola* (Torino: G.B. Paravia, 1868), and republished in Vincenzo Spampanoto, *Vita di Giordano Bruno, con documenti editi e inediti* (Messina: Casa Editrice Principato, 1921).

[38] Angelo Mercati, *Il sommario del processo di Giordano Bruno con appendice di documenti sull'eresia e l'inquisizione a Modena nel secolo XVI*, Studi e Testi, vol. 101 (Vatican City: Biblioteca Apostolica Vaticana, 1942).

[39] For an assessment of Bellarmine's role in the Bruno case, see Xavier-Marie Le Bachelet, S.J., "Bellarmin et Giordano Bruno," *Gregorianum* 4 (1923): 193–210.

[40] Émile Namer has made a speculative attempt to reconstruct these eight propositions in his *Giordano Bruno* (Paris: Seghers, 1966), 29–30. His fifth propo-sition deals with the motion of the earth, but whether this was actually included in Bellarmine's own list at the trial is impossible to decide. However if Namer is correct on this point, then Bellarmine had already concluded that heliocentrism was heretical long before Galileo came upon the scene, which would be a very significant finding.

the decision; and Bruno was given over to the secular authorities for execution as an obstinate and impenitent heretic. The execution took place on 17 February 1600 in the Campo dei Fiori.[41]

Bellarmine had a dual role in the Bruno trial, first as a consultor who helped to prepare the critically important list of eight propositions which Bruno was asked to renounce as heretical, and later as one of the Cardinal Inquisitors who judged the case. Whatever may come to be known in the future if new documents come to light, these were very substantial roles in the proceedings.

It seems to be highly likely that Bellarmine would have clearly remembered, and would have been personally influenced by, his experiences in the difficult Bruno affair when he came to deal with Copernicanism and Galileo in 1615–16. This would have been unavoidably part of what Bellarmine personally brought to the latter case. But how did it affect him? Did it make him more cautious? Less tolerant? Personally anguished? We simply do not know, although the experience of taking part in condemning a man to execution could hardly fail to leave its mark, especially if it is true that Bruno exclaimed to his judges, "You perhaps pronounce sentence against me with a fear greater than that with which I receive it," as the contemporary witness Gaspar Schopp reported.[42] Le Bachelet, who is the main modern authority on Bellarmine, quotes his servant as saying that Bellarmine was personally very upset "at seeing a man condemned by the Holy Office perish without repentance."[43] According to Le Bachelet, that man was Giordano Bruno.

THE RESOLUTION OF THE CONTROVERSY
OVER GRACE AND FREE WILL

Bellarmine played a central role in bringing the theological controversy over God's power and free human choice to a conclusion. The debate was a purely theological one, with no scientific overtones

---

[41] A statue of Bruno, peering scornfully from under his monk's cowl, was erected on the site in 1889 with much fanfare in the Risorgimento spirit of opposition to the conservative Catholic Church of that period.

[42] Vincenzo Spampanato, *Documenti della vita di Giordano Bruno* (Florence: Leo S. Olschki, Editore, 1933), Documenti romani XXX, 202.

[43] Le Bachelet, "Bellarmin et Giordano Bruno," 210.

whatsoever. It formally ended in 1607, just three years before the first theological shots were fired in Galileo's direction. Thus it was not only a part of the immediate ecclesiastical background, but may also have been a painful forewarning to Bellarmine and Pope Paul V, who were among the principal actors in both dramas, not to allow another destructive theological dispute to get out of hand. Paul V's resolution of the conflict, in effect a moratorium along lines originally suggested by Bellarmine, is in sharp contrast with his decisions in 1616 in dealing with Copernicanism.

In briefest outline the theological issue was how could one reconcile genuine human freedom with the universally efficacious power of God's grace.[44] Both sides admitted to the reality of human freedom and to the total power of God; the problems lie in understanding these concepts and in maintaining a delicate balance between them. The dispute began in 1588 with the publication of *Concordia liberi arbitrii cum gratiae donis* by the Jesuit theologian Luis Molina (1536–1600), who leaned toward an emphasis on human freedom. This brought sharp attacks from the Dominican Domingo Bañez (1528–1604), a former student of Cano, who leaned more toward an emphasis on divine power. Previous rivalries between the Jesuits and the Dominicans, with the former centered at the University of Alcala and the latter at the University of Salamanca, flared into hostile theological attacks, with frequent charges of error and heresy hurled by both sides. The bitter conflict continued for twenty years until Paul V declared a moratorium on the dispute in 1607. In so doing, he decided to employ the advice originally given by Bellarmine at the request of Clement VIII in a report submitted to that pope in 1597. The relevant part of Bellarmine's report reads as follows:

> It does not seem that the present dissensions can be healed by a decision on the theories in dispute, for the matter with which they deal is a most serious and important one that would require many years and protracted investigations for its elucidation, especially since both parties have dealt with it in book after book. . . . Therefore it is vain

---

[44] For a convenient overview of this dispute, see James Brodrick, S.J., *The Life and Work of Robert Francis Cardinal Bellarmine, S.J.* (London: Burns Oates and Washbourne, 1928), vol. II, 1–69.

to hope for an end of the controversy by a definite decision on the points of dispute. It seems to me, then, with due deference to better judgments, that the dissensions and scandals could be stopped, that both parties could be satisfied, the security of doctrine maintained, and the Holy See relieved of great trouble and uneasiness, if the Pope would deign to issue an edict to the following effect: First, he would seriously and paternally exhort the contending parties to be mindful of brotherly charity in their mutual relations, to avoid dangerous teaching, and to turn their literary weapons against the enemies of the Church alone. Secondly, he might forbid each Order in virtue of holy obedience, or if it be thought well under pain of excommunication, to qualify the teaching of the other as temerarious or erroneous, much less heretical, in lectures, disputations, sermons, or even in public or private conversation. Each party, however, would be permitted to refute the opinions of which it did not approve, by solid arguments. In this manner all opportunity for unseemly quarrelling would be removed. . . . [45]

In terminating the dispute in this way Paul V said that he would announce his decision on the matter at an appropriate later date. He never did so; nor has any other pope since.

During the first phase of the Galileo affair (1610–16) which immediately followed this, were Paul V and Bellarmine apprehensive that another bitter and fruitless dispute was getting under way? Were their actions motivated in part by parallels to the grace–free will dispute? Did Bellarmine see enough similarities between the two disputes to prompt him to suggest the same method of resolution again? Did he ever actually make that suggestion? How would Paul V have reacted to such advice from Bellarmine? Would the moratorium solution have worked in the case of Copernicanism? The evidence at hand is silent on these questions. When Paul V and Bellarmine established the Church's stance on Copernicanism in 1616, they must have remembered how the conflict over freedom and grace had been resolved a decade earlier in a different way. It is ironic that both decisions were made by the same men.

Oddly enough Pope Paul's 1607 declaration of a moratorium in this purely theological dispute over the reconciliation of God's

---

[45] From ibid., II, 52. Also in Brodrick's revised edition; *Robert Bellarmine, Saint and Scholar*. (Westminster, Md.: Newman Press, 1961), 204–205.

grace and human free will had significant consequences for some of the participants in the heliocentricism dispute a few years later. After the pope's declaration, the Jesuit General Claudius Aquaviva (1543–1615) was highly sensitive to the possibility that the Society of Jesus might be plunged into disfavor with the pope if the conditions of the moratorium would be seen to be violated by new writings by Jesuits on the dispute, and especially by the treatise *De gratia efficaci* . . . (1610) by the Belgian Jesuit Leonard Lessius (1554– 1623). This book caused a complex controversy[46] within the Society which culminated in Aquaviva issuing orders in 1611 to the Jesuits to observe what he called "uniform and solid doctrine." By this phrase he prescribed the following of Thomism in theology and Aristotelianism in philosophy in all Jesuit schools and publications. The Aristotelianism included geocentricism in natural philosophy, an unwelcomed restraint on the Jesuit astronomers at the time. Thus a deliberate effort to avoid involvement in a purely theological dispute ironically had the inadvertent effect of creating a crisis in science for some Jesuits.

In summary Bellarmine was quite elderly and near the end of his long career when the issue of Copernicanism arose in the Catholic world. His reactions to this last great controversy during his life would have been unavoidably influenced by his earlier ideas and experiences. Also as one of the prime architects of Counter-Reformation theology, Bellarmine helped to set the immediate religious framework within which heliocentricism was to be debated. All of this was already in place before Galileo entered the scene.

---

[46] For a detailed analysis of this controversy, along with a wealth of previously unpublished correspondence and documents on the issues involved, see Xavier-Marie Le Bachelet, S.J., *Prédestination et grâce efficace: Controversies dans le Compagnie de Jésus au temps d'Aquaviva (1610–1613)*, 2 vols. (Louvain: Museum Lessianum, 1931). There is clear documentary evidence that Aquaviva's order of uniform and solid doctrine, at least as applied to the controversy over Divine power and human free will, was known to, and approved by, Pope Paul V. See vol. II, 243–245.

3

Galileo's Detour into Biblical Exegesis

The timing of the central events involved in the Church's condemnation of Copernicanism in 1616 is quite peculiar. For the first seventy years after the publication of Copernicus's book in 1543 the institutional Church expressed no official concern. Some of the better informed Catholic scholars had, of course, commented on it, usually in passing, and usually in opposition rather than in support of Copernicanism. One could say that during this long period of seventy years the relationship of the new astronomy to the older understanding of the Bible was not only *not* a primary concern, but not even a secondary concern, for churchmen.

Then in a casual, and perhaps an accidental, conversation after a sociable breakfast at the royal house in Pisa in December 1613, the Grand Duchess Christina raised the issue of the religious orthodoxy of Copernicanism with one of Galileo's closest friends and colleagues, a Benedictine priest named Benedetto Castelli (1578–1643). On hearing of this conversation in his absence, Galileo quickly wrote down his thoughts on the matter in what has come to be called the *Letter to Castelli*.[1] In March 1615 this letter was denounced as heretical in a letter to the Holy Office by a Dominican priest, Niccolò Lorini, but the complaint was quickly dismissed. This was the first official involvement of the Church in the case. At about the same time Galileo considerably expanded his earlier comments to Castelli into an elaborate *Letter to the Grand Duchess*

---

[1] *Le Opere di Galileo Galilei*, Edizione Nazionale, cura et labore A. Favaro (Florence: G. Barbèra, 1890–1909; reprinted 1929–39; 1964–66, 20 vols.), V. 281–288. Hereafter referred to as *Opere*. For an English translation, see Appendix IV.

Christina,[2] which was destined to become a landmark in the literature on biblical exegesis, written oddly enough by a layman and a scientist with no formal training in theology. By the first month of the next year, the issue held top priority in the Holy Office; a decision on the matter was made in February, and Copernicanism was condemned by a Decree of the Congregation of the Index on 5 March 1616. So seventy years of near silence on the question of the relation of Copernicanism to the Bible is followed by a period of a little more than two years (December 1613 to March 1616) in which the issue evolves quickly from a casual after-breakfast topic of conversation to a formal condemnation.

This timing is odd. What were the reasons for the long initial period of lack of official concern, and what happened to bring this to an end? Why did events at the Holy Office then happen so quickly, in one year's time (in effect from March 1615 to March 1616), on an issue which was to become a major source of embarrassment to the Church ever since? The institutional Church usually moves slowly, and had long before learned the wisdom of letting the passage of time help in resolving disputes; why did this not happen here? Many prior centuries of experience in biblical exegesis dating back to the Fathers of the Church, and especially to St. Augustine, had more than adequately equipped the Church with principles of interpretation to respond to this new challenge from the astronomers, as Galileo pointed out repeatedly. An objective and historically informed observer at the Grand Duchess's breakfast gathering would certainly have predicted that the outcome would have eventually been a new accommodation between the biblical tradition and the new cosmology. It could have happened that way; it should have happened that way, but it did not. Why?

BLOCKING THE PATH OF INQUIRY

The answers to the above questions lie buried in the concrete details of the views of the major actors in the drama about the

---

[2] *Opere* V, 309–348. For English translations, see S. Drake, *Discoveries and Opinions of Galileo* (New York: Doubleday, 1957), 173–216; and Maurice A. Finocchiaro, ed., *The Galileo Affair: A Documentary History* (Berkeley: University of California Press, 1989), 87–118.

meaning and the uses of Scripture. In the first two chapters we have described the impact of the decrees of Trent on subsequent Catholic theology and the specific views of Cardinal Bellarmine before the issue of Copernicanism arose. It is now time to examine the immediate events leading up to the condemnation of heliocentricism.

At a first step let us look at Kepler's potential contribution to the dispute. We say "potential" because for obvious reasons of religious rivalries, he is not directly quoted by the participants in Italy. In 1609 Kepler published his most important contribution to science, the *Astronomia nova*. In many ways modern astronomy begins with this book, which announced Kepler's first two laws of planetary motion (the planetary paths are elliptical; the radius line from the sun to the planet sweeps out equal areas in equal times). We know that Galileo was aware of this book, but we do not know how closely he may have read it. One of the many ironies in the Galileo story is that he never in later years made use of Kepler's laws. However, if Galileo had read through at least the Introduction,[3] he would have found Kepler's lengthy discussion of the scriptural objections to a moving earth, and Kepler's arguments against these objections.

Kepler points out first that human language is inextricably tied to the presence of visual imagery in our experience. Because of this dominance of vision, we often say things which we know are literally false, but we automatically adjust the meaning accordingly. Thus even the geocentric astronomers speak of the sun's solstice, although they do not mean that the sun actually stops moving. The language of the Bible, for example in Joshua's command to the sun to stand still, also speaks to us in such human-oriented, vision-dominated phrases, which need not thereby always be taken as literally true. Second, the purpose of the Bible is to make manifest to us the power and the glory of God and to give us moral guidance. It is not its intention to teach us about the nature and structure of the world around us. Kepler supports this autonomy claim for astronomy

---

3 Johannes Kepler, *Gesammelte Werke*, Band III, *Astronomia nova* (München: C. H. Beck'sche Verlagsbuchhandlung, 1937), "Introductio ad hoc opus," 18–36. For a complete English translation of Kepler's "Introductio ad hoc opus" by Owen Gingerich, see *The Great Ideas Today 1983*, ed. Mortimer J. Adler and John van Doren (Chicago: Encyclopaedia Britannica, 1983), 309–323.

by presenting a lengthy discussion of the six days of creation in Genesis 1, which he argues illustrates his point. Third, granting this autonomy claim, he then argues that astronomy provides a second means to see the power and glory of God, and thus it complements the goals of religion. Furthermore, truth in religion is based on the word of God in Scripture, while truth in natural knowledge is based on evidence and reason.

> I also implore my reader, when you have returned from church and are engaged in the study of astronomy, not to forget the goodness of God bestowed on men, which the sacred writer invites us above all to consider. Praise and celebrate with me the wisdom and magnitude of the creator, which I lay open before you by means of a deeper explanation of the structure of the world, by the search for its causes, and by the identification of the errors of vision. . . .
>
> For those who are too dull to be able to understand the science of astronomy, or are too weak to believe Copernicus with an unhindered conviction, I give the following advice. Having dismissed the study of astronomy, and having condemned whatever opinions of the philosophers you wish, stay with your own business. Having abandoned a worldly sojourn, stay at home and carefully cultivate your own little field.
>
> Let me say this about the authority of the sacred writings. To the opinions of the saints about their nature, I reply with one word. In theology the influence of authority should be present, but in philosophy it is the influence of reason that should be present. St. Lactantius denied that the earth is round; St. Augustine conceded its roundness but denied the antipodes; today the Holy Office concedes the smallness of the earth but denies its motion. But for me the holy truth has been demonstrated by philosophy, with due respect to the Doctors of the Church, that the earth is round, that its antipodes are inhabited, that it is quite despicably small, and finally that it moves through the stars.[4]

Galileo may well have read these rather strong words, and he may have found himself tending to agree with them. A good case could be made that these remarks of Kepler had some degree of influence on Galileo's own writings on the topic a few years later. But we will likely never know for sure about this since it would have been

---

[4] Ibid., 33–34.

suicidal for Galileo to refer to the Protestant Kepler on this topic at the height of the Counter-Reformation. As far as we have been able to determine in the surviving sources, even Galileo's bitterest enemies never made this charge of disloyal religious sympathies.

Galileo was soon to experience personally for the first time a scriptural objection to his scientific findings. It was a trivial incident, but worth reporting if only because it was the first. In 1610 Galileo published the *Sidereus nuncius*,[5] a work which permanently established him as a scientist of international repute. In it he reported the first results of observing the heavens with his newly developed telescope. Among these results were his sensational observation of four of the moons of Jupiter which his telescope was able to detect. He named them the "Medicean stars" in honor of his patron, the Medici family of Florence. The next year a fellow Tuscan named Francesco Sizzi (1585?–1618) published a small booklet entitled *Dianoia astronomica*, which attacked Galileo's findings. In particular Sizzi argued that the Medicean stars cannot exist because we know from Scripture that God created only seven planets (i.e., the sun, moon, and five visible planets), which the Greek, Latin, and Hebrew exegetes all agree are symbolized by the seven lamps of the golden candelabra described at Exodus 25:37 and Zechariah 4:2.[6] Galileo chose not to respond to Sizzi's booklet, according to Stillman Drake,[7] because of his personal regard for the promising young Sizzi. At this early date he may also have hesitated to enter into biblical terrain, especially over such an inconsequential point.

On the other hand Galileo did not refrain on a number of later occasions from supporting his own views by referring to Scripture. In one instance he was even corrected in such a maneuver by the ecclesiastical censor. This incident occurred in December 1612 as the *Letters on Sunspots* (1613) were being prepared for publication. In that work one of Galileo's conclusions from the fact of sunspots

---

[5] A new English edition of this treatise, along with an Introduction, Conclusion, and Notes by Albert van Helden, has been recently published: Galileo Galilei, *Sidereus nuncius, or the Sidereal Messenger* (Chicago: University of Chicago Press, 1989).

[6] *Opere* III–I, 213.

[7] Stillman Drake, *Galileo at Work: His Scientific Biography* (Chicago: University of Chicago Press, 1978), 467.

is that the heavens are not inalterable, as the Aristotelian system taught. As an additional support for this conclusion he claimed in his original text that the mutability of the heavens is attested to by the Scriptures.[8] Thus one early version of the contested paragraph began with the sentence, "How could anyone who has seen, observed, and considered these things [i.e., sunspots] (and who has set aside all doubts that could be caused by apparent physical arguments) fail to embrace this opinion [i.e., the mutability of the heavens] which conforms so well to the indubitable truth of the Sacred Scriptures which in so many places openly and clearly refer to the unstable and failing nature of celestial matter?" The censor objected to the first two versions of this paragraph in Galileo's text, both of which make basically the same point, and the issue of scriptural support was completely dropped from the text as finally printed, and replaced with the argument that Aristotle himself would have changed his mind if he had known of the new evidence of sunspots. Galileo had personally experienced the censor's red pen.

It is interesting to note in passing that this censor did *not* object to an earlier passage in this work where Galileo declares for the first time in print his commitment to the truth of Copernicanism. In discussing the newly observed phases of Venus Galileo had declared, "With absolute necessity we shall conclude, in agreement with the theories of the Pythagoreans and of Copernicus, that Venus revolves about the sun just as do all the other planets."[9] The censor's attention was focused more on scriptural than on astronomical claims.

---

[8] The passage in dispute is located at the beginning of the second last paragraph of Galileo's Second Letter to Welser (which begins with the words "Ora, per raccòr qualche frutto . . . " in the Italian text [*Opere* V, 138] and with "Now, in order that we . . . " in Drake's translation in his *Discoveries and Opinions of Galileo*, 118. For the two earlier versions of this paragraph which were censored, see *Opere* V, 138–140; and for the dispute with the censor, see Cesi's letters to Galileo of 10 November 1612, 14 December 1612, 28 December 1612, and 26 January 1613, and Galileo's letter to Cesi of 5 January 1613. For a discussion of this issue, see William R. Shea, "Galileo and the Church," in *God and Nature: Historical Essays on the Encounter between Christianity and Science*, ed. David C. Lindberg and Ronald L. Numbers (Berkeley: University of California Press, 1986), 118–119.

[9] Drake's translation from his *Discoveries and Opinions of Galileo*, 94.

Meanwhile, a much more ominous series of developments was already under way. The main actor in this new drama was Ludovico delle Colombe (1565–1616?) who, together with Niccolò Lorini, O.P. (b. 1544) and Tommaso Caccini, O.P. (1574–1648), led a group centered at Florence (dubbed the "pigeon league" by Galileo's friends since the Italian word "colomba" means "pigeon") that bitterly opposed Galileo.[10] The central concern of this group was the preservation of the doctrines and status of the Aristotelian academic community at that time, for which they had an implacable commitment.

Colombe had been frequently involved in disputes with Galileo for almost ten years, beginning with the controversy over the new star or nova of 1604 and later over Galileo's discovery of mountains on the moon, over his views on floating bodies, and in general over the Copernican notion of a moving earth.[11] Many of Colombe's arguments were quite unsophisticated and self-serving. For example, the new star of 1604 had always been there but became momentarily visible because it was magnified temporarily by the positions of the rotating crystalline spheres; thus Aristotle's immutability of the heavens is preserved. Again the mountains on the moon are encased below a transparent and smooth glass envelope; thus the sphericity of Aristotle's celestial bodies is maintained. Drake has suggested[12] that because of this type of argumentation, Colombe provided Galileo with the prototype of the character of Simplicio in the *Dialogue Concerning the Two Chief World Systems* (1632), where Simplicio's argument generally follows the defense of Aristotelianism in Colombe's treatise *Contro il moto della terra* (1611).[13]

---

[10] Giorgio de Santillana describes this group as follows: "The 'conspiracy' of which Galileo so often speaks is not imagined. It called itself a "League." There were several men in the outfield, engaged in more or less concerted action, like [Cosimo] Boscaglia, [Giorgio] Coresio, and [Arturo Pannocchieschi Count] D'Elci in Pisa, the astronomer [Giovanni Antonio] Magini in Bologna, [Vincenzo di] Grazia and the Archbishop [Alessandro Marzimedici] in Florence, and a number of nameless Dominicans in Rome. But the aggressive leadership belonged to the Lorini-Caccini-Colombe triumvirate. . . ." *The Crime of Galileo*, 38.

[11] For an account of these disputes between Galileo and Colombe, see Drake, *Galileo at Work*, 117–120, 214–219.

[12] Ibid., 488.

[13] *Opere* III–I, 253–290.

In this latter treatise Colombe raised the stakes in the dispute considerably by directly challenging Galileo on scriptural grounds. As the title indicates, this treatise is a long set of pro-Aristotelian arguments against the Copernican notion of a moving earth, mostly from a rigid, defensive, and unimaginative point of view. No mention of Scripture is made until the second to last paragraph, where Colombe maintains that it is better to believe biblical writers, who cannot err, than to believe secular authors, who can and do err. This is followed by a flood of scriptural quotations to prove that the earth is at rest in the center of the universe: "You fixed the earth on its foundations" (Psalm 104:5); "God made the orb immobile" (1 Chronicles 16:30); "He suspended the earth above nothingness, that is, above the center" (Job 26:7); "Before the mountains were constituted with great weight" (Proverbs 8:25); "Who has weighed the mountains in a scale and who has measured the mass of the earth within three finger-widths" (Isaiah 40:12); "The heaviness of stone, the weight of sand" (Proverbs 27:3); "Heaven is up, the earth is down" (Proverbs 30:3); "The sun rises, and sets, and returns to its place, from which, reborn, it revolves through the meridian, and is curved toward the North" (Ecclesiastes 1:5); "God made two lights, i.e., a greater light and a smaller light, and the stars, to shine above the earth" (Genesis 1:17).

Then in the last paragraph Colombe states his challenge to Galileo in terms which leave no doubt about the theological threat intended.

> Could those who are unhappy about this perhaps have recourse to an interpretation of Scripture different than the literal sense? Definitely not, because all theologians, without exception, say that when Scripture can be understood literally, it ought never be interpreted differently, realizing meanwhile that the mystical sense surpasses all philosophy and turns all science on its head. Hence as Cano says in his book *De locis theologicis*, and as all modern commentators on the First Part of St. Thomas's *Summa* also say, in dealing with the senses of Scripture, whenever something is affirmed contrary to the universal opinion of the Fathers, then one should say that that proposition is reckless. Furthermore the theologians say that it is a universal rule that a great error in philosophy is then to be suspected by theology,

and especially if it is something of which the Scripture does speak, as in this case.[14]

These words are menacing. Here we have a philosopher and a layman raising the threat of theological heresy and ecclesiastical censorship against Galileo, who also was neither a theologian nor a cleric. Colombe's ploy was cleverly conceived. Galileo was gradually being maneuvered into a dilemma. If the scriptural objection is allowed to stand, the path of inquiry into the new astronomy has been closed and the special Aristotelian interests of the League have been preserved. On the other hand, if Galileo chooses to respond, he finds himself defending a non-traditional point of view on a theological ground for which he is not professionally trained, and on which he could be criticized for preempting the prerogatives of the bishops to interpret or reinterpret Scripture, as the Fourth Session of Trent had already declared. Colombe's challenge was intended to leave no room to maneuver. The literal reading of Scripture and the universal opinion of the Fathers were stated as unqualified exegetical standards. That would need to be challenged in any credible reply.

Galileo chose not to reply specifically to Colombe, neither in 1611 nor at any later date. He must have seen the trap being set, and Colombe's treatise was not in any way a good occasion to try to remove the roadblock to inquiry. Galileo's personal sense of animosity toward the pigeon league was indeed well-founded. But another occasion to deal with these increasingly pressing issues would have to be found. Meanwhile Colombe was provoked by Galileo's silence. In a treatise published the next year entitled *Discorso apologetico*,[15] which was a sustained attack on Galileo's *Discourse on Bodies in Water* (1612), Colombe refers to his earlier essay against the motion of the earth, and defies Galileo to reply, "You have read it, and have not replied a single thing to us."[16] In a marginal note, which he then crossed out, Galileo called this a "most unexpected outburst

---

[14] *Opere* III-I, 290.
[15] *Opere* IV, 313–369.
[16] *Opere* IV, 340.

of temper"[17] against himself. Castelli reports in 1615 in his published notes on Colombe's *Discorso* that Galileo said his reasons for not replying were that Colombe's essay against the motion of the earth was not published but was circulated privately, that Colombe does not mention Galileo by name, and that he did not want to draw attention to the many errors in a treatise written by a fellow Florentine.[18] These are the more polite reasons for avoiding a confrontation; Galileo must have also remained silent for reasons of theological safety.

The very same scriptural challenge issued by Colombe appears a few years later in a treatise by Francesco Ingoli (1578–1649), entitled *De situ et quiete terrae contra copernici systema disputatio*,[19] which was directed against Galileo by name in the subtitle. This unpublished anti-Copernican tract was written in late 1615 or in 1616, at the climax of the showdown over Copernicanism. The first half of this pamphlet deals with the position of the earth, and the second half with its motion. Each topic is evaluated with three sets of arguments, i.e., mathematical, physical, and scriptural-theological. Ingoli's scriptural argument for the location of the earth at the center of the universe is based on Genesis 1:14, "God said: Let there be lights in the vault of the heavens," where "vault" implies an extended spread as the location of the sun and the moon. His theological argument for the same conclusion is that hell or the abode of the damned is located in the center of the earth, which must therefore be at the maximum distance from the heavens or the abode of the blessed. In the second half of the treatise he poses a more interesting set of scriptural-theological arguments against the motion of the earth. He says that there is an infinite set of such arguments, but that the best are the following. The theological argument is based on the authority of the Church in its decision to use a verse in a hymn at vespers on the Third Ferial Day which says that the earth is immobile! But the scriptural argument is a literal reading of Joshua's command to

---

[17] *Opere* IV, 586.

[18] *Opere* IV. 587.

[19] *Opere* V, 403–412.

the sun to stand still. It is at this point that Colombe's old challenge emerges explicitly.

> Replies which assert that Scripture speaks according to our mode of understanding are not satisfactory: both because in explaining the Sacred Writings the rule is always to preserve the literal sense, when that is possible, as it is in this case; and also because all the Fathers unanimously take this passage to mean that the sun which was moving truly stopped at Joshua's request. An interpretation which is contrary to the unanimous consent of the Fathers is condemned by the Council of Trent, Session IV, in the decree on the edition and use of the Sacred Books. Furthermore, although the Council speaks about matters of faith and morals, nevertheless it cannot be denied that the Holy Fathers would be displeased with an interpretation of Sacred Scriptures which is contrary to their common agreement.[20]

Once again the emphasis is on the literal reading of the Scriptures and on the unanimous consent of the Fathers, the latter now with the important qualification that the Council of Trent had restricted its decree to matters of faith and morals. In 1616 Galileo was in no position whatsoever to reply to this personally directed challenge. However in 1624, at the beginning of the much more open-minded papacy of Urban VIII, he did write an extensive *Reply to Ingoli*,[21] although he remained silent on the scriptural-theological arguments.

In summary, from 1611 to 1616 the scriptural and theological objections against Copernicanism grew in force and in specificity. During precisely those same years Galileo was making some of his most important scientific discoveries, especially with the newly developed telescope, which tended to confirm Copernicanism. It is reasonable to speculate that the entrenched Aristotelians, who originated most of the scriptural objections, did so as a defense against the new ideas of Galileo to serve their own vested interests. It was neither the first nor the last time that a polemical group would use the censoring and inquisitorial procedures of the Catholic Church as weapons to fight for their own goals. Their efforts were aided by

---

[20] *Opere* V, 411.

[21] *Opere* VI, 509–561. English translation in M. Finocchiaro, ed., *The Galileo Affair: A Documentary History*, 154–197.

the fact that as the years had passed after the Council of Trent, the decree of the Fourth Session had come to be interpreted more and more in terms of a strict literalism regarding the scriptural texts and a strict traditionalism regarding the authority of the Church Fathers in common agreement. By the middle of that decade all these forces reached a climax.

Meanwhile Galileo was faced with the dilemma which these events imposed upon him. Should he remain silent in the face of the scriptural objections, and thus allow the path of the new scientific inquiry to be blocked in his Catholic part of the world, or should he speak out against them, and thereby risk ecclesiastical censure for either his views or for his presumption to speak on matters reserved for the bishops and their theologians?

GALILEO'S INITIAL RESPONSE

In the midst of these events Galileo received some startling news from his friend Castelli who had recently been appointed to the chair of mathematics at Pisa. His letter to Galileo of 14 December 1613 reads in part:

> Thursday morning I breakfasted with our Patrons, and when asked about the university by the Grand Duke I gave him a complete account of everything, with which he showed himself much pleased. . . . Finally, after many, many things, all of which passed with decorum, breakfast was over. I left, but I had hardly come out of the palace when I was overtaken by the porter of Madame Christina, who had recalled me. But before I tell you what followed, you must first know that while we were at table Dr. Boscaglia had had Madame's ear for a while, and while conceding as real all the things you have discovered in the sky, he said that [in what you claimed] only the motion of the earth had in it something of the incredible, and could not occur, especially because the Holy Scripture was obviously contrary to that view.
>
> Now, getting back to my story, I entered into the chambers of her Highness, and there I found the Grand Duke, Madame Christina and the Archduchess, Don Antonio, Don Paolo Giordano [Orsini], and Dr. Boscaglia. Madame began, after some questions about myself, to argue the Holy Scripture against me. Thereupon, after having made suitable disclaimers, I commenced to play the theologian with such

assurance and dignity that it would have done you good to hear me. Don Antonio assisted me, giving me such heart that instead of being dismayed by the majesty of their Highnesses I carried things off like a paladin. I quite won over the Grand Duke and his Archduchess, while Don Paolo came to my assistance with a very apt quotation from the Scripture. Only Madame remained against me, but from her manner I judged that she did this only to hear my replies. Professor Boscaglia said never a word.

Everything that took place at this meeting during a good two hours will be recounted to you by Sig. Niccolò Arrighetti.[22]

Despite Castelli's exuberant feelings, Galileo must have seen a threatening stratagem in this letter. Dr. Cosimo Boscaglia (1550–1621) was a professor of philosophy at Pisa, a well-known Plato scholar, and a favorite of the Grand Duke. He was also a member of the Pisa branch of the pigeon league. Castelli explicitly says that it was Boscaglia who had first raised the scriptural objection to the motion of the earth in a private side conversation with the Grand Duchess during the meal. It is likely that, among other things, he brought up the famous passage about Joshua's command to the sun to stand still at the battle of Jericho (Joshua 10:12) which, as we know from Galileo's reply to Castelli, was central in the long second discussion after Castelli had been called back to the private royal chambers. In fact Drake suggests that concern over that passage was the reason why Castelli was recalled.[23] At any rate the prominence of the Joshua objection in the Galileo case grows out of this incident, although that passage had, of course, been quoted against Copernicus seventy years earlier. Boscaglia's silence during the second conversation, where scriptural objections were discussed at great length, must have seemed ominous to Galileo. Was Boscaglia attempting to undermine the court's support of Galileo, who held the title of Philosopher and Mathematician to the Grand Duke Cosimo II? Galileo could not take this chance, even though Castelli had reported that the Grand Duke was in agreement and the Grand Duchess had pressed the point primarily out of interest to see where the argument would go.

---

22 Drake's translation from his *Galileo at Work*, 222–223.
23 Drake, *Galileo at Work*, 230.

A challenge from Colombe was one thing; a challenge at court was something else.

The alacrity of Galileo's response indicates the degree of his concern. Within a few days he had received a more detailed verbal report of the incident from Niccolò Arrighetti (1586–1639), and exactly one week after the date of Castelli's letter, he wrote a long reply to Castelli. This *Letter to Castelli*[24] (21 December 1613) was the first formal statement of Galileo's views on the science-Scripture issue. Its content requires close analysis, since it also sets the framework for his later and more expanded *Letter to the Grand Duchess Christina* (1615). It is impossible to say whether Galileo intended his letter to Castelli as a purely private communication or as a statement to be read, copied, and discussed by others, at least by his friends. The latter was not an uncommon custom in his day when formal publication was costly, time consuming, and impeded by ecclesiastical censorship requirements. At any rate it was copied, by enemies as well as friends, and used against him in a complaint to the Holy Office more than a year later. For this reason the content of the letter is worthy of careful consideration.

Although the *Letter to Castelli* was written within one week, it is obvious that Galileo had been considering the matter for a much longer time. Except for the passage from Joshua specifically mentioned by the Grand Duchess, and which he even then discusses only hypothetically, he carefully refrains from direct exegesis. He keeps himself strictly at the meta-level, discussing only the principles involved in approaching the reading of the Bible. His strategy will serve him well. His main point is disarmingly simple. He begins with the ancient argument that God is the author both of nature and of the Scriptures. Thus we know initially that truths from the two areas cannot contradict each other. Further, although the content of revelation in the Bible is inviolably true, Galileo immediately adds that later interpreters of the Scriptures can and do err. The parallel claim, which is not explicitly mentioned, would be that although the laws of nature are also inviolably true, still the interpreters of nature can and do err. So far the parallel is exact. Then Galileo introduces the key point. The language used in the Bible is accommodated to

---

[24] See Appendix IV for a full English translation of this letter.

the understanding of the common person so that he may know what is needed for salvation. Hence the Scriptures often speak in commonsense terms which, if taken at face value, would be erroneous (e.g., God's right hand or anger.) The main reason why exegetes err is that they often fail to take account of such overly literal language. On the other hand God's revelation of himself in nature does not involve a parallel accommodation to human understanding since a knowledge of the laws of nature is not in any way needed for salvation. Nature does not care whether we understand her or not, and thus her secrets, although often hidden deeply, are not metaphorical or equivocal. The net result of this analysis is that the language of the Bible is often ambiguous while that of nature is not.[25]

If this be granted, then important consequences follow about the relations of science and Scripture. In regard to the articles of religious faith and what one needs to know for salvation, science has nothing to say, and thus cannot present any challenge to the certain truths of salvation. The reason given is that such matters are completely beyond human reason, and can thus be known only by the revelation of God.[26] On the other hand, in cases of disputes relating to our knowledge of the natural world, Galileo concludes that if science has established from experience and rational proof that a natural proposition is *certain*, then the exegetes should interpret the Bible accordingly. In such a case the Scriptures take the last place in the dispute, not the first, which is reserved to science. From this follows a piece of practical advice on scriptural exegesis: do not declare that a passage in the Bible has a definite particular

---

[25] It would seem to follow from this analysis that, if God had decided to speak without any ambiguity and human accommodation in the Scriptures, then the latter's content in regard to natural phenomena would be of direct scientific value. In short the Bible would then be, among other things, a partial textbook for natural science. Galileo alluded to this idea years later when he summarized his argument in a letter to Diodati (15 January 1633). See *Opere* XV, 23–26.

[26] Galileo's argument here is too facile. The traditional theological view was that Divine revelation contains two kinds of knowledge needed for salvation, i.e., some truths which are altogether beyond human reason (e.g., the trinitarian nature of God) and other truths which reason can determine (e.g., the existence of God) but only with great difficulty (cf. St. Thomas Aquinas, *Summa Theologiae* I, 1, 1). If so, then the latter area provides a field for possible conflict between science and revelation which is overlooked here.

meaning if that meaning is based on a claim in natural knowledge which *might* later be proven by science to be false. Galileo makes this even more sweeping: do not try to fix the meaning of Scripture beyond the areas of the articles of faith and what one needs to know for salvation. For the Holy Spirit, in giving us the revelation in the first place, intended to deal with only those areas, and not to teach us about nature where we are to discover the laws of God in other, properly human, ways. This is particularly true in the case of astronomy, for the Bible only infrequently discusses cosmology, not even mentioning the names of the planets. The net result of this position is peace between science and revelation at the price of a full dichotomy between them; Scripture dealing with the articles of faith and salvation which are beyond human reason, and science with natural laws which sense experience and reason can determine with certitude in at least some cases. In religion revelation takes the first place and reason the last place; in science the roles are reversed. Galileo's analysis is certainly contrary to the growing tendency after Trent to take every statement in the Bible as literally true, if possible. His theological contemporaries who represented that view were bound to be offended by the *Letter to Castelli*.

Galileo's comments about Joshua 10:12 at the end of the *Letter* are a genuine *tour de force*. If we insist on a literal reading of Joshua's command to the sun to stand still, and if we assume Ptolemaic astronomy, then the day would have been shorter (by up to four minutes), not longer, and thus the ancient astronomy is proven to be incorrect on biblical grounds. For the sun's proper motion in the geocentric model is its annual motion toward the east (at a slow rate) which is contrary to the much faster daily western motion of the whole heavens, including the sun. To lengthen the day Joshua should have commanded the first sphere to stop, thereby stopping all the others; but the common person cannot be expected to know Ptolemaic astronomy, so the command was to the sun whose proper motion seems to be toward the west. On the other hand in the Copernican model the sun is at the center and it rotates on its own axis, as Galileo knew from his recent discovery of the sunspots. Its axial rotation causes (in some unspecified way) the rotations of all the other heavenly bodies. So if its revolution stops, the whole heavens stop, and the day is longer. Thus the literal reading of Joshua's command is congruent with Copernicanism. Galileo must have enjoyed this debater's argument, for he uses it again in an expanded version at the end of the *Letter to the Grand Duchess Christina*. The entire discussion is rhetorical, however, and would carry no weight at all, granted his own principles of scriptural exegesis.

THE SHADOW OF HERESY

The next year, 1614, was so quiet that Galileo may well have thought that the issue had been put to rest. But actually a storm was brewing just over the horizon. On the fourth Sunday of Advent, the Sunday before Christmas,[27] a Dominican priest named Tommaso Caccini (1574–1648), who seems to have been a thoroughly nasty person as well as a member of the pigeon league, delivered a sermon in the Church of Santa Maria Novella in Florence in which he railed against Copernicanism, the Galileists, and all mathematicians in general. It was one of a series of talks on the Book of Joshua, and the immediate text was the famous chapter 10. Tradition has it that Caccini began his remarks by quoting from Acts 1:11, "Ye men of Galilee, why stand you looking up into the heavens?" — which is too good not to be true, and which Drake wryly suggests may have been Caccini's only clever thought.[28] The affront to Galileo was so blunt and offensive that Caccini's religious superior, Luigi Maraffi, O.P., sent Galileo a formal apology.[29]

Shortly after Caccini's sermon Niccolò Lorini, O.P. (b. 1544) somehow obtained a copy of Galileo's *Letter to Castelli*, which he submitted to an evaluation by his fellow Dominicans at their convent at San Marco's. They decided that the *Letter* appeared to be "suspect and reckless." As a result Lorini sent a letter, dated 7 February 1615, to Paolo Cardinal Sfrondrato, an Inquisitor General in Rome, to lodge a complaint against Galileo. Since this letter expresses so forcefully the specific charges against the *Letter* and also reveals so clearly the menacing atmosphere of the dispute, we quote it here in full.

---

[27] The date was 21 December 1614, exactly one year to the day from the date of the *Letter to Castelli*.

[28] Drake, *Discoveries and Opinions of Galileo*, 154.

[29] *Opere* XII, 127–128.

In addition to the common responsibility of every good Christian, there is an infinite duty placed on the shoulders of all the monks of St. Dominic, who have been appointed by the Holy Father as the black and white dogs of the Holy Office, and especially the theologians and preachers. For this reason then do I, the least of all and your most devoted and special servant, stand before you. I am sending you a copy of a document which all are coming to read, produced by those who call themselves Galileists and which affirms that the earth moves and the sun stands still, following the views of Copernicus. The judgment of all the Fathers of this most religious convent of San Marco is that this document contains many propositions which appear to us to be suspect and reckless. For example, it says that certain modes of speech in the Sacred Scriptures are improper, and that in disputes about natural effects Scripture holds the last place, and that its interpreters are often in error in their exegesis, and that Scripture itself ought to be concerned only with the articles of faith, and that philosophical or astronomical proof has more force in natural matters than sacred or divine proof, as is shown by the propositions which I have underlined in the attached document, which is a true copy; and finally that when Joshua commanded the sun to stand still, this command should be understood to be addressed to the first sphere and not to the sun itself. It is clear that not only is this document in the hands of everyone, without any permission of the superiors, but also that they wish to interpret the Scriptures in their own way and contrary to the common interpretation of the Holy Fathers, that they defend a view which is apparently completely contrary to the Sacred Scriptures, that they speak with little respect for the ancient Holy Fathers and St. Thomas, that they trample upon the whole philosophy of Aristotle (which has served scholastic theology so well), and in sum that they display their cleverness by saying many impertinent things which they spread throughout our whole city, whose Catholocism has been maintained so strongly by your good nature and vigilance. As a result I have resolved to come before you, as I said, so that you, who are full of holy zeal and who, together with your colleagues, have the assignment of keeping a close watch on such things, can, if it appears that there is need here for corrections, provide whatever remedies which are judged to be necessary, lest "a small error in the beginning become a large error at the end." I could have also sent you a copy of some notes composed in this convent about that document, but modesty has bid me to abstain, knowing that I have written to you, who knows so much, and that

I have written to Rome where, as St. Bernard says, the holy faith "has the eyes of a lynx." I agree that all of those who call themselves Galileists are good Christians and men of means, but they are smart alecks to some extent and rigid in their opinions. I also say that in this business I am moved only by zeal; and I request that this letter of mine (I am not speaking of the document) be held in secret by you, as I am certain it will be, and that it not be used as a judicial deposition, but only as kindly advice between you and me as between a most illustrious master and a servant. You should also know that the occasion of this letter was one of two public talks given in our Church of Santa Maria Novella by Father Tommaso Caccini commenting on the book of Joshua, and in particular chapter 10 of that book. Thus I end, asking for your sacred blessing, kissing your garment, and requesting a small place in your prayers.[30]

The copy of Galileo's *Letter to Castelli* which Lorini attached to the above letter was both incomplete (it would have been obvious to any reader that some introductory material was abridged) and significantly inaccurate (which would not have been obvious).[31] Following normal procedures, Cardinal Sfrondrato submitted Galileo's letter to an unnamed theological adviser of the Holy Office for an opinion. The whole matter was ultimately dropped, due at least in part to the following undated judgment by that adviser.

> In the document shown to me today I have found nothing to note except the following three points.
> On the first page it is said, "Many propositions are found in the Scriptures which, in respect to the bare meanings of the words, are false . . . " [Galileo's text reads: "give an impression different from the truth"]. Although these words can be taken in a correct way, still at first sight they seem to be offensive. For it is not good to use the word "false," which should not be attributed in any way to the Sacred Scriptures, whose truth is complete and infallible.

---

[30] Lorini's letter to Paolo Cardinal Sfrondrato, 7 February 1615, in *Opere* XIX, 297–298. Lorini may have died shortly after this date since, despite the seriousness of his complaint to Rome against Galileo, he played no further role in the Galileo affair.
[31] For these differences compare Galileo's original text of the *Letter to Castelli* in *Opere* V, 281–288, with Lorini's copy in *Opere* XIX, 299–305. For the major changes in Lorini's text, see our footnotes to Appendix IV.

Next on the second page it is said, "Scripture does not refrain from perverting [Galileo's text "faintly sketching"] its most important dogmas. . . ." The words "refrain" and "pervert" sound offensive when attributed to Sacred Scripture, for these words refer to evil (for instance, we refrain from evil, and it is a perversion when a just man becomes unjust).

Also the words on page four, "Let it be granted and conceded for now . . . " sound offensive. For in this statement it seems that the author wishes to maintain that it is only a historical truth that the sun was stopped by Joshua in the text of the Sacred Scripture, although from what follows these words can be taken in a correct way.

Otherwise, although this document sometimes uses words improperly, it does not deviate from the narrow path of Catholic expression.[32]

It is virtually certain that Galileo never saw Lorini's letter quoted above. But within a few days he had learned of the incident, because on 16 February he wrote in an agitated vein to his friend in Rome, Monsignor Piero Dini (1570?–1625), for help in protecting his interests.[33] He was truly incensed. Lorini and Caccini were revealed to be part of a conspiracy attempting to manipulate the censorship powers of the Holy Office into humiliating Galileo by a condemnation of Copernicanism as heretical. Galileo writes that some of his adversaries are so devious as to have even encouraged the impression that he was the author of the book by Copernicus, who had died seventy years earlier and who, moreover, undertook his work in astronomy at the request of a pope to assist in the reform of the calendar. Galileo suspects, with good reason, that Lorini had submitted an inaccurate copy of the *Letter to Castelli* to the Holy Office,[34] and so he forwarded a true copy to Dini. His main suggestion to Dini is to try to elicit the support of the Jesuits, who had honored Galileo so lavishly a few years earlier for his discoveries with the telescope, in particular Father Christopher Grienberger

---

[32] *Opere* XIX, 305.

[33] See Appendix V for a full translation of the Galileo-Dini correspondence.

[34] In its turn the Holy Office also made several attempts to obtain the original copy of Galileo's letter, since their copy was obviously incomplete. On these efforts, see Drake, *Galileo at Work*, 244–249.

(1561–1636), who had succeeded Clavius at the Collegio Romano, and, if possible, Cardinal Bellarmine.

Dini vigorously pressed Galileo's case in Rome, and was soon able to send a reply which included a summary of his audience with Cardinal Bellarmine, who did not say what Galileo wanted to hear.[35] The cardinal did not believe that there was any danger of Copernicanism being condemned, the issue being of little concern at present. "The worst thing that could happen to Copernicus would be that some marginal notes might be added to the effect that his doctrine was introduced to save the appearances, or some such thing, similar to those who have introduced epicycles but do not believe in them." With such qualifications one could speak out on Copernicanism under any circumstances. In his second letter to Dini,[36] Galileo reacts sharply to this suggested compromise. He points out that this is not what Copernicus himself thought; moreover, although the Aristotelian spheres are not physically real, all past and present astronomers know that eccentric and epicyclic motions actually occur in the heavens. He concludes that "it is necessary either to condemn it all or to leave it be by itself," leaving no middle ground for a hypothetical status for the new cosmology, in the contemporary sense of that term.

In the meeting with Dini, Bellarmine also had remarked that "it does not appear at present that there is anything in the Scriptures which is more contrary than the passage, 'He exulted like a hero to run his course'." The full text at issue is Psalm 18:5–6, which was traditionally read as a statement of geocentricism. It reads as follows:

> High above, he pitched a tent for the sun,
> who comes out of his pavilion like a bridegroom,
> exulting like a hero to run his race.
> He has his rising on the edge of the heaven,
> the end of his course is its furthest edge,
> and nothing can escape his heat.

Through Dini Bellarmine had invited Galileo to send him whatever biblical reflections he may wish for the cardinal's reactions.

---

[35] See Appendix V, B.

[36] Appendix V, C.

Galileo seized upon this offer, and included in his second letter to
Dini a long reflection on Psalm 18:5–6 from a heliocentric perspective. His strongly neo-Platonic cosmological model, which he says
is his personal conviction, is in outline the following: The universe
as a whole is vivified by a special caloric spirit, distinct from light,
which originates somehow from outside or from the far edges of
the universe, and which focuses in the sun where it is considerably
strengthened and then re-emitted to warm and vivify all bodies,
living and non-living. Thus the sun must be at the center of the
universe, and its axial rotation, attested to by the motion of the
recently discovered sunspots, somehow moves all the other bodies
in the heavens. This last notion had already appeared at the end
of the *Letter to Castelli* in the discussion of Joshua's command to
the sun. Galileo then tries to show how the individual terms and
phrases used in Psalm 18:5–6 can be understood in terms of this
heliocentric model. His elaborate gloss on this passage must have
been intended to persuade Bellarmine that this "most contrary" text
was not inimical to Copernicanism.

Meanwhile Galileo had also written to another friend in Rome,
Giovanni Ciampoli (1590?–1643), for his help after the Lorini incident. On 28 February Ciampoli sent the following disquieting report.

> Cardinal Barberini, who, as you know from experience, has al-
> ways admired your talents, told me just last evening that in regard
> to these opinions he thinks that greater caution is needed in dealing
> with the arguments of Ptolemy and Copernicus, and that one should
> not exceed the limits of physics and mathematics, because *the expli-
> cation of the Scriptures is restricted to theologians who deal with such
> matters*. . . . To avoid the slander of others in this situation, it is quite
> necessary to proclaim frequently that *one submits to the authority of
> those who have jurisdiction over human reason in the interpretation
> of the Scriptures*.[37]

Writing again three weeks later Ciampoli reports on a long
conversation with Cardinal Bellarmine.

> He [Bellarmine] concluded that there ought not to be any con-
> tradiction when one treats the system of Copernicus and his demon-
> strations without entering into Scripture, *the interpretation of which*

---

[37] *Opere* XII, 146, emphasis added.

is to be reserved to the professors of theology who are approved by the public authority. But still it is difficult to admit statements about Scripture, however ingenious, when they disagree so much with the common opinion of the Fathers of the Church. Briefly, to avoid repeating myself, the reasons given were very similar to those which I reported in my other letter about Cardinal Barberini.[38]

These two powerful cardinals, both central in the Galileo case, were in effect raising Trent's principle of interpretive authority, i.e., decisions on the meaning of Scripture are reserved to the Church in its bishops and the pope. Lower-level theologians, much less laymen, should not presume a role in this territory. That is what the Reformation and the Counter-Reformation had been about.

GALILEO'S FINAL RESPONSE

In his first letter to Dini, Galileo had said, in discussing the relations of science and religion, "On these topics I have drafted a very extensive treatise but I do not yet have it in a finished enough form to be able to send you a copy." This treatise was the *Letter to the Grand Duchess Christina*,[39] on which he continued to work despite the unfavorable developments in the spring of 1615, and which he completed in midsummer. The *Letter* was widely copied, distributed, and discussed in Italy but was never published by Galileo.[40] In a sense it was already too late.

Galileo begins the new *Letter* with a bitter account of the injustices perpetrated against him by Caccini and Lorini, who are depicted as using the Bible in an attempt to silence him by causing

---

[38] *Opere* XII, 160, emphasis added.

[39] *Opere* V, 307–348. For a full English translation, see Drake, *Discoveries and Opinions of Galileo*, 175–216. Page references to, and quotations of, the *Letter to the Grand Duchess Christina* are from the Drake translation. One of the key sources used by Galileo in writing this *Letter* was Pereyra's commentary on Genesis; see our discussion of Pereyra's four rules for interpreting Scripture in chapter 1 for the evidence connecting Galileo and Pereyra.

[40] The *Letter to the Grand Duchess Christina* was first published after Galileo's trial in Strasbourg in 1636 in a Latin-Italian edition. It later appeared as an appendix in various editions of Galileo's *Dialogue* published in Northern Europe. For a detailed analysis, see Jean Dietz Moss, "Galileo's Letter to Christina," *Renaissance Quarterly* 36 (1983): 547–576.

the Church to condemn two propositions which Galileo professes to
be true, i.e., "I hold the sun to be situated motionless in the center
of the revolution of the celestial orbs while the earth rotates on its
axis and revolves about the sun."[41] These same two propositions, in
a somewhat less felicitous wording, were to be submitted for evaluation and then judged to be heterodox by a panel of theologians at
the Holy Office in February 1616. Galileo uses his previous letters
to Castelli and to Dini, especially the former, as a working basis
for the new *Letter*, and as a result one can find in it some *verbatim* repetitions and, even more frequently, considerably expanded
paraphrases of the earlier writings along with extensive supporting
quotations from St. Augustine, the classic source for Catholic biblical exegesis. The framework remains at the meta-level, and the
principles of exegesis discussed above from the *Letter to Castelli*
reappear in the new *Letter*, albeit with some quite important differences. God is the author of both nature and the Bible, and thus no
contradiction is possible (Principle of the Unity of Truth) if both, and
especially the Scriptures, are properly understood. But revelation is
often stated in ambiguous language (which causes many interpretive
errors) in order to speak to the common person. For the common
person this causes no problem (which was the purpose of the Holy
Spirit in the first place) since he thinks and speaks in commonsense
terms. But for the educated person interpretation is needed to remove ambiguity and to reconcile a passage in dispute with either
other Scripture passages or with natural knowledge. When science
is *certain* in its conclusions, it takes precedence over Scripture in
natural disputes (The Priority Principle), and in such cases Scripture
should be interpreted or reinterpreted accordingly. In other cases
where science falls short of certitude, the advice is not to fix the
meaning of Scripture one way or the other lest later proof contradict the option taken (The Pragmatic Rule). The intention of the
Holy Spirit in dictating the Scriptures is to give us the knowledge
needed for the faith and for salvation (The Principle of Scriptural
Intention) which, being beyond human reason, can thereby never
be in conflict with the findings of natural knowledge. These are the

---

[41] Drake, *Discoveries and Opinions of Galileo*, 177.

exegetical principles from the *Letter to Castelli* which are carried over into the *Letter to the Grand Duchess Christina*.[42]

To this Galileo adds some quite important expansions and modifications. First, as a loyal member of the Counter-Reformation Catholic Church, he explicitly advocates what we have called Trent's Principle of Interpretive Authority. If everyone interpreted Scripture according to his own personal light, there would be endless disputes and multiple erroneous authorities imposing credal obligations, even concerning the natural world; this argument had played a central role in Bellarmine's *De controversiis*. "Let us therefore render thanks to Almighty God, who in his beneficence protects us from this danger by depriving such persons of all authority, reposing the power of consultation, decision, and decree on such important matters in the high wisdom and benevolence of most prudent Fathers, and in the supreme authority of those who cannot fail to order matters properly under the guidance of the Holy Ghost."[43] There can be no doubt that Galileo recognized the decisive interpretive authority of his Church on matters of biblical meaning and truth.

Second, Galileo adds three centrally important comments on the increasingly prominent issue of whether a proposition is true *de fide* (i.e., is contained in the body of required and certain religious beliefs) because it is universally agreed to by the Fathers of the Church. This point refers to those components of the revealed faith located in tradition more than in Scripture. Galileo's points are: (1) this applies only to cases where the Fathers have actually considered and debated an issue explicitly, as distinct from its being merely an unreflective *façon de parler* of their times (but the Fathers had no occasion in particular to consider reflectively the stability or motion of the sun and the earth); (2) this applies only to matters of faith and morals, as was expressly stipulated by the Fourth Session of the Council of Trent (but the motion or rest of the sun and the earth

---

[42] For a helpful discussion of the relations between the two *Letters* and for a schematic summary of Galileo's principles of exegesis, see Fabris, *Galileo Galilei e gli orientamenti esegetici del suo tempo*, 12–22. Fabris emphasizes the need to distinguish two levels of discussion in the two *Letters*: (1) Galileo's general principles of exegesis, and (2) his interpretations of specific biblical passages, the latter not always being consistent with the former.

[43] Drake, *Discoveries and Opinions of Galileo*, 190–191.

is not a matter of either faith or morals); (3) as a matter of fact the Fathers were not in universal agreement in what little they did say about astronomical matters in the Bible.[44]

Next there are several passages in the *Letter to the Grand Duchess Christina* where Galileo argues that, when it happens in cases of natural phenomena that science falls short of certain demonstrated truth, then one should prefer Scripture over science, when they overlap, to determine the truth of the matter. This seems to be an explicit rejection of his own Pragmatic Rule in the earlier writings.

For instance, Galileo maintains:

> Yet even in those propositions which are not matters of faith, this authority [i.e., the Bible] ought to be preferred over that of all human writings which are supported only by bare assertions or probable arguments, and not set forth in a demonstrative way. This I hold to be necessary and proper to the same extent that divine wisdom surpasses all human judgment and conjecture.[45]

And again:

> In the books of the sages of this world there are contained some physical truths which are soundly demonstrated, and others that are merely stated; as to the former, it is the office of wise divines to show that they do not contradict the holy Scriptures. And as to the propositions which are stated but not rigorously demonstrated, anything contrary to the Bible involved in them must be held undoubtedly false and should be proved so by every possible means.[46]

And again:

> Among physical propositions there are some with regard to which all human science and reason cannot supply more than a plausible opinion and probable conjecture in place of a sure and demonstrated knowledge; for example, whether the stars are animate. Then there are other propositions of which we have (or may confidently expect) positive assurances through experiments, long observation, and rigorous demonstration; for example, whether or not the earth and the heavens move, and whether or not the heavens are spherical. As to

---

44 Ibid., 202–205.
45 Ibid., 183.
46 Ibid., 194.

the first sort of propositions, I have no doubt that where human reason cannot reach — and where consequently we can have no science but only opinion and faith — it is necessary in piety to comply absolutely with the strict sense of the Scripture. But as to the other kind, I should think, as said before, that first we are to make certain of the fact, which will reveal to us the true senses of the Bible, and these will most certainly be found to agree with the proved fact (even though at first the words sounded otherwise), for two truths can never contradict each other. I take this to be an orthodox and indisputable doctrine, and I find it specifically in St. Augustine. . . . [47]

These passages appear to constitute a significant and troublesome change from Galileo's earlier statement of what we have called the Pragmatic Rule in the *Letter to Castelli*. For if these remarks are taken at their face value, and if Copernicanism was not a demonstrated truth at the time (which it was not), then Galileo seems to be saying that we should reject it, for now at least, in favor of the commonsense astronomy of the Bible.[48] Did Galileo say this simply as a rhetorical concession to mollify his theological readers? That seems hardly likely, since it would have been a concession of the heart of the matter. Did he simply commit a major conceptual blunder, not seeing the consequences of these remarks. That is not impossible, of course, but again is hardly likely in a man so accustomed to rigorous thought and who knows that he is writing on a critically important topic. Did he think that Copernicanism was already demonstrated, and thus his main concern would remain unaffected by this concession? Again that is possible, but not very likely. He was still searching for a conclusive proof, as evidenced by the fact that his ill-fated argument from the tides was yet

---

[47] Ibid., 197.

[48] Ernan McMullin, in the Introduction to his *Galileo: Man of Science* (New York: Basic Books, 1967), 3–51, has argued that Galileo held two views which are flatly contradictory: (1) that incidental physical statements in the Bible are irrelevant as a source of truth about nature, and (2) that revelation, as a higher truth, is always to be preferred over science regarding natural facts when that science is less than certain. He maintains that Galileo's personal conviction was (1), but that he compromised on (2) "confident in the belief that he could in any event provide the necessary demonstration of the earth's motion" p. 34.

to enter the scene.[49] He correctly argued in many places that the Ptolemaic system had been conclusively falsified (especially by the evidence of the phases of Venus), but that did not prove heliocentricism, for there was the third alternative of the Tychonic model (which Galileo discussed only rarely but of which he certainly was well aware.) And even if he had thought that Copernicanism was proven as certain, why give away all the other unproven parts of science to scriptural determination, an unwise price to pay to win the present battle?

To the modern reader, steeped in the present universal conviction that science is essentially hypothetical,[50] Galileo's plight is due to his failure to realize this fact about science. If he had realized this, he would indeed never have made the concession under discussion. However, although Galileo disagreed with his Aristotelian contemporaries on many doctrines, he shared with them the view that science can and should attain full certitude to count as

----

[49] This argument (to the effect that the tides are caused by the compounding of the double motion of the earth) was first written down by Galileo in January 1616 as a conclusive [actually it is defective] proof of heliocentricism, and became the main focus of the Fourth Day of his *Dialogue* (1632). The earlier version appears in his *Discorso sopra il flusso e reflusso del mare* (*Opere* V, 377–395); English translation in Finocchiaro, ed., *The Galileo Affair: A Documentary History*, 119–133.

[50] Where "hypothesis" means a likely or probable state of affairs in nature which is worthy of further study to verify or falsify by means of the hypothetical-deductive method. But in Galileo's day the term was more likely to carry the meaning of a "fictional or unreal state of affairs which however, if assumed, is an aid to computation." Cf. McMullin, *Galileo: Man of Science*, 35. For a detailed justification of the claim that Galileo's meaning for "hypothesis" is "quite foreign to the use of 'hypothesis' in the hypothetical-deductive methodology that is currently associated with modern science," see William A. Wallace's critically important "Aristotle and Galileo: The Uses of HUPOTHESIS (Suppositio) in Scientific Reasoning," in *Studies of Aristotle*, ed. Dominic J. O'Meara (Washington, D.C.: Catholic University of America Press, 1981), 47–77.

An extensive and very helpful discussion of the multiple meanings of "hypothesis" and its cognates in the Galileo era can be found in Guido Morpurgo-Tagliabue, *I processi di Galileo e l'epistemologia* (Milano: Edizone di Comunità, 1963). Morpurgo-Tagliabue's main thesis is that pervasive ambiguities over this notion at that time caused persistent misunderstandings at multiple levels which led in turn to the condemnation of Copernicanism and the trial of Galileo.

science.[51] His reasons for this related to the mathematical structure of nature, not to Aristotelian essential definitions; but that is not relevant, the resulting certitude requirement is the same.[52] Hence our contemporary solution was not really available to him.

On the other hand Galileo may well reply to us that we moderns do not sufficiently appreciate the force of religious belief in the Scriptures which was characteristic of his day. As a Counter-Reformation Catholic it is most likely that he believed that every statement in the Bible is actually true, granting that its meaning has been correctly established. Moreover this truth is fully certain because it is the truth of the word of God. Now it is not the purpose of the Bible to teach science, or as Galileo put it, quoting Cardinal Baronius, "The intention of the Holy Ghost is to teach us how one goes to heaven, not how the heavens go."[53] But in carrying out its proper role of teaching the faith and the way to salvation, the Bible incidentally mentions many natural and historical facts. This is an extra dividend of knowledge which we would be foolish to ignore, especially since these pieces of information are certain truths. However, if science has fully proven the contrary of such a surplus scriptural claim to be true, then we must admit that we have misunderstood the meaning of that biblical statement, and we must reinterpret it according to the demonstrated natural truth. So far, so good.

But when science falls short of certitude, two situations arise. As the passages quoted earlier indicate, in some cases we are dealing with natural phenomena "where human reason cannot reach" and "no more than plausible opinion and a probable conjecture" is possible. In that case the preferred course is always to reject that opinion as false if it is contrary to a truth of the Bible, which is overwhelmingly stronger. The question that remains is what to do in the case of a natural truth stated in the Bible for which it is *possible* for science to prove conclusively either it or its opposite at some time in the

[51] For a detailed and illuminating discussion of this claim, see William A. Wallace, *Galileo and His Sources* (Princeton, N.J.: Princeton University Press, 1984), especially chapter 3.

[52] For an account of this point, see William R. Shea, "La Controriforma e l'esegesi biblica di Galileo Galilei," in *Problemi religiosi e filosofia*, ed. A. Babolin (Padova: Garagola, 1975), 55–57.

[53] Drake, *Discoveries and Opinions of Galileo*, 186.

future (this was the status of Copernicanism at that time). Although the passages quoted earlier are definitely ambiguous in distinguishing these two cases of non-demonstrated truths, we would argue that Galileo was willing to accede to Scripture, for reasons of the Bible's superior certitude, in cases where demonstration was *impossible*. But in cases where demonstration was *possible*, he intended to opt for the Pragmatic Rule of the *Letter to Castelli*, i.e., in such cases do not declare that a passage in Scripture has any particular meaning if that meaning is based on a claim in natural knowledge which *might* later be proven by science to be false. For otherwise there always could occur a scandal to the faith, as Augustine had warned. Granting this, the central question then would be what criteria are to be used to distinguish presently undemonstrated scientific claims into (a) those which are indemonstrable in principle, and (b) those which are demonstrable but not yet actually demonstrated. Galileo gives us no clues as to what criteria he would suggest.

It is also important to remember that the basic issue was not the interpretation of Scripture (it already had a detailed history of interpretation for centuries on the disputed passages) but its reinterpretation; i.e., what standards should be used to decide on a *change* in the previously accepted reading, given new developments in other disciplines. Understanding the status of those disciplines was as equally important as the exegetical principles involved, and in 1615 the notion of science was very much in transition.

Our analysis of the *Letter* has the merit of preserving consistency in Galileo's view and of not compromising his commitment to Copernicanism, while at the same time taking account of his requirement for certitude in science and the even higher certitude of the Scriptures properly understood. At least all can agree that it is quite unfortunate that there is such textual ambiguity (i.e., between indemonstrable vs. yet-to-be-demonstrated natural science claims) at the critical point of the argument in Galileo's most mature statement on the relations of science and the Bible. What was ultimately at stake was whether the scriptural blockade erected in the path of scientific inquiry by Colombe and his friends could be removed. Galileo's ambiguity made the blockade more formidable than it really was.

Although Galileo was fated to lose this battle, he ultimately won the war. In modern times the Catholic Church has reasserted his exegetical principles and their Augustinian roots. Thus Pope Leo XIII in *Providentissimus Deus* (18 November 1893) quotes precisely the same passages from St. Augustine used by Galileo to justify the same conclusions.

> If dissention should arise between them [the theologian and the physicist], here is the rule also laid down by St. Augustine, for the theologian: — "Whatever they can really demonstrate to be true of physical nature, we must show to be capable of reconciliation with our Scriptures; and whatever they assert in their treatises which is contrary to these Scriptures of ours, that is to Catholic faith, we must either prove it as well as we can to be entirely false, or at all events we must, without the smallest hesitation, believe it to be so." To understand how just is the rule here formulated we must remember, first, that the sacred writers, or to speak more accurately, the Holy Ghost "Who spoke by them, did not intend to teach men these things (that is to say, the essential nature of the things of the visible universe), things in no way profitable to salvation." Hence they did not seek to penetrate the secrets of nature, but rather described and dealt with things in more or less figurative language, or in terms which were commonly used at the time, and which in many instances are in daily use at this day, even by the most eminent men of science.[54]

Galileo's distinction between proven and unproven scientific claims is reflected in Pope Pius XII's *Humani generis* (12 August 1950):

> It remains for Us to speak about those questions which, although they pertain to the positive sciences, are nevertheless more or less connected with the truths of the Christian faith. In fact, not a few insistently demand that the Catholic religion take these sciences into account as much as possible. This certainly would be praiseworthy in the case of clearly proved facts; but caution must be used when there is rather question of hypotheses, having some sort of scientific foundation, in which the doctrine contained in Sacred Scripture or in Tradition is involved. If such conjectural opinions are directly or

---

[54] Claudia Carlen, *The Papal Encyclicals, 1878–1903.* (Wilmington, N.C.: McGrath, 1981), 334–335.

indirectly opposed to the doctrine revealed by God, then the demand that they be recognized can in no way be admitted.[55]

Finally Pope John Paul II, addressing the Pontifical Academy of Sciences on 10 November 1979, was considerably more candid and explicit in stating the Church's view of Galileo:

> The greatness of Galileo is recognized by all, as is that of Einstein; but while today we honor the latter before the College of Cardinals in the apostolic palace, the former had to suffer much — we cannot deny it — from men and organizations within the Church. . . . I hope that theologians, scientists, and historians imbued with a spirit of sincere collaboration, will more deeply examine Galileo's case, and by recognizing the wrongs, from whatever side they may have come, will dispel the mistrust that this affair still raises in many minds, against a fruitful harmony between science and faith, between the Church and the world. . . . Galileo formulated important norms of an epistemological character that are indispensable for reconciling Holy Scripture and science. In his letter to the Dowager Grand Duchess of Tuscany, Christine of Lorraine, he reaffirms the truth of Scripture: "Holy Scripture can never lie, provided its true meaning is understood, which — I do not think it can be denied — is often hidden and very different from what a simple interpretation of the words seem to indicate" (national edition of the works of Galileo, vol. V, p. 315). Galileo introduces a principle of interpretation of the sacred books that goes beyond the literal meaning but is in accord with the intention and type of exposition proper to each of them. It is necessary, as he affirms, that "the wise men who explain it should bring out their true meaning.[56]

The Church's failure in 1615–16 to use its own exegetical inheritance from Augustine, even after having this pointed out by Galileo, can be understood only as an aberration due to the excessively defensive mind-set of the Counter-Reformation. The Principle of Interpretive Authority so strongly focused attention against private interpretation that it overshadowed a much more complex situation. There was no way that the Church would have granted to Galileo what it had denied to Luther. But, of course, this was in no way

---

[55] Claudia Carlen, *The Papal Encyclicals, 1939–1958.* (Wilmington, N.C.: McGrath, 1981), 181.

[56] *Science* 207 (14 March 1980): 1166–1167.

what Galileo was seeking. Ironically he was advocating a return to the tradition of the Church on how to read the Scriptures.

On the other hand modern science was still in its infancy and did not yet fully understand its own epistemology, and especially the strength of its truth claims. Like his Aristotelian contemporaries, but for different reasons, Galileo conceived of natural science as capable of attaining full certitude. This left undemonstrated scientific claims (including heliocentricism at that time) in a sort of epistemological limbo. Bellarmine's advice to consider Copernicanism "hypothetically" meant that its non-reality would be conceded, i.e., one would take it only counterfactually as a convenience for calculations. That Galileo could not accept. On the other hand the modern sense of "hypothesis" as a claim which is probably true in the light of past evidence (and hence likely to be real) and which is thus worthy of further examination, would have been a most helpful model for the goal and nature of science. But it would be an anachronism to say that Galileo took that step. The result was an epistemological framework not really adequate for the issues being raised.

In short the evolving character of *both* the newly born natural sciences and of post-Trent theology, especially regarding biblical exegesis, put the participants in the disputes over Copernicanism in a position from which it was highly unlikely that they could have resolved the issues satisfactorily for both sides. The easy wisdom of hindsight should not blind us to the genuine difficulties of their situation.

4

Foscarini's Bombshell

The early months of 1615 were trying times for Galileo and his circle of friends. The flow of events was not in their favor. Although Lorini's complaint about Copernicanism had been dismissed by the Holy Office, it had the effect of sharpening sensitivities in official Rome to the scriptural orthodoxy of the new astronomy. Along with this came a stiffening of attitudes in the direction of a more literal reading of the Bible and a preservation of its traditional interpretations. Stirrings were beginning to be felt of a new challenge to the Tridentine principles of scriptural interpretation and authority.

In the midst of this unsettled situation there occurred a devastating surprise to all concerned. For Galileo an initial reaction of exhilaration must have been quickly followed by a sense of foreboding. On 7 March Prince Cesi wrote to him from Rome: "I am sending you . . . a book which has just been published, namely, a letter by a Carmelite Father, who defends the opinion of Copernicus by reconciling it with all the passages of Scripture. This book could not have appeared at a better time, unless it be harmful to increase the anger of our adversaries, which I do not believe."[1] Two weeks later, on 21 March, Ciampoli wrote from Rome: "I understand that a booklet has recently been published in Naples which maintains that the opinion of the motion of the earth and the stability of the sun is not contrary to Sacred Scripture and to the Catholic religion. Since the book definitely enters into the Scriptures, as I have said,

---

[1] *Opere* XII, 150.

it runs a great risk of being condemned by the Congregation of the Holy Office, which will meet here in a month."[2]

The long title of this short book was *A Letter concerning the opinion of the Pythagoreans and of Copernicus about the mobility of the earth and the stability of the sun and the new Pythagorean system of the world, to the Most Reverend Father Sebastiano Fantone, General of the Carmelite Order, in which it is shown that that opinion agrees with, and is reconciled with, the passages of Sacred Scripture and theological propositions which are commonly adduced against it.*[3] Its author was Paolo Antonio Foscarini, a native of Montaltro Uffugo in Calabria, about whom surprisingly little is known.[4] He was a Carmelite priest, was trained as a theologian who later served as a professor of theology, was twice appointed as Provincial of the Carmelite Order in Calabria, and was reputed to be a

---

[2] *Opere* XII, 160.

[3] *Lettera sopra l'opinione de' Pittagorici e del Copernico* . . . (Napoli: Lazzaro Scoriggio, 1615) [Hereafter referred to simply as *Lettera*.] The *Lettera* is dated 6 January 1615. The Italian text was reprinted in Fiorenza (1710), in Milano (1811), and in Firènza (1850). The latter is the text used in our translation, and is located in *Opere de Galileo Galilei, prima edizione condotta* . . . ed. by d'Alberi (Firenza, 1842–56), vol. 5, 466–494. It is not merely odd but inexplicable that Favaro did not include Foscarini's *Lettera* in his twenty-volume modern edition *Le Opere di Galileo Galilei* (Florence: 1890–1909), which is probably the major cause of the contemporary neglect of the *Lettera*. A Latin translation of the *Lettera* by David Lotaeus, who abridged brief remarks acknowledging the authority of the pope, was published in Northern Europe after Galileo's trial in *Systema cosmicum di Galileo Galilei*, which appeared in numerous editions between 1636 and 1699. Thomas Salusbury's English translation in his *Mathematical Collections and Translations* (London: Wm. Leybourn, 1661), vol. I, 473–503, was made from the Latin text, and thus contains the same omissions. This English version, in a difficult, archaic, and florid style for the modern reader, is the only other English translation before ours, which is printed in Appendix VI.

[4] Foscarini's birth is given variously in 1565 or in 1580, and his death in 1615 or on 10 June 1616. There is disputed evidence to the effect that Paolo Antonio's original surname was "Scarini," but that he changed it to "Foscarini" in order gainfully to associate himself with the prominent and noble Foscarini family of Venice. For this evidence and both sides of the dispute, see Antonio Favaro, "Serie nona de scampoli galileiana #63: Paolo Antonio Foscarini," in *Accademia Patavina de Science, Lettere, ed Arti, Atti e Memorie* (Padua) 10 (1894): 33–36; and P. Anastase de Saint-Paul, "Paul-Antoine Foscarini," in *Dictionnaire de théologique catholique* (Paris: Letouzey et Ané, 1933), vol. 12, 53–55.

widely learned man, whose knowledge included mathematics and astronomy.[5] From his *Lettera* it is clear that, although he was not technically a professional astronomer, he was rather well informed about recent developments in that field, including the telescopic discoveries of Galileo, for whom he had a great admiration. We have been able to find no information at all as to how or why he decided to write the *Lettera*, which, as Ciampoli had predicted, was destined to be condemned in short order. Although everyone on both sides of the dispute was taken completely by surprise, the reactions were quick and decisive.

SCIENCE AND SCRIPTURE IN THE LETTERA

Foscarini is unmistakably clear about his goals in writing the *Lettera*; namely, he explicitly says in many places, including the title, that he wishes to show that the newly revived heliocentric model of the universe is contrary neither to any of the passages in the Scriptures which seem to say otherwise nor to certain select theological views of his day which also may seem contrary. If he can succeed in establishing this, then, he argues, if heliocentricism is proven to be true at some point in the future, the Church would be in a position to use his reinterpretations to avoid the scandalous impression that there is error in the Bible. In the process of carrying out this project, he of course spends some time in reflecting on his principles of exegesis. But unlike Galileo's writings on the same general topic, Foscarini does not attempt to keep his discussion at this safer meta-level. Rather his primary focus is to deal directly with the relevant passages of Scripture and to undertake their reinterpretation from a heliocentric perspective. Although the main contribution of, and contemporary interest in, Foscarini's *Lettera* was at this level, it thereby was also vulnerable to the charge that it violated the restriction of scriptural interpretation to the institutional Church in its

---

[5] For a general discussion of Foscarini's writings, see Stefano Caroti, "Un sostenitore napoletano della mobilità della terra; il padre Paolo Antonio Foscarini," in *Galileo e Napoli*, A cura di F. Lomonaco et M. Torrini (Napoli: Guida, 1987) 81–121. On the *Lettera*, see R. J. Blackwell, "Foscarini's Defense of Copernicanism," in *Nature and Scientific Method,* ed. Daniel O. Dahlstrom (Washington, D.C.: Catholic University of America Press, forthcoming).

pope and bishops, as the Fourth Session of the Council of Trent was understood in his day. We will argue in more detail later that this was the main reason why the *Lettera* was condemned in the decree of the Congregation of the Index in March 1616.

At the time he wrote the *Lettera* Foscarini was quite aware that he was making a bold and daring move. He explicitly says, "As far as I know, and may it be pleasing to God, I am without doubt the first one to undertake this project."[6] He sees the traditional geocentric view of the universe as thoroughly engrained in the minds of his contemporaries in the form of habits of thought which can be changed only with great effort, so he opens by reviewing the history of the new view to show that it also has an ancient lineage. He points out that modern minds are at least as inventive as the old sages, especially in this case with the recent discoveries about the heavens with the telescope (a clear reference to Galileo, who is mentioned by name a few pages later). He also reminds his readers that the traditional views about the antipodes and the inhabitability of the tropics had already been changed (these same examples had previously been used by Kepler in his Introduction to the *Astronomia nova*, which Foscarini may have read), and that the new model of the universe is neither more strange nor more paradoxical. Approximately twenty percent of the text at the beginning of the *Lettera* is devoted to these softening preliminary moves.

Foscarini also uses his introductory historical survey to present his view that the Copernican theory is at least as probable as the Ptolemaic theory. In fact, in his view, the latter has recently experienced a decrease in its likelihood, and the former an increase, largely due to the observations made by Galileo. It is clear throughout the *Lettera* that, although he professes neutrality,[7] Foscarini's sympathies are with the new heliocentric view, and he concludes by saying, "it is very clear that the opinion of Pythagoras and Copernicus is so probable that it is perhaps more likely than the common

---

[6] Appendix VI, 223.
[7] Appendix VI, 226.

opinion of Ptolemy."[8] But nowhere does he claim that Copernicanism has been proven true.[9] But that *might* happen in the future,
and that eventuality and its consequences are his main reasons "to
undertake this project."

Unfortunately Foscarini is much less clear in his views about the
relation between natural knowledge and revelation. In several places
he gives the impression that the former can never attain certitude
but only some degree of probability; if so, then natural knowledge
should always given way to the superior certitude of revelation when
a conflict arises.[10] Thus he says,

> What is central in this matter is that if something is found to be
> contrary to divine authority, and to the sacred words dictated by the
> Holy Spirit, and to its inspired interpretation by the Sacred Doctors,
> then in that case one ought to abandon not only human reason but also
> sense itself. If all the best conditions and best possible circumstances
> are given, and if something contrary to divine authority is presented
> to us (even if it is so clear that one cannot evade it), one still ought to
> reject it, and judge with certainty that what is presented is a deception
> and that it is not true. For knowledge through faith is more certain
> that any other knowledge which we have from any source or means.[11]

If this passage is taken as decisive, then Foscarini would have to
conclude that no matter what degree of probability could be attained
by human sense and reason, including full certitude ("even if it is so
clear that one cannot evade it"), one must nevertheless reject this
natural knowledge as a deceptive error if it conflicts with Scripture as
traditionally interpreted. Does Foscarini say this to express his own

---

[8] Appendix VI, 247.

[9] Caroti argues ("padre Paolo Antonio Foscarini," 86) that Foscarini likely
became personally convinced of the truth of Copernicanism in about 1614, but he
treats it as only probable in his writings to avoid controversy.

[10] Since Galileo possessed a copy of Foscarini's *Lettera* when he wrote his
Letter to the Grand Duchess Christina, it is possible that he adopted from Foscarini
the idea of the priority of the Bible over science when the latter falls short of
demonstrated truth.

[11] Appendix VI, 220.

real convictions, or to bow to the authority of his religious superiors? At any rate this notion of scriptural hegemony seems to express one side of Foscarini; namely, his role as an obedient theologian.

On the other hand there are numerous passages in the *Lettera* where Foscarini indicates that it is possible for natural knowledge, and specifically an astronomical theory, to attain full certitude; but then in the context of this eventuality he argues for the Augustinian principle that the Bible should be reinterpreted accordingly. The clearest such passage is the following:

> Hence, if the Pythagorean opinion is true, then without doubt God has dictated the words of Sacred Scripture in such a way that they can be given a meaning which agrees with, and is reconciled with, that opinion. This is the motive which has led me (given that that opinion already is clearly probable) to look and search for ways and means to accommodate many passages of Sacred Scripture with it, and to interpret these passages, with the aid of theological and physical principles, in such a way that they are not openly contradictory. As a result, if by chance this opinion should in the future become explicitly established as a certain truth (although now it is taken as only probable), no obstacles would arise which would worry or hinder anyone, and thus unfortunately deprive the world of that venerable and sacred association with truth which is desired by all good people.[12]

If this passage is taken as decisive, then scriptural hegemony should give way to a reinterpretation of the Bible in regard to whatever has been proven to be certainly true in natural knowledge.

Consequently there seems to be an unresolved tension in Foscarini's mind between these two critically different views of the relation between revelation and natural knowledge. In our opinion the second view must have overcome his initial tendency toward theological hegemony, and must have been more dominant in his mind, at least when he wrote the *Lettera*, for otherwise he should have condemned Copernicanism rather than favored it. As a result we disagree with Bruno Basile who argues that Foscarini maintained that no cosmological theory could ever be established as definitely

---

[12] Appendix VI, 222–223.

true.[13] Foscarini's own explicitly stated reason for proceeding with the reinterpretation of Scripture was that if and when Copernicanism were to be established as true, this could produce a scandal for the faithful (since the Bible would thus be shown to contain error) unless the Church were already prepared with new readings of Scripture consistent with heliocentrism. If cosmological systems could in principle never go beyond degrees of probability, such a scandal could never occur, and Foscarini's stated motivation would not have made sense. At any rate it is unfortunate that Foscarini seems to have been of two minds on this central issue. He seems to share Galileo's ambiguity on the status of the truth claims of the natural sciences.

However, when Foscarini moves beyond his introductory material and into the main argument of the *Lettera*, he adopts a quite clear strategy to accomplish his purposes. First he lists six categories of scriptural passages and theological doctrines which contain in his view all the apparent objections against Copernicanism. He then gives six interpretive principles (the two groups of six do not correspond to each other one-to-one) which he argues are adequate to explain away these seemingly contrary biblical passages and theological doctrines. Once this negative phase is completed, i.e., when all the religious objections to Copernicanism have been resolved, the last quarter or so of the treatise is devoted to positive biblical passages and theological doctrines which actively support heliocentricism.

The six groups of objections to Copernicanism consist of scriptural passages and/or theological doctrines which in some way say the following (the fourth and sixth groups are not biblical but theological):

(1) The earth is stationary and does not move.
(2) The sun is moved and rotates around the earth.

---

[13] Bruno Basile, "Galileo e il teologo 'copernicano' Paolo Antonio Foscarini," *Rivista di Letteratura Italiana* 1 (1983): 63–96; esp. pp. 73–76. On the other hand Basile is quite correct in his main thesis; namely, that there was a close and profound relationship between Foscarini and Galileo, although Galileo was forced by prudence to remain silent on this because of the strong negative reaction at the time to Foscarini's *Lettera* and because of its subsequent condemnation.

(3) The heavens are at the top and the earth at the bottom.
(4) Hell is in the center of the earth.
(5) The earth is contrasted to the heavens as a center to a circumference.
(6) After judgment day the sun will stop in the east and the moon in the west.

When Foscarini turns next to his principles of interpretation to account for the above groups of contrary passages, and thus comes to the core of his argument, something rather peculiar happens. Only his first principle is a theological principle of biblical exegesis. The remaining five principles are purely philosophical standards, and are thus principles taken from natural knowledge. But philosophical interpretations of Scripture should be required to satisfy the same standards as scientific interpretations; namely, the Augustinian requirement that any such principles first be established as true with certainty before one procedes to interpret the Bible accordingly. It is rather ironic that Foscarini completely misses this parallel. If one or more of his philosophical principles were to be rejected, which is not difficult to imagine, his argument is seriously weakened. The veteran status of scholastic philosophy as compared to the neophyte status of science in his day may well have been the reason why Foscarini sees no problem with his principles of exegesis.

His one and only theological principle of interpretation is quite traditional and breaks no new ground.

> The first and most important principle is the following. When Sacred Scripture attributes something to God or to any creature which would otherwise be improper and incommensurate, then it should be interpreted and explained in one or more of the following ways. First, it is said to pertain metaphorically and proportionally, or by similitude. Second it is said . . . according to our mode of consideration, apprehension, conception, understanding, knowing, etc. Thirdly, it is said according to the vulgar opinion and the common way of speaking; the Holy Spirit frequently and deliberately adopts the vulgar and common way of speaking. Fourthly, it is said under the guise of some human aspect.[14]

---

[14] Appendix VI, 226–227.

After applying this principle to numerous passages from the Scriptures, including an extended discussion of the six "days" of creation in Genesis 1, Foscarini draws his main conclusion.

> Coming thus to our main point, and using the same argument, if the Pythagorean opinion were true, it would be easy to reconcile it with those passages of Sacred Scripture which are contrary to it, and especially those passages of our first and second groups, by using our principle; that is, by saying that in those places Scripture speaks according to our mode of understanding, and according to appearances, and in respect to us. For thus it is that these bodies appear to be related to us and are described by the common and vulgar mode of human thinking; namely, the earth seems to stand still and to be immobile, and the sun seems to rotate around it.
>
> And hence Scripture serves us by speaking in the vulgar and common manner; for from our point of view it does seem that the earth stands firmly in the center and that the sun revolves around it, rather than the contrary. The same thing happens when people are carried in a small boat on the sea near the shore; to them it seems that the shore moves and is carried backwards, rather than that they move forwards, which is the truth.[15]

The example of the perception of relative motion by observers in a boat departing from the shore, at the end of the above quotation, was picked up by Bellarmine in his reply to Foscarini[16] and by Galileo in his notes on Bellarmine's reply.[17] A few pages later, in a clear reference to the Fourth Session of Trent, Foscarini makes the much more significant point that, "The Church . . . cannot err, in matters of faith and our salvation only. But the Church can err in practical judgments, in philosophical speculations, and in other doctrines which do not involve or pertain to salvation."[18] In his reply to this claim Bellarmine makes a crucial and crippling pronouncement on the meaning of "matters of faith," which in turn provoked a sharp observation from Galileo. Under his first principle of interpretation Foscarini also claims that in the Scripture the Holy Spirit speaks to each person at his own level, and that "God's only intention is to

---

15 Appendix VI, 232.
16 Appendix VIII.
17 Appendix IX, A.
18 Appendix VI, 234–235.

teach us the true road to eternal life."[19] It is then that God will reveal the truths of natural knowledge to us *a priori*, which we now know so imperfectly—one of the several places where Foscarini's hesitation about attaining real truth in natural knowledge makes its appearance. His first principle receives a longer discussion and application than the other five taken together.

These last five philosophical principles[20] are worthy of a quick summary if only to illustrate how completely the mode of argumentation changes. Foscarini's second principle is that God has implanted in all things an immutable law governing their being, nature, and motions. Thus the motions of the earth are stable and fixed in this sense, which is what the Scriptures mean when they say that the earth is immobile! The third principle is that if only a part of a thing moves, it cannot be said to be moved simply and absolutely. For example, if a glass of sea water is moved, the sea itself cannot be said to have moved. So when the earth changes in substance, quality, or quantity, as in the cycle of life and death, it itself is not changed as a whole. Thus the earth is immobile. The fourth principle is that nothing as a whole can be moved from its natural place, although its parts can be so moved violently. Now the natural place of the earth is in the fixed path of the third orbit; so again the earth is immobile, as the Bible says. The fifth is that the earth is a perpetual, not a contingent, creature. Thus its parts cannot be separated from itself as a whole, and hence it is stable and immutable. This is coupled with a long digression on heaviness as due to the natural tendency of parts to unite with their proper wholes, in which Foscarini expresses some pride in his anti-Aristotelianism. The sixth and last principle is that a comparative predicate is properly attributed to a thing when it is related to the whole (or nearly all) of its class. For instance, a person is said to be tall in relation to the average height of all humans, not to just pigmies. Hence the earth is said to be low in

---

[19] Appendix VI, 233.

[20] Caroti ("padre Paulo Antonio Foscarini,"104–107) has shown that these five principles are based on Foscarini's reading of Copernicus's *De revolutionibus*, Book I, esp. chapter 8. It may be significant to note that this same chapter 8 of Copernicus's book was to be abridged *in toto* according to the corrections issued by Rome in 1620 in the aftermath of the condemnation of Copernicanism.

comparison to the whole universe, and not just in relation to a few of the planets. Thus the Scripture properly says that the earth is low because it is rather close to the center even though it is above the sun, Venus, and Mercury. This is also used to explain how Christ could "descend" to earth, and "ascend" into heaven, and the sense in which hell is in the center of the earth.

The last pages of the *Lettera* contain a neo-Platonic description of the sun as a majestic god ruling in the center of the three heavens and an arcane discussion of a whole series of biblical passages which supposedly indicate heliocentricism, including a long analysis of the six-branched candelabra constructed for the Temple in Exodus 25:31–35, which we have met earlier in Sizzi's *Dianoia* as an objection to Galileo's observation of the moons of Jupiter.

But despite the rather disjointed character of the discussion toward the end of the *Lettera*, Foscarini did not lose sight of his main objective, as is clear when he draws his final conclusion.

> From these principles and their delineation it is very clear that the opinion of Pythagoras and Copernicus is so probable that it is perhaps more likely than the common opinion of Ptolemy. For from it one can derive the most precise system, and the hidden constitution, of the world in a way which is much more solidly based on reason and experience than is the common opinion. It is also quite clear that the new opinion can be explained in such a way that there is no longer any need to be concerned whether it is contrary to passages of Sacred Scripture or to the justification of theological propositions.[21]

Galileo must have read the last sentence of the above quotation with a mixture of hope and skepticism. When Foscarini's *Lettera* was published and first debated, Galileo was in the early stages of the writing of his own *Letter to the Grand Duchess Christina*. There is no doubt that the *Lettera* influenced Galileo's thinking in this area, despite the lack of specific documentation due, according to Basile,[22] to the need for Galileo and his friends to avoid association with a document which they correctly expected to be condemned. Of the two letters, Galileo's is the more sophisticated, both in respect to his awareness that a complex set of biblical exegetical principles needs

---

[21] Appendix VI, 247.
[22] Basile, "Galileo e il teologo 'copernicano'."

to be taken into account, and in respect to his greater sense of the historical roots of the theological issues back to St. Augustine. And it is important to note that both authors share an ambiguity, albeit for different reasons, at the heart of their arguments over the attainment of certitude in science. The storm caused by Foscarini's *Lettera* beginning in the spring of 1615 must have contributed to Galileo's decision not to publish his *Letter to the Grand Duchess Christina*. It might be interesting to speculate what would have happened if Foscarini had never written his letter and Galileo had published his. But such speculation would be idle. What we do know is that the publication of Foscarini's *Lettera* provided a near perfect occasion for the churchmen to protect their interests by making a move against Copernicanism without directly confronting Galileo. By the summer of 1615 it was already too late for Galileo's *Letter to the Grand Duchess Christina* to change the course of events.

MATE, CHECKMATE, AND TOBIAS'S DOG

When Ciampoli wrote to Galileo on 21 March 1615 to announce the publication of Foscarini's book, he added that he expected it to be condemned soon by the Holy Office. That prediction may not have been pure speculation. He may have heard that a complaint against the book had already been brought before that body. There is no direct documentary evidence of such a complaint, but it can reasonably be inferred from the fact that there does exist a document giving a theologian's opinion on the orthodoxy of the *Lettera*, which was the usual initial step in response to a complaint. That document,[23] which is the unsigned and undated,[24] was also made known to Foscarini, who quickly wrote a strongly worded

---

[23] Appendix VII, A.

[24] The unidentified theologian's report was probably written sometime during the second half of March. It could not have been written before 6 January (the date of Foscarini's *Lettera*) nor after 12 April (the date of Bellarmine's letter of reply to Foscarini). Foscarini's *Defense*, which is also undated, had to come between the theologian's report and Bellarmine's letter of 12 April. To allow adequate time for the composition of these documents, and in light of the fact that the issue of Foscarini's *Lettera* was of growing interest during March of that year, it seems reasonable to date these documents in late March or very early April at the latest.

Defense[25] of his *Lettera* which replied directly to the unnamed theologian's report.

Sometime later, probably in April, Foscarini sent a copy of his *Defense* and of his original *Lettera* to Cardinal Bellarmine for his evaluations.[26] Bellarmine's return letter, dated 12 April 1615, was a succinct and devastating response directed at the heart of the matter. This letter of Bellarmine, which mentioned Galileo by name, in time became known to Galileo, who prepared a detailed set of private notes on it,[27] apparently for use by Foscarini who later that spring and into the summer was composing a revised and more complete treatise which he hoped would put a final end to the dispute. This last treatise by Foscarini was never published, and no working draft has been found. Meanwhile early that same summer Galileo completed his *Letter to the Grand Duchess Christina*, but did not publish it.

The net result was that Foscarini's original *Lettera* gave rise to a complex series of replies and counter-replies which clearly reveal the state of the question in the spring of 1615. It also brought significant discussion of the substance of the issues involved to an effective, and unfortunate, culmination.

The first document in this series, the unnamed theologian's judgment, is quite disappointing. It seems to have been written by a comparative amateur in both theology and astronomy, and does not do justice to Foscarini's arguments. The first paragraph simply declares that the motion of the earth and the immobility of the sun is a "rash opinion" (which infuriated Foscarini), and is clearly not even probable because it is contrary to the Scriptures. In the midst of disagreeing on the interpretation of a few isolated biblical passages, the theologian states his general conclusion that "his [Foscarini's] reconciliation contorts the Sacred Scriptures, and explains them contrary to the common explication of the Holy Fathers, which agrees with the more common, indeed the most common, and most true opinion

---

[25] Appendix VII, B.

[26] These are the documents which Bellarmine refers to in the first sentence of his letter to Foscarini of 12 April 1615: "I was pleased to read the letter in Italian and the treatise in Latin which Your Reverence sent to me." See Appendix VIII.

[27] Appendix IX, A.

of almost all astronomers."[28] We receive no more analysis than this from an obvious advocate of the reigning point of view. The only point of interest is the last paragraph where the author insists that the Book of Tobit teaches that the heavens are solid and dense, not thin and tenuous: interesting because if Bellarmine read this report, he would have seen a scripturally based rejection of his own life-long conviction that the heavens are fluid.

Foscarini's *Defense*,[29] which long has been overlooked by Galileo scholars, is an energetic and impassioned response to the criticisms in the theologian's report. Its first sentence already shows his irritation, "It is not easy for me to accept the characterization of rashness with which the opinion that the earth moves has been branded . . . ", a tone which permeates the document. In many ways the *Defense* is a more substantive treatise than the original *Lettera*. It is more attentive to the full range of principles of biblical exegesis which are involved; it develops in much more detail the historical roots of these principles in the Catholic tradition; and it is much clearer on the relation between science and religion. It was Foscarini's finest hour in this dispute, and as it turned out, also his last public statement.

He begins by rejecting bluntly the "rashness" charge by showing that none of the senses of that term identified by Cano apply to his *Lettera*. He then confronts at length what is perhaps the central question, "What is the authority of the Fathers of the Church in

---

[28] Appendix VII, A.

[29] It is important to note that there are two different manuscript versions of the *Defensio*. The differences consist in several omissions, made by an unknown person, in the manuscript held at the Biblioteca Corsiniana in Rome, which are clearly designed to soften the force of Foscarini's argument. [This assumes that Caroti ("padre Paolo Antonio Foscarini," 117) is correct in maintaining that the longer manuscript, held at the Archivio Generale dell'Ordine Carmelitano in Rome, is the original text and is not the product of additions.] The shorter version was published by Domenico Berti in his "Antecedenti al processo galileiano e alla condanna della dottrina copernicana," in *Atti della R. Accademia dei Lincei*, 1881–1882, Serie terza, *Memorie della classe di scienze morali, storiche e filologiche*, vol. 10 (Roma; Salvicuci, 1882), 49–96. (Text of the *Defensio* is on pp. 73–78.) The longer version is scheduled to be published by Emanuele Boaga, O. Carm., in *Carmelus* 37 (1990) Fasc. 1 (forthcoming). For a discussion of the two manuscript versions, see Caroti, "padre Paolo Antonio Foscarini," 113–121, and E. Boaga.

this case of heliocentricism?" He answers by insisting on a clear distinction between matters of faith and morals on the one hand and natural knowledge on the other. The motion of the earth and the stability of the sun belong to the latter category. Furthermore it is quite evident that the Fathers concerned themselves with matters of faith and morals, and not with natural knowledge, which some of them even deliberately avoided to devote themselves completely to the word of God. Thus when they happen on occasion to speak on such topics their authority is no greater than what natural human reason itself can attain, as Cano has explained.[30] As a result one not only can, but should, disagree with the opinion of the Fathers on matters of natural knowledge whenever evidence and reason so indicate. This is not scandalous, and in no way detracts from the authority of Scripture or of the Fathers in their proper area of faith and morals. He then adds his critical argument: this is precisely what has been defined by the Church itself at the Council of Trent.

> But this latter restriction [i.e., to matters pertaining to faith and morals] is most correctly stated by the Council of Trent, Session IV, and before that by the Lateran Council, Art. 11, under Leo X, and by many other councils, with the urging and assistance of the Holy Spirit. For all the councils declare that the very words which I introduced above [i.e., the authority of the Holy Fathers prevails] should be understood as referring to matters which pertain to faith and morals.
>
> However in matters which pertain to the natural sciences and which are discovered and are open to investigation by human reason, the Sacred Scriptures ought not to be interpreted otherwise than according to what human reason itself establishes from natural experience and according to what is clear from innumerable data.[31]

---

[30] The third paragraph of Foscarini's *Defense* is an extended quotation from M. Cano's *De locis* VII, 3. This passage is Cano's discussion of the first of his six criteria for determining the types and degrees of the authority of the Fathers of the Church. See chapter 1 for a discussion of these six points.

[31] Appendix VII,B. Immediately after this quotation Foscarini refers to Augustine's *De Genesi ad litteram* I, 18 and 21, for further support. Exactly these same passages are quoted in Galileo's *Letter to the Grand Duchess Christina* and in Pereyra's earlier *Commentary on Genesis*. See footnote 26 in chapter 1.

When he wrote the *Defense* Foscarini must have already planned to send it, with a copy of the *Lettera*, to Bellarmine for his evaluation. The above quotation is in effect a direct request to Bellarmine to make a statement on the *de fide* status of Copernicanism in the light of the Fourth Session of the Council of Trent, a challenge which Bellarmine did not ignore.[32] In the context of this same discussion Foscarini also uses the Augustinian argument of the lack of wisdom in rigidly interpreting the Scriptures in light of a body of natural knowledge which may itself change, thus casting suspicion for some on the truthfulness of the word of God.

> From this it is clear that if the arguments of philosophy and mathematics have established a system contrary to the Ptolemaic system, which has been accepted up to the present, we ought not to affirm emphatically that the sacred writings favor the Ptolemaic system or the Aristotelian opinion, and thus create a crisis for the inviolable and most august sacred writings themselves. Rather we ought to interpret those writings in such a way as to make it clear to all that their truth is in no way contrary to the arguments and experiences of the human sciences (as Pererius says).[33]

The same point is made more eloquently a few pages later:

> In matters pertaining to the sciences acquired by human effort, no one ought to be so addicted to a philosophical sect, or to defend some philosophical opinion with such tenacity, that he thinks that the whole of Sacred Scripture should henceforth be understood accordingly. For otherwise, since something new is always being added to the human sciences, and since many things are seen with the passage of time to be false which previously were thought to be true, it could happen that, when the falsity of a philosophical opinion has been detected, the authority of the Scriptures would be destroyed since that authority has been based on an interpretation which we had thought was true or correct (but nevertheless it was not). Therefore we should not be so tenaciously committed to the philosophy of Aristotle or to Ptolemy's

---

[32] In his letter to Bellarmine accompanying the copies of the *Lettera* and the *Defense*, Foscarini explicitly requested Bellarmine's judgment on the issues involved. For excerpts from this unpublished letter, see Caroti, "padre Paolo Antonio Foscarini," 118–121.

[33] Appendix VII, B. The reference to Pereyra seems to be to his Fourth Rule in his *Commentary on Genesis*, given in chapter 1.

world system that we seem to wish to defend them as we would home and hearth.[34]

At any rate the appeal to the doctrine that *only* "matters pertaining to faith and morals" are to be taken as *de fide* in the Scriptures and in the Fathers is the core of Foscarini's defense. And in making this his central defense, he in effect focused future attention in this dispute primarily on this key point. He adds, moreover, some further remarks regarding his first (and only theological) principle of exegesis in the *Lettera*; namely, that the Holy Spirit speaks in the Scriptures in the language of the common man and is accommodated to the understanding of all. First, he correctly points out that this principle has long been used by all the Fathers and scholastic theologians. Second, he adds the important point that the use of this principle does not abandon the literal sense of the texts. The literal sense is what is signified by the words themselves. But when the words signify both properly and figuratively, the literal sense is the figurative sense. Thus "God's arm" does not mean that God has a physical arm as a bodily part (proper sense) but rather this signifies God's power (figurative sense). In these remarks Foscarini is providing room for the contemporary exegetical view that every sentence in the Scriptures has a literal meaning, and is true when taken in the correct literal sense. When Bellarmine read this part of Foscarini's *Defense*, he could not have failed to recognize this account of literal meaning as identical with his own teaching in his *De controversiis* I, I, 3, 3.[35] Foscarini had decided to play for high stakes in his appeal to Bellarmine, by using the cardinal's own teaching in his defense, along with the ultimate authority of the Council of Trent.

The general lack of attention by Galileo scholars to the content of Foscarini's *Lettera*, and even more so to the text of his *Defense*, has resulted in a failure to appreciate fully the significance of Bellarmine's famous letter to Foscarini of 12 April 1615.[36] It is essential to read this letter of Bellarmine in the context of the two documents by Foscarini which are mentioned in its very first sentence. In fact,

---

[34] Appendix VII, B.

[35] Appendix III.

[36] Appendix VIII.

although Bellarmine's letter has been widely commented upon in the literature, in our judgment its main point has been simply missed.

Bellarmine must have studied Foscarini's documents with considerable care, for each point in his brief letter is of substantive importance. He begins by congratulating Foscarini (and Galileo by name, even though Galileo was not a party to the correspondence) for having "acted prudently in being satisfied with speaking in terms of assumptions [*ex suppositione*] and not absolutely, as I have always believed Copernicus also spoke." In reality this sentence is a piece of almost direct advice masquerading as ironic praise. He must have known that both Foscarini and Galileo actually held the stronger view of the Copernican opinion, that is, that it describes the world as it actually is. The terms of the cardinal's advice are made quite specific. There is "nothing dangerous" in treating Copernicanism as a fiction which happens to be quite useful in calculating celestial motions—and that is all that is needed by astronomers. But it is a "very dangerous thing" to treat that theory as the real structure of the world, because this would be offensive to philosophers and theologians, but much more importantly because it is destructive of religious faith by making out the Scriptures to be false. Bellarmine asserts himself here in his primary responsibility and authority as a cardinal to protect the integrity of the faith from the imputation of error in the word of God. To Foscarini's claim that his *Lettera* has shown how to avoid such falsity by reinterpreting the Scriptures from the heliocentric perspective, Bellarmine replies that his attempts have been only partially successful because many biblical passages remain which do not, and likely cannot, receive such a reinterpretation. Without citing any such passages, Bellarmine in effect states that Foscarini has failed in his primary objective in the *Lettera*.

The second point is even more critical. Bellarmine begins by saying that all are agreed that the Fourth Session of Trent has forbidden the interpretation of Scripture contrary to the common agreement of the Fathers, who in this case all say that the sun rotates around an immobile earth at the center of the universe. He then addresses a rhetorical question to Foscarini. "Ask yourself then how could the Church, in its prudence, support an interpretation of Scripture which is contrary to all the Holy Fathers." Foscarini had, of course, already answered that question in his *Defense* by saying that this applies only to matters of faith and morals. Bellarmine is also ready with his reply to this.

> Nor can one reply that this is not a matter of faith, because even if it is not a matter of faith because of the subject matter [*ex parte objecti*], it is still a matter of faith because of the speaker [*ex parte dicentis*]. Thus anyone who would say that Abraham did not have two sons and Jacob twelve would be just as much of a heretic as someone who would say that Christ was not born of a virgin, for the Holy Spirit has said both of these things through the mouths of the Prophets and the Apostles.

These remarks expand the concept of "matters of faith" considerably by introducing a startling standard of exegesis, which was new to the debate. We will call this the principle of *de dicto* truth. *The mere fact that something has been said in the Scriptures* makes it not only certainly true but a "matter of faith,"[37] assuming that its meaning is clearly established. The subject matter in the biblical statement is irrelevant. If this is granted, Foscarini's *Defense* is demolished. Bellarmine's example leaves no room for doubt about what he is saying. The historical fact that Abraham had two sons and Jacob twelve is just as much a "matter of faith" as the virgin birth of Christ. As a result every statement in Scripture, once its correct literal meaning has been established, is a *de fide* truth. And, of course, the power to determine the correct literal meaning is ultimately located in the Church.

Bellarmine indeed would say that he is in agreement with the words of the Council of Trent when it says that a Catholic is bound to believe the Scriptures as commonly interpreted by the Fathers on matters of faith and morals. Except now "matters of faith" has been expanded beyond its usual restriction to religious issues to include also all historical and empirical matters in the Bible on which there

---

[37] This principle was not a new one in Bellarmine's mind. It will be recalled from chapter 2 that much earlier in the *De controversiis* Bellarmine had raised the question of the truth status of information in the Scriptures of things which do not pertain to the faith. His position then was, "But it is necessary to believe them because they were written, as is evident in all the histories of the old Testament . . . " (*De controversiis* I, I, 4, 12) and, "In the Scriptures not only the opinions expressed but each and every word pertains to the faith. For we believe that not one word is useless or not used correctly" (II, II, 12).

happens to be agreement in the Church or among the Fathers as to
the meaning. And the truth in all such cases (be they of a religious
or non-religious content) is determined by the very fact that *that* is
what God has said. As a result geocentricism has become a "matter
of faith" according to the principle of *de dicto* truth! Foscarini and
Galileo had no possibility of a reply to this pronouncement from the
most powerful cardinal of the day. Checkmate.

Bellarmine has traveled a long way beyond the usual restricted
reading of "matters of faith and morals" in the second decree of the
Fourth Session. And in the absence of evidence as to how he made
that journey, we will not speculate further. But there is a logic to
what he is saying. If there is infallible truth in Scripture on matters
of faith and morals (in the usual restricted sense) as commonly understood by the Fathers, then ultimately this is true *de dicto*, i.e.,
simply because the Holy Spirit has said so in the Scriptures. Further
if every statement in the Bible has a literal meaning which is also
true with the certitude of the word of God, then why not extend
the concept of "matters of faith" as far as we can into historical and
empirical matters in the Scriptures where there is found to be common agreement as to meaning? To do otherwise would be to refuse
to accept from God his surplus gift of invincible truth on various
non-religious matters. At any rate Bellarmine's principle of *de dicto*
truth, by far the most significant, albeit overlooked, point in his letter to Foscarini, resolved the cosmological question in dispute in a
way which Foscarini certainly never expected. In effect all significant discussion on the relation of science and Scripture had ended.
Neither Foscarini nor Galileo published again on this topic.

Bellarmine's third and final point in his letter to Foscarini is a
concession of the Augustinian view about proof in science. If something is demonstrated to be certain in natural knowledge, then and
only then should we procede to reinterpret Scripture accordingly,
or at least to say that we simply do not understand a seemingly
contrary passage. But there is at present no such proof of Copernicanism, as Bellarmine correctly points out. So the *status quo* should
be maintained. This challenge to produce the required proof was not
lost on Galileo. To Galileo's ambivalence in the *Letter to the Grand
Duchess Christina* about how to distinguish between the two classes
of non-demonstrated truths, i.e., those which can and those which

cannot receive a demonstration in the future, Bellarmine proffers a *biblical* criterion. The great wise man Solomon has said that, "The sun rises and sets and returns to his place . . . ", and certainly "it is not likely that he would assert something which was contrary to demonstrated truth or to what could be demonstrated."[38] This will not do for Galileo, but the only sure way to change the situation was to provide a strict proof, as Bellarmine had conceded.

There is one additional document to consider in this story. In time Galileo acquired a copy of Bellarmine's letter to Foscarini, and he jotted down a series of notes about it which have survived. These undated, point-by-point notes on the letter were apparently intended for Foscarini's use in preparing a more extensive treatise on the issues first discussed in his *Lettera*.[39] They also reveal Galileo's state of mind on the controversy in approximately the late spring of 1615. We will comment here only on the two main points vis-à-vis Bellarmine's letter.

First Galileo concedes to Bellarmine that there is no conclusive proof yet of the motion of the earth, and "we do not ask anyone to believe this point without a demonstration. . . . If the proponents were to have no more than ninety percent of the arguments on their side, they would be rebutted." It is clear again that Galileo's model of science includes the old Aristotelian requirement of full certitude. But on the other hand the arguments of those who deny the motion of the earth have largely been shown to be false; so the heliocentric model should not be denigrated or ignored simply because to date it has not been proven. When this is kept in mind, it is easier to understand Galileo's high hopes in January 1616 that the argument for the motion of the earth as the cause of the tides would serve as the needed demonstration.

Second Galileo responded to Bellarmine's crucial principle of *de dicto* truth in the Scriptures,

> It is replied that then everything which is in Scripture is a "matter of faith because of who said it," and thus in this respect ought to be included in the regulations of the council. But this is clearly not the case, because then the Council ought to have said, "The

---

[38] Appendix VIII.
[39] Appendix IX, A.

interpretations of the Fathers must be followed for every word in the Scriptures," rather than "in matters of faith and morals." Thus having said "in matters of faith," it seems that the council's intention was to mean "in matters of faith because of the subject matter." It would be much more a "matter of faith" to hold that Abraham had sons, and that Tobias had a dog, because the Scriptures say so, than to hold that the earth does not move, granting that the latter is found in the Scriptures themselves. The reason why the denial of the former, but not of the latter, would be a heresy is the following. Since there are always men in the world who have two, four, six, or even no sons, and likewise since someone might or might not have dogs, it would be equally credible that someone has sons or dogs and that some-one else does not. Hence there would be no reason or cause for the Holy Spirit to state in such propositions anything other than the truth, since the affirmative and the negative would be equally credible to all men. But this is not the case concerning the mobility of the earth and the stability of the sun, which are propositions far removed from the apprehension of the common man. As a result it has pleased the Holy Spirit to accommodate the words of Sacred Scripture to the capacities of the common man in such matters which do not concern his salvation, even though in nature the fact be otherwise.[40]

These remarks are significant. Galileo correctly points out that on Bellarmine's principle *everything* in the Scripture becomes a matter of faith. If so, then the council would have said this explicitly, but it did not do so. Elsewhere he says, "Let me add that it seems to be abundantly clear that the Council [of Trent] obliges agreement with the common explanation of the Fathers *only* 'in matters of faith and morals, etc.',"[41] i.e., Galileo advocates taking that key phrase in its restricted sense. But it is one thing to say this in private, unpublished notes, and quite a different thing for a layman to dispute this point publicly with the most powerful and learned cardinal of the day. He would not dare to enter the latter arena.

But he could express his irritation privately. On Bellarmine's grounds, belief that Tobias had a dog has become a matter of faith; an example chosen no doubt for its utter insignificance and irrelevance

---

[40] Appendix IX, A.
[41] Appendix IX, B, emphasis added.

to religious concerns.[42] Galileo goes on to develop a mocking and ironic argument to the effect that denying the existence of Tobias's dog would indeed be a heresy, given Bellarmine's principle. For such a purely contingent and obvious matter of fact could be equally true or false, and we must accept on face value whatever the word of the Holy Spirit tells us in such a case. But the mobility or immobility of the earth is far removed from obvious common sense. Hence the denial of the immobility of the earth is not a heresy, for in this case the Holy Spirit has said that the earth moves only to accommodate his words to the common man, even though the fact is otherwise. In short the meaning in the case of Tobias's dog is properly literal, but in the case of the immobility of the earth it is only figurative. As a result Tobias's dog is correctly said to be a matter of faith but the immobility of the earth is not. This mocking reduction to absurdity of Bellarmine's principle of *de dicto* truth vented Galileo's irritation privately but would have been suicidal if stated publicly, as Galileo certainly understood.

Meanwhile Foscarini continued work on his new treatise. As late as 20 June Cesi wrote to Galileo from Rome with great optimism.

> Until the Father [Foscarini] has finished his work, which will be a full and detailed treatise in Latin, the necessary caution will be to remain silent here, by not dealing any more with this opinion, and elsewhere also to treat it very little, so as not to awaken in the meantime the passions of the most powerful Aristotelians. . . . The treatise by the Father will arrive soon, and will be a great help because of the care which he has taken to reply fully to all the objections raised here to the contrary and because of the great number of passages of the Holy Fathers which he will reconcile. I believe that this will be enough permanently to end and settle the matter and to reduce the adversaries to silence.[43]

But Foscarini's new treatise never did arrive in Rome. For unknown reasons it was never published, and no working drafts have been found. At this point Foscarini disappeared from the scene as

---

[42] Tobias's unnamed dog is merely mentioned, and then only twice (Tobit 6:1 and 10:4), in a completely incidental way.

[43] *Opere* XII, 190.

suddenly as he had arrived six months earlier. The *Lettera* was condemned by the Congregation of the Index on 5 March 1616; and
three months later Foscarini died, on 10 June 1616,[44] circumstances
unknown, having "strut and fret his hour upon the stage, and then
was heard no more."

---

[44] This date is not certain; some accounts locate his death in 1615.

5

The Bible at Galileo's Trial

Galileo's trial was an immensely complex affair. To fully understand it one would need to examine the trial and its antecedents at many levels: the scientific, theological, and philosophical issues involved, the legal basis and procedural rules which governed it, the ecclesiastical politics and intrigues behind the scenes, and the personalities of the main actors. It is beyond the scope of this book to take on an examination of all these factors.[1] Rather we will limit ourselves to a discussion of only one of the theological issues involved; namely, the role of the Bible in the proceedings against Galileo.

The situation is further complicated by the fact that there were really two trials, separated by seventeen years, or perhaps better, two quite distinct phases of what was really one and the same trial. The first took place in 1616, and focused on the indictment and judgment of Copernicanism as false and clearly contrary to the Scriptures, with Galileo being involved only indirectly. The second took place in 1633, and focused on Galileo personally over the question of whether he had disobeyed an injunction placed on him individually as part of the proceedings of 1616. This two-phase character of the trial had the effect of neatly separating the conceptual issues regarding the relation of science and the Bible from the question of Galileo's

---

[1] For the documents relating to the 1633 trial, the reader is referred to *Opere*, volume XIX, and to Pagano, *I documenti del processo di Galileo Galilei*. For a convenient English translation of most of these documents, see Finocchiaro, *The Galileo Affair: A Documentary History*. There are numerous over-all discussions of the trial in English: see especially Santillana, *The Crime of Galileo* and Jerome J. Langford, *Galileo, Science, and the Church* (Ann Arbor, Mich.: University of Michigan Press, 1966).

personal responsibility and culpability, a separation which does not appear to have happened accidentally.

THE ORIGIN OF THE CHARGES AGAINST COPERNICANISM

The Catholic Church decided to brand Copernicanism as erroneous in February 1616. The roots of this calamitous decision went back exactly one year, to 7 February 1615, when Lorini initiated the first involvement of the Holy Office with his complaint against the orthodoxy of Galileo's *Letter to Castelli*. Lorini's specific complaint was dismissed, but unfortunately that episode did not end the affair. Tommaso Caccini then went to Rome and met with Cardinal Aracoeli to arrange an appearance before the Holy Office to testify about events which had occurred in Florence. On 19 March Pope Paul V ordered the Holy Office to conduct an interrogation of Caccini because he was "informed about the errors of Galileo, and insists on testifying about them to exonerate his conscience."[2] The interrogation took place the next day in Rome in the great hall of the Holy Office before Fr. Michelangelo Sighizzi, O.P. (1585–1625), the Commissary General of the Roman Inquisition.

As was customary, a scribe, who remains unnamed in this case, prepared a deposition of the substance of the interview, which was then signed by the witness to verify its authenticity. The resulting document is thus not a strictly *verbatim* account of the witness's testimony, but its accuracy on content is quite dependable. A close examination of Caccini's deposition[3] explains a great deal about the condemnation of Copernicanism one year later.

The first topic on which Caccini testified was his sermon against Copernicanism in the Church of Santa Maria Novella in Florence on 20 December 1614. He began by relating that the passage of Scripture under discussion on that Fourth Sunday of Advent was the miracle of God's stopping the motion of the sun at Joshua's request, as related in Joshua 10:12. He then continued:

> In regard to this passage, which I first interpreted in its literal sense and then in its spiritual meaning for the salvation of souls, I

---

[2] Pagano, *I documenti*, 79.
[3] *Opere* XIX, 307–311; Pagano, *I documenti*, 80–85.

took the occasion to reprove, with the modesty proper to the office which I held, a certain opinion maintained and taught, as they say, by Nicholas Copernicus and in our day by the mathematician Sig. Galileo Galilei, and which is very well known in the city of Florence; namely, that *the sun, being according to him the center of the world, is consequently unmoved by progressive local motion, that is, from one place to another.* [Il sole, essendo, secondo lui, centro del mondo, per consequenza e immobile di moto locale progressivo, cioe da un termine all'altro.] And I said that this seemed to be an opinion which was held by the most important writers to be contrary to the Catholic faith, because it contradicts many passages of the divine Scriptures whose literal sense, as determined by the agreement of the Holy Fathers, says and signifies the contrary; for example, the passages of Psalm 18, of Ecclestiastes 1, and of Isaiah 38, in addition to the cited passage of Joshua. And to assure my more intelligent listeners that what I taught did not proceed from my own imagination, I read them the doctrine of Niccolo Serrariò, from his fourteenth question on chapter 10 of Joshua.[4] After saying that this position of Copernicus is contrary to the common judgment of almost all philosophers, of all scholastic theologians, and of all the Holy Fathers, Serrario adds that he does not see how this doctrine could not be heretical because of the scriptural passages indicated above. After making this point I warned that no one is permitted to interpret the divine Scriptures contrary to the sense on which all the Holy Fathers agree, for this has been forbidden both by the Lateran Council under Leo X and by the Council of Trent. [emphasis added]

The import of this testimony is unmistakable. The Fathers of the Church have all interpreted Joshua 10:12, and similar passages, in their proper literal sense, that is, the sun is in motion. Furthermore the Church teaches, specifically at the Council of Trent, Session IV, that one may not interpret Scripture contrary to the common agreement of the Fathers. Therefore Copernicanism is formally heretical, i.e., directly contrary to the explicit word of God. And Galileo is mentioned by name as an advocate of this heresy. Caccini's logic was impeccable.

---

[4] Caccini refers here to N. Serarius, *Josue ab utero ad ipsum usque tumulum* (Maguntiae, 1609–10) II, 235. See our discussion of Serario in chapter 2.

In the above quotation we have emphasized the words of the alleged heresy: "the sun, being according to him the center of the world, is consequently unmoved by progressive local motion, that is, from one place to another." This specific wording, which may have originated from either Caccini or the scribe, is cumbersome, and does not appear to have been spoken by one who was comfortably familiar with Copernicanism. A modified version of this wording was used a year later to state part of the indictment against the heliocentric doctrine.

Caccini then went on to report that although many were pleased with his sermon, some of the disciples of Galileo met later with Caccini's religious superior, Fr. Ferdinando Ximenes, regent of the Church of Santa Maria Novella, to register their complaints. Hearing of this, Caccini reported that he then met with the Inquisitor of Florence, and advised him "that it would be well to put restraints" on these petulant disciples of Galileo, for "Some of them have expressed these three propositions; namely, God is not a substance, but an accident; God is a sensory being because he has divine senses; and the miracles attributed to the Saints are not true miracles." The origin of these three additional allegedly heterodox views is not clear; and they were not attributed directly to Galileo but to some of his followers. Still the intent to embarrass Galileo himself is obvious.

It was only after these events, according to Caccini's deposition, that Lorini showed him a copy of Galileo's *Letter to Castelli* which, seeming unorthodox, was submitted to the Holy Office. Caccini then summarized his testimony up to this point with the following remarks.

> And so I testify to this Holy Office that it is well known that the above-mentioned Galileo holds these two proposition: *the earth moves as a whole, and also with a diurnal motion; the sun is immobile.* [La terra secondo se tutta si muove, *etiam* di moto diurno; Il sole e immobile.] These propositions, according to my conscience and intelligence, are contrary to the divine Scripture as understood by the Holy Fathers, and consequently are contrary to the faith, which teaches us that we ought to believe as true whatever is contained in the Scriptures. [emphasis added]

Again, the emphasized words in this quotation, introduced by either Caccini or the scribe to state the suspect views, will be used a year later in a slightly modified form as part of the indictment against Copernicanism.

At this point in the proceedings Caccini was asked how he knew that Galileo held and taught that the sun is immobile and that the earth moves. His reply was that, in addition to this being public knowledge, he had heard this specifically from Filippo de' Bardi, the Bishop of Cortona, and from Giannozzo Attavanti (c. 1580–1657), a parish priest in Florence, the latter in conversations the previous summer in Fr. Ximenes's room. Caccini then added the critically important remark, "I have also read this doctrine in a book dealing with sunspots which was published in Rome under the name of Galileo, which Fr. Ximenes gave to me."

Although Caccini gave no specific passage as a reference, the *Letters on Sunspots* was indeed the first published work in which Galileo explicitly adopted Copernicanism. This book of Galileo's does not contain the wording emphasized in the above quotations from Caccini's deposition which designated the alleged heresies; so the peculiar wording again seems to be Caccini's or the scribe's. However the heliocentric position was certainly there for Caccini to see. Perhaps he had in mind the following passage from early in the first letter, as Galileo interprets the newly observed phases of Venus.

> These things leave no room for doubt about the orbit of Venus. With absolute necessity we shall conclude, in agreement with the theories of the Pythagoreans and of Copernicus, that Venus revolves about the sun just as do all the other planets.[5]

Or perhaps Caccini was thinking of the commitment to Copernicanism at the end of the third letter.

> And perhaps this planet also [Saturn], no less than horned Venus, harmonizes admirably with the great Copernican system, to the universal revelation of which doctrine propitious breezes are now seen to be directed toward us, leaving little fear of clouds or crosswinds.[6]

---

[5] Drake, *Discoveries and Opinions of Galileo*, 93–94.
[6] Ibid., 144.

Whatever specific passages Caccini may have had in mind, the net effect was the same; namely, that Galileo was suspect of heresy, not only in his privately stated views but also in his published writings.

Later in the interrogation Caccini was asked about Galileo's reputation in Florence as a Catholic. His answer was truly cruel. "Galileo is held by many to be a good Catholic, but others hold him to be suspect in matters of the faith, because they say that he is very intimate with the Servite Fr. Paolo [Sarpi], who is so famous in Venice for his impiety, and they say that even now letters still pass between them." Guilt by association, a sometimes effective ploy. Paolo Sarpi (1552–1623) was the most vigorous critic of the Council of Trent in the Catholic world,[7] and in 1606, as the state theologian in Venice, had bitterly opposed Pope Paul V, and especially Cardinal Bellarmine, who had placed Venice under interdict for the expulsion of the Jesuits from Venetian territory.

All of this evidence in Caccini's deposition makes it clear that he not only questioned Copernicanism as heretical, but also that he attempted to associate Galileo in his person and in his writings as closely as he could with this heterodox position. If successful, this strategy would mean that a condemnation of heliocentricism would also bring down Galileo personally.

Whatever its many faults, the Inquisition was careful and thorough in its methods. As a result, then as now, the wheels of the court system turned slowly. Caccini's deposition required verification, and leads had to be investigated further. The obvious first step was to obtain testimony from Ferdinando Ximenes about Caccini's deposition. But Ximenes had left Florence for Milan at the end of March, and later went to Bologna, as revealed by a complex set of letters from Rome to the Inquisitors in these cities,[8] which failed to secure the needed interrogation. These delays continued up to the middle of November, when Ximenes was finally interviewed in Florence on the thirteenth of that month, and Attavanti on the fourteenth.

---

[7] This reputation was based primarily on Paolo Sarpi's extensive *Istoria del Concilio Tridentino*, which he did not complete until 1616, and which was first published in Northern Europe in 1619, when it was immediately placed on the *Index*.

[8] Pagano, *I documenti*, 87–92.

Ximenes's deposition verified in general what Caccini had told the Holy Office eight months earlier, but also somewhat softened it.[9] He said that he knew that either Galileo or some of his disciples (he was not sure whose opinion it was) had said that the earth moves and the heavens are immobile; that God is an accident and that all things are discrete quantities composed of vacua; that God is a sensory being who laughs and cries. He did not remember them saying that the miracles ascribed to the saints are not true miracles. When asked how he knew this, he mentioned that his source was Giannozzo Attavanti, who many times the previous year had discussed these ideas with him in his room "disputationis gratia" [for the sake of argumentation], and that Attavanti, who was not much of a scholar, was expressing the opinion of Galileo. Ximenes then added that he had immediately warned Attavanti that these ideas were false and heretical, for "the truth is that the earth as a whole is immobile and founded on its own stability, as the prophet says, and that the heavens and the sun move." He ended by saying that he had never seen Galileo, but that his teaching was displeasing "because it does not conform to the orthodox Fathers of the Holy Church, and so is contrary to the truth."

The deposition given the next day by Attavanti, who was a naively innocent bystander in the affair, had the effect of making matters worse. He said that he was not one of Galileo's students, but that he had had conversations with him on literary and especially philosophical matters. When asked whether any of Galileo's views were opposed to the faith, he replied,

> I have never heard Sig. Galileo say anything contrary to Sacred Scripture or to our holy Catholic faith. But in regard to philosophical and mathematical matters, I have heard him say, according to the doctrine of Copernicus, that the earth moves in its center or in its globe, and that the sun also moves around its own center, but does not move forward progressively, according to his writings published in Rome under the title of *On Sunspots*.[10]

This second reference in the records of the Holy Office to the Copernicanism of Galileo's *Letters on Sunspots* must have focused

---

[9] *Opere* XIX, 316–318; Pagano, *I documenti*, 93–95.
[10] *Opere* XIX, 318–20; Pagano, *I documenti*, 95–98.

the attention of the Inquisitors on this point where Galileo was vulnerable. Eleven days after Attavanti's testimony, some unidentified official added this ominous note, dated 25 November 1615, at the bottom of the deposition: "See the writings of Galileo published in Rome with the title *On Sunspots*."[11]

The remainder of Attavanti's testimony dealt with the other charges previously mentioned (God is an accident, and is a sensory being). He asserted that he and Ximenes had debated these views for the sake of the argument; but they were interrupted on several occasions by Caccini, whose room was nearby, who warned of heresy, and who said that he planned to preach against Copernicanism.

There apparently are no further documents relevant to the Galileo case in the records of the Holy Office between 25 November and the following February. So we must, in effect, use the three depositions (by Caccini, Ximenes, and Attavanti) to throw whatever light is possible on the propositions formulated in Italian on 19 February 1616 for judgment by the Consultors of the Holy Office. These propositions were:

(1) That the sun is the center of the world, and consequently is immobile of local motion. [Che il sole sii centro del mondo, et per consequenza immobile di moto locale.]

(2) That the earth is not the center of the world nor is it immobile, but it moves as a whole and also with a diurnal motion. [Che le terra non e centro del mondo ne immobile, ma si muove secondo se tutta, *etiam* di moto diurno.][12]

The primary question before the eleven consultors (who functioned as theological experts for the Holy Office) was whether either of these statements was contrary to the faith. The statements were to be considered separately. The first thing to be noted is the strong similarity in the Italian wording between these two propositions and the words we have emphasized in the quotations given earlier from Caccini's deposition. It seems to be virtually certain that whoever in the Holy Office composed these two propositions made explicit and direct use of Caccini's testimony, even though no reference is

---

[11] Pagano, *I documenti*, 98.
[12] *Opere* XIX, 320–321; Pagano, *I documenti*, 99–100.

made to his deposition. The cumbersomeness of the wording of the final charges, on which many scholars have commented, was due to their having originated from either Caccini or his scribe, who were not trained in astronomy. Given the gravity of the decision at hand, one would have hoped that a more authentic source had been used. At any rate the powerful impact of Caccini's testimony cannot be denied.

Second, the propositions to be judged were purely astronomical in character. All three of the depositions had also mentioned other suspect views of a theological character (i.e., God is an accident; God is a sensory being; and the miracles of the saints are not true miracles), but all this was dropped. This does not mean that the Holy Office would not have been concerned with these theological views. Rather it illustrates that at the time the evidence relating to these other charges must have been considered insignificant, and that the overwhelming concerns of the cardinals in the Holy Office were cosmological. It also meant that the decision would directly pit religious authority against natural scientific knowledge without qualifying or softening conditions.

Third, it should be noted that neither Copernicus nor Galileo nor any of their writings were mentioned in the statements to be judged. The conceptual issues of astronomy were completely separated from the persons and the publications associated with them. The consultors were asked to judge only the former. Copernicus, Galileo, and their writings were to be dealt with separately.

The issue thus was whether or not each proposition, taken in isolation and at face value, was contrary to the faith.

THE VERDICT AND THE DECREE

Four days later, on 23 February, the consultors met and reached a unanimous decision, which was then communicated to the Holy Office the next day in a brief report in Latin. It may seem that the consultors acted too quickly—only four days for research and deliberation on such a fateful issue—but that is not really true. The question had been under discussion at length for a full year in Church circles, and little, if anything, new was left to be said. Langford lays blame for the decision primarily on the consultors,[13] but their decision was virtually automatic, given the contemporary literalism in biblical exegesis which we have seen. There was little room at that time for advocating new metaphorical readings of Scripture. Moreover the cardinals constituting the Holy Office could have rejected the judgment of the consultors if they wished, but they did not. Instead they accepted the following recommended censures.

(1) The sun is the center of the world, and is completely immobile by local motion.

Censure: All agreed that this proposition is foolish and absurd in philosophy and is formally heretical, because it explicitly contradicts sentences found in many places in Sacred Scripture according to the proper meaning of the words and according to the common interpretation and understanding of the Holy Fathers and of learned theologians.

(2) The earth is not the center of the world and is not immobile, but moves as a whole and also with a diurnal motion.

Censure: All agreed that this proposition receives the same censure in philosophy; and in respect to theological truth, it is at least erroneous in faith.[14]

The wording of the censured propositions, now given in Latin, is a literal rendition of the Italian texts discussed earlier. Each of the propositions is first evaluated philosophically, and each receives the same judgment of being "foolish and absurd." The philosophical standards used here are not mentioned, but obviously were those of the scholasticized Aristotelianism of the day. Its built-in geocentricism had to be in conflict with Copernicanism; so given these standards, the consultors made the "correct" and predictable decision. More significant is the ease with which an ecclesiastical body passed judgment on philosophical grounds, showing no concern that that philosophy might itself be erroneous, even though at the time this very philosophy was coming under question.

Much more importantly, each proposition also received a theological censure, albeit of a different character. The first proposition

---

[13] Langford, *Galileo, Science, and the Church*, 90
[14] *Opere* XIX, 320–321; Pagano, *I documenti*, 99–100.

was declared to be "formally heretical," and the reason is spelled out explicitly. It directly contradicts the word of God in the Scriptures as found in its literal meaning and as commonly understood in the Church. The specific passages so contradicted are not mentioned, but this was unnecessary because they were so well known from the prior years of dispute. Again, given the extremely literalistic principles of exegesis of the times, the consultors chose to criticize Copernicanism, not their own exegetical principles; and as a result they made the "correct" and predictable decision, even though they were disastrously wrong. There is no way of knowing whether the consultors made use of what we have called Bellarmine's principle of *de dicto* truth in Scripture; but if they did, they would have been even less open to judge in favor of the propositions they were considering. It is likely that they considered the first proposition as a simple "open and shut" case.

The charge of formal heresy applied to the first proposition was the strongest category of ecclesiastical censure. We might recall from chapter 1 that the first of Melchior Cano's rules for the identification of the content of faith was that "in cases where the meaning is clear and plain, . . . then Scripture itself is the standard, . . . while if the meaning is obscure, then the true meaning of Scripture is the meaning of the Church." Thus heliocentricism in its literal sense (i.e., the sun is in the center of the universe) was hit with the heaviest possible blow.

The second proposition received the considerably weaker theological censure of being "at least erroneous in faith." This means that no explicit statements are to be found in the Scriptures which directly contradict the claim that the earth is not in the center of the universe and that it moves with both an annual and a diurnal motion. But one can *infer* that the latter claim is false by using premises from Scripture and/or commonly accepted theological doctrines. This is a use of the last and second last categories on Cano's list of rules for the identification of matters of faith, where he defines a "theological conclusion" as "what is deduced by a certain and firm inference from the principles of this science."[15] The specific inference(s) used by the consultors to draw the theological conclusion that the earth does

---

[15] See our discussion of Cano's rules in chapter 1.

not move is (are) not given. The general idea is clear enough, but we will not attempt to reconstruct this inference since it could conceivably have been done in quite a few different ways, depending on what scriptural passages and/or theological doctrines were employed as premises, including the logical opposite of the first proposition just censured.

The acceptance of this double censure recommended by the consultors had the clear effect of identifying Copernicanism as contrary to the faith. The verdict was unequivocal. All the proceedings up to this point had been held in secrecy. The only remaining legal transaction was to publish the above verdict publicly. This was done by a Decree from the Congregation of the Index, dated 5 March 1616. The relevant section of this Decree reads as follows:

> It has come to the attention of this Sacred Congregation that the Pythagorean doctrine of the mobility of the earth and the immobility of the sun, which is false and completely contrary to the divine Scriptures, and which is taught by Nicholas Copernicus in his *De revolutionibus orbium coelestium* and by Diego de Zuñiga in his *Commentary on Job*, is now being divulged and accepted by many. This can be seen from the letter published by a Carmelite priest, entitled *Letter of Fr. Paolo Antonio Foscarini on the Opinion of the Pythagoreans and of Copernicus on the Mobility of the Earth and the Stability of the Sun and on the New Pythagorean System of the World*, Naples: Lazzaro Scoriggio, 1615. In this letter the said Father tries to show that the above-mentioned doctrine of the immobility of the sun in the center of the world and of the mobility of the earth is both in agreement with the truth and is not contrary to Sacred Scripture. Therefore, lest this opinion spread further and endanger Catholic truth, it is ordered that the said Nicholas Copernicus's *De revolutionibus orbium* and Diego de Zuñiga's *Commentary on Job* are suspended until corrected; also that the book of the Carmelite Father Paolo Antonio Foscarini is completely prohibited and condemned; and also that all other books teaching the same thing are prohibited, as the present Decree prohibits, condemns, and suspends them all respectively.[16]

---

[16] *Opere* XIX, 322–323; Pagano, *I documenti*, 102–103. It is possible, but in our opinion rather unlikely, that Tommaso Campanella's (1568–1639) elaborately

The first sentence of the portion of the Decree quoted above announced publicly for the first time the prior decision of the Holy Office that Copernicanism is false because it contradicts the Scriptures. The document had the primary effect of placing the three books mentioned on the *Index of Forbidden Books*. The primary offender was Foscarini's *Lettera*,[17] which not only advocated the condemned doctrine but dared to proceed to an actual reinterpretation of Scripture accordingly (an undertaking which the Fourth Session of Trent had reserved to the pope and the bishops). There were no saving graces here, and the *Lettera* was condemned *in toto* and without any qualifications or hope of emendations. A much lesser condemnation was meted out to Copernicus's *De revolutionibus* and Diego de Zuñiga's *Commentary on Job*; namely, suspension until corrected. For the latter this amounted only to eliminating the few pages of the commentary on the passage at Job 9:6.[18] The corrections for Copernicus's book, not announced until four years later,[19] consisted of (1) omitting a disrespectful comment about Lactantius in the Dedicatory Preface, (2) dropping isolated assertions that the

---

argued plea for a reconciliation between the Bible and Copernicanism had an influence on the deliberations leading up to this Decree. His *Apologia pro Galilaeo mathematico florentino* was first published in Frankfurt in 1622. The date of its composition is unknown, and there is considerable dispute among scholars as to whether it was written before or after the condemnation of Copernicanism in this 5 March 1616 Decree. Campanella wrote his *Apologia* in response to a specific request from Cardinal Boniface Caetani for an evaluation of the new astronomy in relation to the Scriptures. Cardinal Caetani was the curial official charged with formulating the needed corrections to Copernicus's *De revolutionibus* mentioned in the Decree. On this, see Bernardino M. Bonasea, "Campanella's Defense of Galileo," in *Reinterpreting Galileo*, ed. William A. Wallace (Washington, D.C.: Catholic University of America Press, 1986), 205–239, and James R. Langford, "Science, Theology, and Freedom: A New Look at the Galileo Case," in *On Freedom* ed. Leroy S. Rouner (Notre Dame, Ind.: University of Notre Dame Press, 1989), 108–125.

  17 Appendix VI.

  18 Appendix II.

  19 *Monitum Sacrae Congregationis ad Nicolai Copernici lectorem* (1620). *Opere* XIX, 400–401. English translation in Finocchiaro, *The Galileo Affair*, 200–202. Owen Gingerich has recently published, with commentary, a little-known document in the Vatican Library (Codex Barberiniano XXXIX.55), probably written by Cardinal Caetani, which served as a working document for the Congregation of the Index in its preparation of the *Monitum*, and which throws considerable light

earth moves, and (3) eliminating the whole of Book I, Chapter 8, which is devoted to refuting the accumulated Aristotelian-Ptolemaic arguments for an earth at rest in the center of the universe. The drastically sharper sanction against Foscarini as compared to Copernicus also shows that the integrity of Scripture was the ultimate concern of the Holy Office, and that the scientific theory was objectionable because of its impact in that direction.

No mention was made in the Decree of Galileo or any of his writings. But he could hardly have missed the message. The pointedly harsh treatment of Foscarini made it permanently impossible for Galileo to publish his own *Letter to the Grand Duchess Christina*. For those of us who, unlike Galileo, have read the three depositions leading up to the decision and the Decree, the condemnation of "all other books teaching the same thing" clearly would have included Galileo's *Letters on Sunspots*. But Galileo must have been able to infer this on his own. Was it the case that, given Galileo's international reputation as a scientist, the Holy Office decided that it could not diplomatically afford to risk making him a martyr by including him or his writings in the Decree? The interests of the Church always came first. But they could make the implication abundantly obvious, which they did. By contrast, Foscarini's relative obscurity and clerical status made him the perfect instrument for the Holy Office to assert its authority with less risk to the Church. Too bad that they apparently were unable to see the devastating impact of their actions beyond their Roman world and beyond their own small place in time.

But these remarks towards clarification of the Decree are far from adequate. Nagging questions remain. Why did the Church not simply end the matter here without anything further involving Galileo? He clearly would have recognized that the Decree applied

---

on the significance of the "corrections" announced in 1620. See his "The Censorship of Copernicus' *De revolutionibus*," *Annali dell'Instituto e Museo di Storia della Scienza di Firenza* 6 (1981) Fasc. 2: 45–61. Gingerich's interesting map showing the European distribution of censored copies of Copernicus's *De revolutionibus* and the relatively minimal effect outside of Italy of the 5 March 1616 Decree of the Congregation of the Index, is reprinted on p. 135 of his "The Galileo Affair," *Scientific American* 247 (no. 2) (August 1982): 132–143.

to anything he might write in the future on the topic. And if some specific inclusion of Galileo was thought in order, then why not treat him in the same way that Copernicus had been treated? The Church could have easily placed the *Letters on Sunspots* on the *Index* "until corrected," and the corrections would have been few and easy to identify. They must have thought of this, because it was indirectly suggested twice in the depositions. But that was not what happened. Instead it was decided, apparently at the highest level, to separate the person of Galileo from the doctrine of Copernicus. It was determined that Galileo's loyalty and obedience were to be tested.

THE ORDER TO OBEY

Except for the Decree of 5 March, Galileo, of course, would not have known anything firsthand about the interrogations and documents discussed earlier in this chapter. They were all secret proceedings of the Holy Office. But he may well have been suspicious that things were going against his interests because, contrary to the advice of the Tuscan ambassador at Rome and of several friends, Galileo went to Rome in December 1615 specifically to argue his case. Had he somehow heard that his *Letters on Sunspots* had been denounced just a few weeks earlier by Attavanti?

Galileo's main maneuver at the time was to try to formulate a definitive proof of heliocentricism. To that end he wrote out in January 1616 a first version of his hopefully conclusive (but defective) argument to explain the tides by the double motion of the earth,[20] which was later to become the foundation of the Fourth Day of the *Dialogue*. He managed to persuade the young Cardinal Alessandro Orsini (1593–1626) to present this document to Pope Paul V in the hope of winning the pope's support. This maneuver had exactly the opposite effect; yet as late as early February Galileo was still optimistic.

On 25 February, the day after the consultors submitted their censures of the two suspect propositions, the results were reported to

---

[20] *Discorso sopra il flusso e reflusso del mare* (1616), in *Opere* V, 377–395. English translation in Finocchiaro, *The Galileo Affair*, 119–133.

the pope, who immediately ordered Cardinal Bellarmine to arrange a private meeting with Galileo on the issue of Copernicanism. His instructions to Bellarmine were quite specific.

> The Most Holy has ordered the illustrious Cardinal Bellarmine to call before him the said Galileo and to advise him to abandon the said opinion; and if he should refuse to obey, the Commissary, before a notary and witnesses, should impose upon him an injunction to abstain completely from teaching or defending that doctrine and opinion or from discussing it; and if he should not agree, he is to be imprisoned.[21]

The pope's instructions to Bellarmine were very explicit. He envisioned three successive steps. First Bellarmine was to inform Galileo of the condemnation of heliocentricism by the Holy Office and to ask Galileo to drop his commitment to that position. If Galileo agreed to obey, the meeting was to be concluded. Second, if he refused to obey, then the Commissary General was to place Galileo under an injunction to obey. If Galileo accepted the injunction agreeably, then the meeting would be over, with Galileo restrained by the injunction. Third, if Galileo opposed the injunction, he was to be imprisoned.

The meeting between Bellarmine and Galileo took place the next day at the cardinal's residence. The Commissary General mentioned in the pope's instructions and also present at the meeting was Michaelangelo Seghizzi, O.P., the same official who had presided at Caccini's deposition one year earlier.

What happened at that meeting? Did Galileo agree to abandon Copernicanism in light of the Church's condemnation when initially asked to do so? If so, the meeting should have ended at that point. Or did Galileo object and refuse to obey? If so, Galileo should have been placed under an injunction. Did that happen? If so, who issued the injunction, Seghizzi or Bellarmine? Was the injunction served legally? What were the specific orders contained in the injunction placed on Galileo?

---

[21] *Opere* XIX, 321; Pagano, *I documenti*, 100–101.

We do not know the answers to these questions. The meeting certainly took place; and we also know that the order of imprisonment in step three of Pope Paul's instructions was not given. However it is significant to note that even at this early stage the pope had envisioned the possibility of imprisoning Galileo, and he must have been prepared to carry out such a drastic action. Galileo's obedience was a serious matter.

The reason for our lack of knowledge of precisely what happened is that the two surviving documents summarizing the meeting are flatly inconsistent with each other. Furthermore one of the documents is ambiguous at the critical point of delineating what happened just after Bellarmine's initial request of Galileo.

These documents originated as follows. In the next two months after the meeting the rumor mills of Rome carried the report that Galileo had abjured his opinion and that he had been censured and punished. To clear his reputation Galileo very prudently asked Bellarmine for his help in the form of a letter to certify what had happened at the meeting. Bellarmine had no hesitations in supplying Galileo with the following letter:

> We, Robert Cardinal Bellarmine, hearing that it has been calumniously rumored that Galileo Galilei has abjured in our hands and also has been given a salutary penance, and being requested to state the truth with regard to this, declare that this man Galileo has not abjured, either in our hands or in the hands of any other person here in Rome, or anywhere else as far as we know, any opinion or doctrine which he has held; nor has any salutary or any other kind of penance been given to him. Only the declaration made by the Holy Father and published by the Sacred Congregation of the Index has been revealed to him, which states that the doctrine of Copernicus, that the earth moves around the sun and that the sun is stationary in the center of the universe and does not move east to west, is contrary to Holy Scripture and therefore cannot be defended or held. In witness whereof we have written and signed this letter with our hand on this twenty-sixth day of May, 1616.[22]

---

[22] *Opere* XIX, 348; Pagano, *I documenti*, 138. Translation is from Langford, *Galileo, Science, and the Church*, 102–103. For a photo reproduction of the autograph of this letter, see Baldini and Coyne, *The Louvain Lectures*. Changes made

Meanwhile another account of the meeting, a memorandum written apparently by an unnamed scribe in attendance at the session, was placed in the file of the Holy Office. This document,[23] which is irregular in some significant ways, reads as follows:

> At the Palace, the usual residence of the aforenamed Cardinal Bellarmine, the said Galileo, having been summoned and standing before His Lordship, was, in the presence of the Very Reverend Father Michael Angelo Seghiti de Lauda, of the Order of Preachers, Commissary-General of the Holy Office, admonished by the Cardinal of the error of the aforesaid opinion and that he should abandon it; and later on—*successive ac incontinenti*—in the presence of myself, other witnesses, and the Lord Cardinal, who was still present, the said Commissary did enjoin upon the said Galileo, there present, and did order him (in his own name), the name of His Holiness the Pope, and that of the Congregation of the Holy Office, to relinquish altogether the said opinion, namely, that the sun is in the center of the universe and immobile, and that the earth moves; nor henceforth to hold, teach, or defend it in any way, either verbally or in writing. Otherwise proceedings would be taken against him by the Holy Office. The said Galileo acquiesced in this ruling and promised to obey it.[24]

The ambiguity in the documents referred to above resides in the words "successive ac incontinenti," which Langford translates as "and later on."[25] This phrase, which has been interpreted in many

---

by Bellarmine in this autograph reveal that he revised the original version to make the letter more protective for Galileo.

[23] It seems that there are almost as many speculative reconstructions of the meeting described in this document are there are Galileo scholars. It has even been argued, although it is not now generally accepted, that this document is a later forgery designed to entrap Galileo and that the meeting it describes did not actually take place. For access to this literature, see Langford, *Galileo, Science, and the Church*, 93–97; Santillana, *The Crime of Galileo*, 125–131; L. Geymonat, *Galileo Galilei*, trans. S. Drake (New York: McGraw-Hill, 1965), esp. Drake's "The Galileo-Bellarmine Meeting: A Historical Speculation," 205–220; and Morpurgo-Tagliabue, *I processi di Galileo*, 19–27.

[24] *Opere* XIX, 321–322; Pagano, *I documenti*, 101–102. Translation is from Langford, *Galileo, Science, and the Church*, 92.

[25] For example, Finocchiaro (*The Galileo Affair*, 147) translates this as "And therefore, indeed immediately"; Joseph Clark, S.J., has translated it as "and over,

ways, introduces the critical discussion of what happened after Bellarmine had carried out stage one of the pope's instructions.

But of much greater importance is the inconsistency between the two documents. Bellarmine's certificate states that Copernicanism "cannot be defended or held." Galileo reasonably took this to mean "defended as true" and "held to be true," which would still allow discussion of the arguments pro and con. However the memorandum at the Holy Office contained the much stronger wording, "nor henceforth to hold, *teach*, or defend it *in any way, either verbally or in writing*." The added, emphasized words ruled out any and all discussion of the topic rather unequivocally.

Assuming that the injunction placed on Galileo was issued legally, which of the above did it order? No one knows. Unfortunately the crux of the trial in 1633 turned precisely on this point. And the one man whose mere word would have conclusively settled the issue at the trial, Cardinal Bellarmine, had died in 1621. The crucial development in many ways was the original decision made in 1616 which led to all this; namely, the decision to put Galileo to an explicit test of obedience to the Decree of 5 March, rather than simply to include his *Letters on Sunspots* for correction in that Decree, or better yet, to let Galileo read it on his own and infer its unavoidable application to his own work. Unfortunately in conducting the private session with Galileo, an ambiguous and dangerous situation was created which was to haunt all concerned for years to come.

THE BIBLE IN THE COURTROOM

Galileo, of course, had no way of knowing about the memorandum in the secret files of the Holy Office. For him Bellarmine's certificate defined the practical ground rules of what was and was not permitted under the Decree of 1616. Even at that, however, he did not broach the topic of Copernicanism for the next eight years.

Then the scene changed significantly for the better. In 1623 Galileo's acquaintance and admirer, Maffeo Cardinal Barberini of Florence, was elected pope and took the name of Urban VIII. The

---

and over, and over again, and since the aforesaid Galileo was uncontrollably voluble on the matter . . . " (see Langford, *Galileo, Science, and the Church*, 96n).

new pope was a well-educated man of letters and friend of artists and intellectuals. Encouraged by this development, Galileo journeyed to Rome, where he was warmly welcomed, and where he engaged in six long conversations with Urban VIII, who was comfortable with him taking up the topic of Copernicanism again, albeit hypothetically. The pope himself thought that such matters could never be demonstratively settled, since there are no restrictions on the power of God to create whatever kind of world that he might choose to create.

Galileo returned to Florence with the confidence and resolve to undertake his postponed book on the structure of the world. This project consumed the next eight years of his life, interspersed with many delays due to his chronic ill health and to protracted negotiations with the printers and with the censors for required permissions. Finally in February 1632 the book was published in Florence, with ecclesiastical permissions from the censors in both Rome and Florence. It was Galileo's masterpiece, his *Dialogue Concerning the Two Chief World Systems, Ptolemaic and Copernican.*

The book caused an immediate storm of protests over everything from personal effrontery to serious charges of religious heterodoxy. The latter were due mostly to the fact that the Copernican side clearly seems to win the argument among the interlocutors of the *Dialogue*, despite the author's claims to a balanced neutrality. Sales of the book were stopped, and copies confiscated, by the summer of 1632.

In September a Special Commission appointed by Urban VIII to look into the matter discovered the 1616 memorandum in the files of the Holy Office. Even the pope was surprised. A trial became unavoidable. For the publication of Galileo's book had rather clearly violated the injunction not "to hold, teach, or defend it in any way, either verbally or in writing." Various delays pushed the trial into the spring of 1633. The proceedings started on 12 April, and ended on 22 June.

Since Galileo's trial was an immensely complex affair, we intend to look only at the role of the Bible in the proceedings. Regarding the events in the first phase of the trial in 1615–16, there is no doubt that the Bible is located at center stage. But when one studies the documents of the 1633 phase of the trial, one finds something unexpected. There is rather little mention of the Scriptures, and then almost always in the context of pointing out that the 1616 Decree had declared Copernicanism to be contrary to the Bible.

In these trial documents one finds little or no mention of the levels of meaning and truth value of the Scriptures, no use of the distinction between literal and figurative passages, no discussion of what is or is not a matter of faith and morals, no analysis of the criteria for determining the unanimous agreement of the Fathers, nor even quotations from Scripture in support of the Church's position. By 1633 all these topics had faded from the picture. The classic questions of biblical exegesis were no longer center stage.

Rather, almost all the references to the Bible are in the context of recalling the condemnation of heliocentricism in 1616; and then the concern is not to reexamine the substance of that decision but to reassert it, with both force and frequency. The proceedings in 1633 were not focused on science and the Scriptures; that issue had been settled beyond recall in 1616. The focus rather was on the person of Galileo. Was he loyal or was he disobedient?

In Galileo's depositions to the court attention is almost exclusively directed to the injunction, the Decree, and what had happened when he obtained the censors' permissions to publish. It was not the time or the place to reargue the views in the *Letter to Castelli*. The dramatic high point came when Galileo produced the testimony of Bellarmine's certificate, which he had prudently saved, to the effect that Copernicanism could "not be defended or held"— period. It then became a case of which documentary account of the Bellarmine-Galileo meeting would predominate. The decision on this key issue was not surprising; but obviously it had nothing to do with the Scriptures.

The Bible did make its appearance in another way, which turned out to be quite damaging to Galileo. Toward the end of the proceedings a summary of the trial was drawn up, by an unknown author, to be sent to the pope and the cardinals who were to judge the case.[26] This document was the main basis for their decisions. But it is an inaccurate account in certain subtle ways designed to reflect negatively on Galileo. The main device used by the author

---

[26] *Opere* XIX, 293–297; Pagano, *I documenti*, 63–68. English translation in Finocchiaro, *The Galileo Affair*, 281–286.

of this document was to recount Lorini's original complaint in 1615 against Galileo, including excerpts from his inaccurate copy of the *Letter to Castelli*, which made it appear that Galileo had said that some statements in the Bible are false and that others pervert important dogmas.[27] Needless to say, those who argue that the 1633 trial was the product of a conspiracy have used this anti-Galileo trial summary as primary evidence.[28]

There is no doubt that this slanted trial summary had its intended effect, for in the preamble to the sentence,[29] Lorini's denunciation and the *Letter to Castelli* are mentioned as Galileo is charged with "interpreting Holy Scripture according to your own meaning in response to objections based on Scripture which were sometimes made to you."[30] Although the Fourth Session of the Council of Trent is not mentioned here, not one of the judges would have failed to see that Galileo had thereby disobeyed the decree of the council. Further the *Letter to Castelli* is said to contain "various propositions against the authority and true meaning of the Holy Scripture."[31]

The Bible is also mentioned in the formal sentence which comes a few pages later. Galileo is judged to be

> vehemently suspected of heresy, namely of having believed and held the doctrine which is false and contrary to the Sacred and Divine Scriptures, that the sun is the center of the world and does not move from east to west and that the earth moves and is not the center of the world; and that any opinion may be held and defended as probable after it has been declared and defined contrary to the Holy Scripture.[32]

Both charges of heresy in this final judgment explicitly mention the Bible. The first is the familiar charge that Galileo has violated the 1616 condemnation of heliocentricism as contrary to the Scriptures, a prior decision which remained unquestionable at the 1633 trial.

---

[27] For the specifics, see the footnotes to Appendix IV and our discussion in chapter 3 of Lorini's adulterated copy of the *Letter to Castelli*.

[28] For example, see Santillana, *The Crime of Galileo*, chap. 14.

[29] *Opere* XIX, 402–406. English translation in Finocchiaro, *The Galileo Affair*, 287–291.

[30] Finocchiaro's translation in his *The Galileo Affair*, 288.

[31] Ibid.

[32] Langford's translation in his *Galileo, Science, and the Church*, 152.

The second judgment goes one step further by asserting that one cannot even claim that heliocentricism is probable.

This is interesting for at least two reasons. First the point being made against Galileo is that he cannot take refuge in saying that the *Dialogue* treated Copernicanism merely as an open possibility. Note that this is quite different from treating it "hypothetically" in the sense of assuming it counterfactually for purposes of calculation. The latter concedes the non-reality of heliocentricism; the former allows that it might be the way things actually exist in the world. But if Copernicanism is contrary to the Bible, then it is not the existential state of affairs in the world, and thus cannot be said to be probable. This is an expansion on the 1616 rejection of Copernicanism.[33]

Second the judges are invoking here what appears to be a methodological principle of biblical exegesis.[34] What has been declared to be contrary to the Scripture is false. But the false cannot be said to be probable. To say otherwise is to conflate truth and falsity, for the probable is that which may well be true. This is not being said, however, primarily for methodological reasons, but for the theological concern to protect the truth status of the Bible from any shadow of falsity. For to say that the Bible contains falsity would surely be a heretical denial of the word of God.

If we step back from the details of Galileo's two-phased trial, we can see that a pattern emerges. In the first stage the problems of the relations of science and religion and of biblical exegesis vs.

---

[33] The fact that Galileo was condemned in part for maintaining Copernicanism as probable strongly indicates that, when Bellarmine, Urban VIII, and others allowed Copernicanism to be taken "hypothetically," by "hypothetical" they did *not* mean the consideration of a theory as probable in the modern sense of that term. Rather they were referring to the *counterfactual* sense of "hypothetical," as explained here and at the end of chapter 3.

[34] In his "The Methodological Background to Galileo's Trial" (in *Reinterpreting Galileo*, ed. William A. Wallace [Washington, D.C.: Catholic University of America Press, 1986], 241–272), Finocchiaro expresses some surprise (pp. 241–242) that this second charge of heresy against Galileo has a methodological character. But it was not methodology as such but the implication here of falsity in the word of God in the Bible that was of concern. We should also note that this second charge of heresy in the judgment against Galileo (i.e., that what is contrary to Scripture cannot be probable) had appeared earlier in 1615 in the first paragraph of the unidentified theologian's censure of Foscarini's *Lettera*. [See Appendix VII A.]

scientific truth in general were central. This stage was characterized
by foundational debates over the conceptual issues involved. This
was followed by a decision (which became quickly unquestionable)
which terminated debate at the conceptual level: Copernicanism is
contrary to the Scriptures. This in turn was followed by a public an-
nouncement of the decision and of the general obligation to accept
and obey it: the Decree of 1616. In the present case Galileo received
in addition personal orders to agree to and observe the condemnation: the disputed injunction. From this point on, discussion of the
merits of the original decision became taboo, and attention focused
on issues of loyalty and obedience. When a violation of the decision
occurred later, or was thought to have occurred, adjudication of the
case was carried out in terms of how the individual responded to
the obligations to agree and obey, and not in terms of the wisdom
of the resolution of the original conceptual issues: the trial of 1633.
This is how the Galileo affair developed. The cultural atmosphere
at the end was quite different from that of the beginning. Cognitive
disputes over truth and falsity gave way to authority disputes over
loyalty and disobedience.

Were these stages of development in the Galileo case merely
accidents of history, a sequence of contingent developments peculiar
to his situation? Or is the pattern described above more deeply
rooted in the character of religious belief? In the last chapter we
will argue the pros and cons of these questions, with an eye on the
possibility that institutionalized religious belief is governed by a logic
of authority, perhaps analogous to the logic of science, which helps
us to understand what happened in the Galileo trial and whether it
could happen again.

6

The Jesuit Dilemma: Truth or Obedience?

Let us return to the year 1614, a time when Galileo and the Jesuits were still on very amicable terms. In June of that year Christopher Grienberger, S.J. (1561–1636), who had succeeded Clavius as Professor of Mathematics at the Collegio Romano, invited Galileo's friend Giovanni Bardi (born c. 1590) to present a lecture and a set of experimental demonstrations before a distinguished audience at the Collegio Romano on the topic of how bodies float on water or move within water when submerged.[1] Bardi's presentation was well received by his audience, including Grienberger's Jesuit scientific colleagues. Even the Aristotelian philosophers at the Collegio were reported to have been persuaded by the experiments.[2]

This topic in hydrostatics had first engaged Galileo's attention three years earlier, and had resulted in the publication in 1612 of his *Discourse on Floating Bodies*, his first published treatise on physics. Galileo's book sparked an immediate and strong set of attempted refutations from the academic natural philosophers of the day who saw the book as inconsistent with some basic Aristotelian principles. Although we need not go into the specifics of this dispute,[3] in

---

[1] For Bardi's account of this lecture, see his Letter to Galileo, 20 June 1614. *Opere* XII, 76.

[2] Stelluti's Letter to Galileo, 28 June 1614. *Opere* XII, 78.

[3] For an account of these details, see Stillman Drake, *Cause, Experiment, and Science: A Galilean Dialogue Incorporating a New English Translation of Galileo's "Bodies that Stay atop Water or Move in It"* (Chicago: University of Chicago Press, 1981), especially the Introduction, pp. xv–xxix.

general Galileo defended the Archimedean emphasis on the relative densities of the bodies involved and rejected the contentions of the Aristotelians that the causes of these phenomena were the resistance of the water and the shape of floating bodies. This latter point had been raised in the dispute by Galileo's old nemesis Ludovico delle Colombe.

Leaving aside the technical merits of the evidence and arguments in this somewhat specialized scientific problem, what is of interest to us is Bardi's report to Galileo about Grienberger's comments on these experiments.

> Fr. Grienberger told me that if the topic had not been treated by Aristotle (with whom, by order of the General, the Jesuits cannot disagree in any way but rather are obliged always to defend), he would have spoken more positively about the experiments because he was very favorably impressed by them. He also told me that he was not surprised that I disagreed with Aristotle, because Aristotle is clearly also wrong in regard to what you [i.e., Galileo] once told me about two weights falling faster or slower.[4]

These remarks are indeed noteworthy. Grienberger admits privately to Bardi that the experimental evidence clearly seems to indicate that the Aristotelian account of floating bodies is erroneous. He adds gratuitously that the same verdict applies to Aristotle's theory of falling bodies. Yet he restrains himself from saying this publicly, and his reason is that the General of the Society of Jesus has ordered the Jesuits to defend Aristotle in all things and not to disagree with him in any way (non possono opporsi niente). Personal conviction has come into conflict with institutional policy.

As a scientist Grienberger undoubtedly had studied this currently topical problem of floating bodies before Bardi's lecture, and those investigations, plus Bardi's additional demonstrations, persuaded him on empirical grounds that the Aristotelian position is wrong. But as a loyal Jesuit priest who accepts the authority of his Society's rules and regulations, he feels obligated not to oppose Aristotle's teachings.

Grienberger's dilemma was not an isolated case. The Jesuit priest-scientists of that period provide an excellent set of concrete

---

[4] Bardi's Letter to Galileo, 20 June 1614. *Opere* XII, 76.

cases for study as to how the newly emerging scientific culture (in which many Jesuit scientists were outstanding contributors at the frontiers, especially in optics[5]) came into conflict with the long-standing religious culture. These Jesuit scientists were, of course, totally sincere in their religious beliefs and in the commitment of their personal lives to the Society which they had joined. At the same time they actively participated as first-class representatives of the new science. How did they try to resolve the tensions in their dual role as both priests and scientists? What impact did this have on later events in the Galileo case, and does this help to explain the gradual loss of friendship between Galileo and the Jesuits after 1616?

SOLID AND UNIFORM DOCTRINE

The passage quoted above reporting Grienberger's comments on Bardi's demonstrations has been noted by various Galileo scholars, but oddly enough no one has explicitly asked about the order issued by the General of the Society forbidding disagreement with Aristotle. What was this order, how did it come about, and what weight would it have carried for members of the Society?

What Grienberger must have had in mind in his conversation with Bardi were two letters for the instruction of the Jesuits written recently by Claudio Aquaviva, S.J. (1543–1615), General of the Society of Jesus. Such letters appeared at irregular intervals and on various topics seen as important by the General for the work and governance of the Jesuits. Aquaviva's first letter,[6] dated 24 May 1611, concerns the need for the Jesuits to return to "solid and uniform doctrine" in their teaching and writing in theology and in

---

[5] For an excellent discussion of the role played by the early Jesuits as scientists, see William B. Ashworth, Jr., "Catholicism and Early Modern Science," in *God and Nature: Historical Essays on the Encounter between Christianity and Science,* edited by D. C. Lindberg and R. L. Numbers (Berkeley: University of California Press, 1986), especially 153–160.

[6] For the Latin text of this letter, see *Epistolae selectae praepositorum generalium ad superiores Societatis* (Romae: Typis Polyglottis Vaticanis, 1911), 207–209.

philosophy.[7] By the turn of the century increased membership in the Society had led to larger numbers of publications expressing a wide variety of differing opinions.[8] Aquaviva saw this situation as dangerous for the maintenance of loyalty to the Church, for attaining the goals of the Society, and for the unity and brotherhood of its members. As the decades had passed after the Council of Trent, the rules of the Society became more rigid and specific, a tendency which reached its strongest form during Aquaviva's tenure as General. The Jesuits were both a product of, and a strong driving force behind, the Counter-Reformation; after the Council of Trent their primary role was the defense of Catholic orthodoxy. The highly defensive tone of Aquaviva's letter reveals his sharp concern that this role was being compromised.

A second, more concrete and more immediate motivation behind Aquaviva's letter was to avoid any shadow of suspicion that the Jesuits had violated the conditions imposed by Pope Paul V in his 1607 moratorium which ended the twenty-year controversy between the Jesuits and the Dominicans over the reconciliation of Divine grace and human free will. In the intervening four years additional Jesuit writings on this topic, and especially Leonard Lessius's *De gratia efficaci* . . . (1610), had opened that possibility. Extensive correspondence within the Society at the time shows an increasing conservatism on this point which culminated in the new regulations issued by Aquaviva.[9]

---

[7] For a helpful discussion of the historical origins of this phrase, which was standardized by Aquaviva in this letter, see Ugo Baldini, "Una fonte poco utilizzata per la storia intellettuale: le 'censurae librorum' e 'opinionum' nell'antica Compagnia di Gesu," *Annali dell'Instituto storico italo-germanico in Trento* 11 (1985): 19–67, especially 21–29.

[8] During Aquaviva's long tenure as General (1581–1615) the Society expanded enormously: from 5000 to 13000 members, from 144 to 372 schools, and from 33 to 123 houses of residence. See William V. Bangert, S.J., *A History of the Society of Jesus*, 2d ed. (St. Louis: Institute of Jesuit Sources, 1986), 98. For a study of the reforms introduced by Aquaviva, see Michel de Cereau, "La réforme de l'intérieur au temps d'Aquaviva," in *Les Jésuites: Spiritualité et activités* (Paris: Beauchesne, 1974), 53–69.

[9] For a history of these developments, supported by a large collection of previously unpublished correspondence and documents, see Le Bachelet, *Prédestination*

His remedy for these problems was to reassert the importance of uniform thinking among Jesuits on an agreed upon common intellectual foundation, a policy which had been consistently recommended in the documents of the Society since its inception.[10] This "solid and uniform doctrine" was defined as the teaching of St. Thomas Aquinas in theology and of Aristotle in philosophy. Aquaviva makes it quite clear that merely avoiding error is not enough; he advocates the positive adoption of a specific theology and philosophy, seen as interwoven, and not merely in their conclusions but also in their principles. This rule is unambiguous and applied to all Jesuits. However the actual observance of it by Jesuit scientists at times fell short of the strictness of the rule itself.

One of the specific places where these instructions were to be carried out was in the censorship of books about to be published and of "opinions" taught in the curriculum of the Jesuit colleges.[11] The

---

et grâce efficace. It is also clear that Pope Paul V knew of, and approved of, Aquaviva's prescription of "solid and uniform doctrine," at least insofar as it applied to the controversy over Divine grace and human free will. (See ibid., II, 243–245)

[10] This was a long-standing concern of Aquaviva. When he was elected General of the Society in 1581, he immediately began a process of reorganizing the Jesuit course of studies on Thomistic foundations, which resulted finally in the definitive 1598 edition of the *Ratio studiorum.* For Bellarmine's considerable contributions to this process, see Xavier-Marie Le Bachelet, S.J., *Bellarmin avant son cardinalat, 1542–1598: Correspondance et documents.* (Paris: Beauchesne, 1911), 493–519.

[11] See Ugo Baldini, "Le 'censurae librorum' e 'opinionum'," for an excellent study of the origins and day-to-day operations of the censorship process among the early Jesuits. This system of censorship, originally suggested by Ignatius in the *Constitutions* of the Society, had evolved into the following form by the beginning of the seventeenth century. At the Curia of the Society in Rome were located the General Revisors (a committee usually of five members) with analogous groups of Provincial Revisors in each of the Jesuit Provinces throughout the world. Certain especially important topics were reserved for judgment by the General Revisors in Rome, who also served as an appellate court of decision when the Provincial Revisors were unable to reach agreement. The General Revisors reported to the General of the Society. One of the effects of the suppression of the Society in 1773 was the apparent loss of all the records of the various Provincial Revisors. However, the records of the General Revisors in Rome have been preserved, and are located in the Archivum Romanum Societatis Iesu (ARSI), Fondo Gesuitico. The latter source contains informative documents on how the Jesuit scientists reacted to the 1616 condemnation of Copernicanism.

Jesuits already had in place an elaborate system of pre-publication evaluations of books written by members of the Society (a device still in use by Jesuits in our day, and analogous to present practices of refereeing technical writing, although the judgment of the Jesuit censors in the early seventeenth century carried much greater force). This focusing of the Society's internal censoring system on "solid and uniform doctrine" had a major impact on Jesuit scientific writings after the Decree of 1616 condemning Copernicanism. Aquaviva's first letter closes with a request that local Provincial officials report back to him in the near future on their efforts to implement this order for solidity and uniformity.

His second letter[12] was dated 14 December 1613, exactly six months prior to Grienberger's conversation with Bardi after the lecture on floating bodies. The reports had been received from the Provincials, and the General was not pleased. He strongly reasserted the need for all to unite on the terrain of "solid and uniform doctrine," reminding his fellow Jesuits of their obligations of obedience. It is no excuse to say that one does not know the mind of St. Thomas, since this is quite clear from either his own texts or from his commentators, which are not to be replaced by anyone's private interpretation. Those who teach novelties are to be removed from their teaching positions and assigned to other ministries of the Society, even in the middle of a course if necessary. There is no doubt that Aquaviva still saw variety and novelty of opinion as distracting the Society from the defense of Catholic orthodoxy. He ordered that his prior letter be read annually at faculty meetings at the beginning of each academic year. He then adds:

> Whoever teaches views contrary to St. Thomas or who introduces new things into philosophy on his own initiative or from obscure authors is ordered to retract them immediately. . . . If a doubt should arise, or if a teacher chooses to defend his own opinion obstinately, the Prefect and the Rector, proceeding with great authority and kindness, will consult on the matter and hand it over to other learned members of our Society for more careful examination. After this they will order the teacher to acquiesce and to let himself be governed, because we

---

[12] *Epistolae selectae praepositorum generalium ad superiores Societatis,* 209–215.

have schools, as is pleasing to God, in which anything which occurs outside the vow of obedience is simply unacceptable.[13]

Although these views are asserted with extra insistence in Aquaviva's letter, they were not new to the Jesuits. In both letters the General refers to earlier legislative authority, especially to Decree 41 of the Fifth General Congregation (1593–94) of the Society of Jesus:

> Our teachers in scholastic theology are to follow the doctrine of St. Thomas; only those who are well acquainted with St. Thomas are to be promoted to the chairs of theology. Those who are not well acquainted with this author, or who disagree with him, are to be barred from the office of teaching. . . . [14]

> In matters of any importance philosophy professors should not deviate from the views of Aristotle, unless his view happens to be contrary to a teaching which is accepted everywhere in the schools, or especially if his view is contrary to orthodox faith. In accordance with the Lateran Council, they should strenuously try to refute any arguments of Aristotle, or of any other philosopher, which are contrary to the faith.[15]

These same directions on the teaching of Aristotelian philosophy were still reaffirmed as late as the middle of the eighteenth century.[16] The original legislation on this had been stated in the Jesuit *Constitutions* (Part IV, Chapter 14) which dates back to St. Ignatius, the founder of the Society. "In logic, natural and moral philosophy, and metaphysics, the doctrine of Aristotle should be followed,

---

[13] Ibid., 212–213.

[14] *Decreta, canones, censurae, et praecepta Congregationum Generalium Societatis Jesu* (Avenione: Ex Typographia Francisci Sequin, 1830), vol. III, p. 339.

[15] Ibid., 341. This second statement about philosophy professors also appears *verbatim* in the 1599 version of the evolving document *Ratio studiorum* which governed the teaching curriculum of the Jesuit colleges. This 1599 edition was the first really official version of the *Ratio*, and it was published under Aquaviva's supervision. For an English version, see Edward A. Fitzpatrick, *St. Ignatius and the Ratio Studiorum* (New York: McGraw-Hill, 1933).

[16] This is located in Decree 36, General Congregation XVI (1730), and in Decree 13, General Congregation XVII (1751). See *Decreta, canones, censurae, et praecepta Congregationum Generalium Societatis Jesu*, vol. IV, pp. 320, 339.

as also in the other liberal arts."[17] This is the regulation which was reinforced by Aquaviva with special vigor.

If we keep all of this legislation in mind, there is little wonder that Grienberger told Bardi that he could not agree with his lecture because the General had ordered the Jesuits to defend Aristotle in all matters. The Jesuit view at the time was that Aristotelian-Thomistic philosophy-theology constituted one fully unified system, or seamless garment in more contemporary language, which had been identified without ambiguity as the "solid and uniform doctrine" they were ordered to defend. A rift in one corner, even though it be a matter of pure physical facts and their interpretation, could and did threaten the whole edifice in their minds. Thus it was that a dispute over how bodies float in water was a threat to Catholic orthodox belief and to the Jesuits' avowed role as its defender. The extreme organic conceptual unity of the Aristotelian-Thomistic system was both its great strength and its great weakness. It is astonishing to realize that a floating cork could shake the walls of St. Peter's. But it did.

Grienberger was not the only Jesuit scientist caught in this dilemma of choosing between his religious commitments and the new anti-Aristotelian science. In fact it became a repeated pattern, with tragic effects for both the Jesuits and the Church in general. When this choice had to be made, the Jesuit scientists not surprisingly opted for their religious world. Jesuit science thus died on the vine, just as the first blossoms had appeared.[18] It could have been otherwise. But governed by unequivocal rules and a fixed mindset intended to fight different battles in the sixteenth century, the Jesuits under Aquaviva's leadership approached the scientific revolution in the seventeenth century as though it were phase two of the Reformation.

---

[17] St. Ignatius Loyola, *The Constitutions of the Society of Jesus*, translated, with an Introduction and Commentary, by George E. Ganss, S.J. (St. Louis: Institute of Jesuit Sources, 1970), 220.

[18] This issue was first brought to my attention by a reading of Ashworth, "Catholicism and Early Modern Science," 155–160.

THE JESUIT TRADITION ON OBEDIENCE

The situation of Grienberger and his fellow Jesuit scientists was made more complex by their religious vows of obedience. By their time the concept of religious obedience had a long and evolving history in the Catholic Church, primarily in the development of the monastic orders. In the most general terms obedience was seen as the response of receptivity to authority. All authority was understood as coming either directly or indirectly from God. As a result the authority of the religious superior was ultimately the authority of God himself, and obedience to the superior was obedience to Christ speaking through that person. As the Scriptures had put it, "He who hears you, hears me; he who despises you, despises me."[19] Thus submission to the order of the superior is a religious act of vanquishing one's will as a sacrifice or holocaust to God.

This general perspective received a distinctively new interpretation at the hands of St. Ignatius, the founder of the Jesuits, in his *Letter on Obedience* (1553). Traditionally obedience was taken to be conformity with a lawful order at least at the level of action, and better, also at the level of personal will or choice, i.e., the execution of what is commanded and an interior willingness to do so. Ignatius added a third level, conformity in thought.

> But he who aims at making an entire and perfect oblation of himself besides his will must offer his understanding (which is a further and the highest degree of obedience), not only willing, but thinking the same as the Superior, submitting his own judgment to his, so far as a devout will can bend the understanding. For although this faculty has not the freedom of the will, and naturally gives its assent to what is presented to it as true, there are, however, many instances when the evidence of the known truth is not coercive, in which it can with the help of the will, favor this or that side. And when this happens every obedient man should conform his thought to the thought of his Superior.[20]

---

[19] Luke 10:16.

[20] St. Ignatius Loyola, *Letter on Obedience*, paragraph 9. Translation is from Father Manuel María Espinosa Pólit, *Perfect Obedience: Commentary on the Letter on Obedience of Saint Ignatius of Loyola* (Westminster, Md.: Newman Bookshop, 1947), 24.

Thus perfect obedience consists of conformity of action, of will, and of thought.[21] The only exceptions allowed were the cases of an immoral order and of a truth known to be coercive.

The full impact of Ignatius's *Letter* was brought out rather clearly by Cardinal Bellarmine in a short treatise which he wrote in 1588 entitled *Tractatus de obedientia, quae caeca nominatur*.[22] This tract was written as a reply to a renegade Jesuit, Julian Vincent of the College of Bordeaux, who had written an essay, falsely attributed to another Jesuit, claiming that the General of the Society was infallible. Vincent then used this essay to attack the Jesuit tradition on obedience. This episode created a scandal, which attracted the attention of the pope, and which led to the trial and imprisonment of the Jesuit who was the supposed author. So the General at the time (who, by the way, was Aquaviva) asked Bellarmine to calm the waters by clarifying the Jesuit notion of obedience.[23]

Bellarmine picked up on the word 'blind', which had been used twice in Ignatius's *Letter*, and explained it as follows.

> By the phrase 'blind obedience' he [Ignatius] understood an obedience which is pure, perfect, simple, and without discussion of what is commanded or why it is commanded, but is satisfied only by the fact that it is commanded. Even if nothing further be said, all this must be taken with an exception, namely, that what is commanded is not sinful, an exception which Fr. Ignatius clearly expressed both in his *Letter on Obedience* and in the *Constitutions*.[24]

---

[21] As a contemporary example of these three degrees of obedience, suppose that a legally established government has a draft law for military service and has just sent me my induction notice. I obey only at the first level if I report for induction, but grudgingly; at the second level, if I report willingly; and at the third level, if I willingly report and also agree, without questioning, with the law's rationale, e.g., a show of strength to discourage a belligerent neighbor from violating our borders.

[22] *Treatise on the Obedience which is Called Blind*. Original autograph texts are in ARSI, Opera Nostrorum, 239. For the Latin text, see Brodrick, *Life and Work of Cardinal Bellarmine*, vol. 1, 485–498.

[23] Brodrick, *Life and Work of Cardinal Bellarmine*, vol. I, 134. For Bellarmine's writings in reply to Julian Vincent, see *Auctarium Bellarminianum*, edited by Xavier-Marie Le Bachelet, S.J. (Paris: Beauchesne, 1913), 386–403.

[24] Brodrick, *Life and Work of Cardinal Bellarmine*, vol. I, 485.

After quoting a string of passages from Ignatius, including parts of the *Letter*, Bellarmine went beyond Ignatius to conclude:

> Thus from all these passages it is clear that sin is an exception, but not doubt. For when doubt exists, one ought to agree immediately with superiors and not with one's own judgment, as is manifestly taught both by true humility and by clear reason.[25]

For Bellarmine the "blindness" of obedience refers to the presence in the subject of an initial inclination to carry out an order because that is what was commanded, rather than a first impulse to question its meaning or the reasons standing behind it. He immediately adds that the one and only exception is that an order is not to be obeyed if what it commands is immoral. Sin is an exception; but doubt is not. In the latter case one should follow the superior's order, for if one settles one's conscience this way but by chance is thereby wrong, one acts out of invincible ignorance,[26] and "it is better to do something less good out of obedience than to do a better thing contrary to obedience."[27] Furthermore, one should not actively search for alternatives to, or difficulties in, a lawful order; perfect obedience is grounded in perfect indifference.[28] If by chance one spontaneously thinks of something contrary to an order, or is concerned about it, the rule of obedience does not forbid bringing this matter up in good faith with a superior, as long as one "maintains indifference before and after this presentation."[29] Referring specifically to paragraph 19 of the *Letter on Obedience*, Bellarmine comments:

> Furthermore Fr. Ignatius adds that it is not contrary to perfect obedience for someone to propose to a superior, with due reverence and humility, what has by chance occurred to him as contrary to the superior's command, granting that he is prepared to conform his will

---

[25] Ibid., vol. I, 486.

[26] *Tractatus de obedientia, quae caeca nominatur*, chap. 5. Brodrick, *Life and Work of Cardinal Bellarmine*, vol. I, 497.

[27] "Sermo tertius in visitatione ecclesiae cathedralis," in R. Bellarmine, *Opera oratoria postuma*, ed. S. Tromp, S.J., 11 vols. (Romae: Aedibus Pont. Universitatis Gregorianae, 1942–69), vol. III, 152.

[28] Ibid., vol. II, 270.

[29] *Letter on Obedience*, paragraph 19. Espinosa Pólit, *Perfect Obedience*, 29.

and judgment with what is judged and willed by the one who stands in the place of Christ.[30]

In one of his sermons Bellarmine carried this a step further with the suggestion that Ignatius extended the virtue of obedience beyond explicit orders to even the wishes of superiors.[31] And, of course, the strongest statement by Ignatius is his famous comment in the *Spiritual Exercises* that, "If we wish to be sure that we are right in all things, we should always be ready to accept this principle: I will believe that the white that I see is black, if the hierarchical Church so defines it."[32] Striking rhetorical examples can indeed be counterproductive, especially for an audience other than the one intended. But there is no doubt that for the founder of the Jesuits defined religious truth took precedence over any other mode of truth determination. This primacy would certainly be included in the conformity of thought found in perfect obedience.

This entire discussion of the Jesuit tradition on obedience from Ignatius and Bellarmine is, of course, at the level of a religious ideal. It is not our intention to evaluate that ideal, but to report it as a framework to help understand the mind of the Jesuit scientists in the seventeenth century. Now it is indisputable that all Jesuits at that time would have been thoroughly familiar with their distinctive tradition on the religious vow of obedience. Whether or not Grienberger and his confreres accepted Aquaviva's letters on "solid and uniform doctrine" with the perfect obedience advocated by the Society is moot and undecidable. If they did so receive it, they would have conformed with Aquaviva's two letters in action, in will, and in thought. The latter would have required them to be intellectually persuaded of the truth of the Aristotelian-Thomistic philosophy-theology which is unequivocally identified as the "solid and uniform doctrine" ordered by Aquaviva. If any of their own scientific work conflicted with this, they would have been obliged as a minimum under religious obedience to maintain a public silence on the matter, which appears to have happened with some frequency.

---

[30] Brodrick, *Life and Work of Cardinal Bellarmine*, vol. I, 486.

[31] Bellarmine, *Opera oratoria postuma*, vol. II, 254.

[32] *The Spiritual Exercises of St. Ignatius*, "Rules for Thinking with the Church, 13," trans. Anthony Mottola (Garden City, N.Y.: Doubleday, 1964), 141.

In a case of conflict empirical truth became secondary to truth by authority.

The only allowable exception to the obligation of obedience was a case of a sinful order. But Aquaviva's order was certainly not seen as immoral by his fellow Jesuits (although one could now construct interesting arguments to that effect which would cut to the heart of the matter). If Grienberger or any of his fellow Jesuit scientists chanced to have a serious doubt about the wisdom of Aquaviva's orders, he could and should have said so, maintaining the proper indifference. And perhaps some Jesuits at the time actually did so, although we know of no evidence to that effect. If they had done so after the General's first letter, that may have contributed to the more insistent tone of the second letter. But no matter what may have happened, it is clear from the tone of the second letter that Aquaviva was not sympathetic with any doubts that may have arisen.

Thus all the ingredients of the Jesuits' dilemma came into place: the new scientific culture, in which some of them were leaders of the first rank, contained elements which were inconsistent with the "solid and uniform doctrine" which they had been ordered to defend by their General under the obligations of religious obedience. Faced with this dilemma their response, not unexpectedly, was to embrace the horn of obedience.[33] This, in turn, diverted Jesuit science further and further from the mainstream. It also reversed their previous friendly relationships with Galileo, and indeed was likely the main cause of later Jesuit antagonisms toward Galileo, although some individual Jesuits, especially Orazio Grassi and Christopher Scheiner, also had independent personal axes to grind.

---

[33] That Grienberger personally did so seems to be implied by a sharp remark by Giovanni Faber in a letter to Galileo, 23 November 1612. "As a child of holy obedience, he [Grienberger] does not dare to state his own opinion" (*Opere* XI, 434). An explicit clash between Jesuit religious obedience and Copernicanism is implied in a report by Piero Dini in a letter to Galileo (16 May 1615) regarding the assessment of Galileo's views on heliocentricism in Rome: "I understand that many Jesuits are secretly of the same opinion, although they remain silent" (*Opere* XII, 181).

BIANCANI'S BATTLE WITH THE JESUIT CENSORS

Aquaviva's mandate for "solid and uniform doctrine" had a direct effect upon the writings of the Jesuit scientists, and this appeared immediately, several years *before* the condemnation of Copernicanism in 1616. Hence the Jesuits were already returning to the older Aristotelian cosmology for their own reasons, an impetus which was then accelerated by the Decree of 1616. This can be conclusively documented from the surviving reports of the Roman Revisors, or censors, of the Society. Their censures were not intended for publication, of course, but by comparing their recommendations with the actually published versions of various scientific treatises, one can easily see the private disagreements which stand behind what otherwise appears to be an undisputed Aristotelianism.

A particularly clear and instructive case of this is the set of censures relating to the physical and astronomical writings of Giuseppe Biancani, S.J. (1566–1624).[34] The Society's records show that Biancani joined the Jesuits in 1592; he studied at the Collegio Romano at the turn of the century, probably under Clavius; and he was appointed professor of mathematics at the Jesuit college in Bologna in 1603, and later in Parma in 1606. In present-day literature he is sometimes depicted as an opponent of Galileo and the new science, but his exchanges in the unpublished sources with several Jesuit censors over his two main books show that quite the opposite was the case.[35] These documents also clearly reveal a split within the Jesuits at that time between the philosophers of orthodox Aristotelian persuasion and a group of mathematicians and astronomers, including Biancani, who advocated the autonomy of astronomy and mathematics and a more quantitative and descriptive approach, which resulted in some quite anti-Aristotelian views. Thus although he disputed some of Galileo's calculations, Biancani agreed that the surface of

---

[34] These censures are located in ARSI, Fondo Gesuitico, 662, 156–176, and 655, 105–121. They have been partially published by Ugo Baldini in his "Additamenta Galilaeana: I. Galileo, le nuova astronomia e la critica all'Aristotelismo nel dialogo epistolare tra Giuseppe Biancani e i revisori romani della Compagnia de Gesu," *Annali dell'Instituto e Museo di Storia della Scienza di Firenze* 9 (1984): 13–43.

[35] For a discussion of this claim and the evidence in its support, see Baldini, "Additamenta Galilaeana," 14 ff.

the moon is mountainous and not a smooth sphere; he also maintained that the heavens were composed of fluid matter, not solid spheres, another anti-Aristotelian view.

The main area of dispute with the censors occurred over his *Aristotelis loca mathematica*,[36] a systematic and highly critical analysis of the passages in Aristotle pertaining to mathematics and its uses in the sciences. This major work was completed by Biancani early in 1614, and sent, as was the custom, to the censors for evaluations prior to publication. The most revealing report,[37] addressed to Aquaviva as General (which was the usual procedure) was submitted by Giovanni Camerota, S.J. (1559–1644), one of the five General Revisors in Rome at the time. With a rather clear nod toward Aquaviva's letters on "solid and uniform doctrine," Comerota complains that the author should not say that Aristotle's views are wrong or that his arguments are defective, nor should he praise heretics like Maestlin, Tycho, and Kepler. He objects to Biancani's approval of Tycho's arguments that comets are above the moon, and therefore that the heavens are changeable; and also to his argument that the heavens are composed of fluid matter, and that the planets move through this fluid by their own motive force, as fish swim through water. This latter point, it should be recalled, was also the lifelong view of Cardinal Bellarmine, which Grienberger was later to point out in Biancani's defense.

In reply to these censures the final published version of the book toned down its critical stance toward Aristotle, but not its praise for Tycho and Kepler. On the other hand the new doctrines in physics and astronomy which seemed contrary to official doctrine were simply reported in the book neutrally and without the author's commitment. Biancani's obedient response was on the minimalist side as far as corrections were concerned.

A bigger problem arose, however, over Aristotle's discussion of floating bodies in the last paragraph of Chapter 6, Book IV, of the *De caelo*. Biancani submitted a sixteen-page addition on this topic, the

---

[36] *Aristotelis loca mathematica ex universis ipsius operibus collecta, et explicata. Accessere de natura mathematicarum scientiarum tractatio* (Bononiae, 1615).

[37] ARSI, Fondo Gesuitico, 662, 162r–163v, dated 15 September 1614. Published in Baldini, "Additamenta Galilaeana," 26–29.

same issue discussed by Bardi and Grienberger in June 1614. In a later report, dated 16 February 1615, Camerota made the following recommendation:

> The addition to Biancani's book about bodies moving in water should not be published since it is an attack on Aristotle and not an explanation of him (as the title indicates). Neither the conclusion nor the arguments to prove it are due to the author [Biancani] but to Galileo. And it is enough that they can be read in Galileo's writings. It does not seem to be either proper or useful for the books of our members to contain the ideas of Galileo, especially when they are contrary to Aristotle.[38]

Biancani protested vigorously to this recommendation, and requested that it be overturned, in two letters written in April 1615 to the soon to be elected new General Muzio Vitelleschi, S.J. (1563–1645) (Aquaviva had died on 31 January 1615). But his protest was rejected, and he was forced to accept the censor's decision. As a result at the appropriate place in Biancani's *Aristotelis loca mathematica* for a discussion of *De caelo* IV, 6, one reads:

> At this point a commentary on the last chapter of the *De caelo* is needed. In its place the reader is referred to the Italian treatise of Galileo Galilei on bodies which float on, or move in, water, where toward the end many things are presented in an explanation of this chapter.[39]

The full sharpness and irony of these remarks can be appreciated only in the light of the Biancani's struggles with the unpublished reports of the Jesuit censors. And all this happened *before* the 1616 condemnation of Copernicanism.

In the meantime Biancani had written another book for which he is more famous and which was directly devoted to astronomy, his *Sphaera mundi, seu cosmographia*.[40] This book must have been

---

[38] ARSI, Fondo Gesuitico, 662, 166r. Printed in Baldini, "Additamenta Galilaeana," 31.

[39] These remarks appear at paragraphs #124–29 in *Aristotelis loca mathematica*, 88.

[40] The full title is *Sphaera mundi, seu cosmographia demonstrativa, ac facili methodo tradita: in qua totius mundi fabrica, una cum novis Tychonis, Kepleri, Galilaei, aliorumque astronomorum adinventis continetur* (Bononiae, 1620).

completed in its penultimate draft form sometime late in 1615, and then submitted to the censors as usual.

Of the numerous reports from the censors on this book, by far the most significant was written by Grienberger, a close friend of Biancani, and who, judging from his comments, must have been personally in agreement with him and also anguishing over the same problems of intellectual freedom. On the second page of his long and undated censure[41] appear the following most significant remarks.

> He [Biancani] says on page 91b, line 14, that astronomers, whom he names, and especially Copernicus, use diagrams in determining and explaining celestial motions, and they call them hypotheses. But in other places Copernicus does not speak hypothetically, but definitely tries to prove that the system of the world is such as he has imagined it to be, and as a result he tries to refute arguments which assert the contrary. This is the main reason why his book has by recent decree been prohibited until corrected, which I understand has been done although it has not yet been promulgated.[42]

The scene has now changed dramatically. The Congregation of the Index decided on its Decree against Copernicanism at its meeting of 3 March 1616. The Decree was published on 5 March. Thus Grienberger's undated report was almost certainly written on 4 March. It is highly likely that he had learned this information about the Decree from Bellarmine, who would have attended that meeting of the Congregation. It is also quite likely that the reason Grienberger gives for the condemnation of Copernicus, namely, that he tried to establish his system of the world as real and not merely as hypothetical, was also shared by Bellarmine, who had reported this to him. Indeed Bellarmine had already explicitly recommended only a hypothetical and not a realistic status for Copernicanism a year earlier in his famous letter to Foscarini [see Appendix VIII]. At any rate the impact on Jesuit scientists of the Decree against

---

[41] ARSI, Fondo Gesuitico, 655, 111r–118v. Partially printed in Baldini, "Additamenta Galilaeana," 32–36.

[42] ARSI, Fondo Gesuitico, 655, 112r. Baldini, "Additamenta Galilaeana," 32. Incidentally this passage clearly also shows that at that time 'hypothesis' meant a statement about a counterfactual or non-real state of affairs, and not the modern sense of a likely real state of affairs for which more evidence is sought, as we have argued earlier.

Copernicanism was certainly immediate, and came on top of several previous years of orders to maintain traditional views.

Grienberger's discomfort with this dramatic turn of events and his sympathy for Biancani's dilemma become more evident as his report continues. He points out that Aristotle's view that the heavens are inalterable is refuted by many changes observed in the heavens in recent years. He mentions that Cardinal Bellarmine himself not only agrees, but also thinks that this is consistent with the Scriptures and its commentators. Motion can just as easily be attributed to the planets and the stars themselves if the spheres are denied, although he grants that their spiral motions through a fluid medium are difficult to understand and explain, a problem with this view which Bellarmine also shared. At the end he adds a plea for intellectual freedom written at a moment of great pressure, but which unfortunately was fated to go unheard.

> A new *Cosmographia* seems to be necessary because the old one has been changed a great deal in our day and many embellishments have been added to it. But the question has been raised as to whether it is proper for us Jesuits to do this. It seems to me that the time has now come for a greater degree of freedom of thought to be given to both mathematicians and philosophers on this matter, for the liquidity and corruptibility of the heavens are not absolutely contrary to theology or to philosophy and even much less to mathematics. . . . It seems that he [Biancani] has not exercised his talents sufficiently in writing the *Cosmographia*. But I am quite willing to excuse him about this. For up to now his hands have been tied, as have ours. Thus he has digressed into many less important topics when he was not allowed to think freely about what is required.[43]

This unheeded plea may well be the beginning of the end of classical Jesuit science. Although Grienberger, the successor to Clavius, was a major player in the scientific circles of his day, he never wrote a major treatise on science. One wonders whether this was the reason. Biancani's book waited four years before it could be published. The language was softened, but all the new ideas and theories were still reported for the reader's information, although in a

---

[43] ARSI, Fondo Gesuitico, 655, 118r–v. Baldini, "Additamenta Galilaeana," 35–36.

neutral vein. When Biancani reached the critical section of his book, "On the Motion of the Earth," he reviewed all the available theories, ancient and modern. Referring specifically to the heliocentric views of Copernicus, Kepler, and Gilbert, he comments:

> By this hypothesis they not only save all the appearances but also think that they have easily answered the arguments of all the adversaries. But that this opinion is false and should be rejected (even though it is established by better proofs and arguments) has nevertheless become much more certain in our day when it has been condemned by the authority of the Church as contrary to Sacred Scripture.[44]

The dilemma of the Jesuit scientists could hardly be made more explicit: truth or obedience. Copernicanism is to be rejected on grounds of religious authority, even though it is "established by better proofs and arguments" than its rivals. The double meaning of these remarks leaps out of the page for those who have read the unpublished reports of the censors. But despite Biancani's struggles for precisely the opposite results, it has been his fate in history to be identified as an enemy of Galileo and the new science. He deserved much better treatment from both sides.

THE ONSET OF INTELLECTUAL RIGOR MORTIS

From this point onward the character of discourse about astronomy among the Jesuit scientists underwent a gradual but distinctive evolution toward rigidity. The *scientific* merits of the observations and theories, both pro and con Copernicanism, slowly began to fade away from center stage. Likewise fading away were substantive discussions of the standards of biblical exegesis, of the history of biblical interpretations, and of the relations of both to the natural sciences, topics which had been actively pursued from the Reformation and the Council of Trent up through Galileo's *Letter to the Grand Duchess Christina*. In their place there first appeared a set of appeals to the Decree of 1616 and to the principle of authority, to settle the issue at least as far as Copernicanism was concerned. This gradually evolved into more elaborate theological, philosophical,

---

44 *Sphaera mundi, seu cosmographia*, Book IV, Chapter 2, p. 37.

and apologetic arguments to establish more precisely the fact, character, and degree of heresy involved. By mid-century the latter emphases had exacted a heavy toll indeed from the earlier originality of Jesuit science.

The beginnings of these developments can be seen in the bitter, prolonged, and unfortunate controversy between Galileo and Orazio Grassi, S.J. (1583–1654), who was the successor to Grienberger in the Chair of Mathematics at the Collegio Romano.[45] In the fall of 1618 three successive comets had appeared which attracted the attention of all who looked at the skies, amateurs and professionals alike, and which were regarded by many as evil portents. The professional astronomers were interested primarily in the physical composition, location, and paths of motions of these comets, problems which at that time were beyond anyone's powers to resolve. Grassi delivered a public lecture on these topics, which was published anonymously the next year. Although it contained nothing which directly challenged Galileo, nevertheless Galileo decided to answer it in an essay published under the name of his associate Mario Guiducci (1585–1643). This led to further replies and counter-replies (with Grassi writing under the pseudonym 'Sarsi') which continued until 1626.[46] Galileo's last contribution to this exchange was *The Assayer* (1623), his most significant writing on what we would now call the philosophy of science.[47]

---

[45] Grassi is also famous as the architect for the Jesuit Church of St. Ignatius in Rome, which was built contiguous to the Collegio Romano, and which is a classic baroque edifice, begun in 1626.

[46] The successive treatises in this exchange (all published in *Opere* VI) were as follows: Grassi's anonymous *De tribus cometis anni MDCXVIII* (1619); Mario Guiducci, *Discorso delle comete* (1619) [actually written by Galileo]; Lothario Sarsi [Grassi], *Libra astronomica ac philosophica* (1619); Mario Guiducci, *Lettera al M. R. P. Tarquinio Galluzzi* (1620); Galileo, *Il Saggiatore* [*The Assayer*] (1623); and Lothario Sarsi [Grassi], *Ratio ponderum librae et simbellae* (1626). For English translations of all except the last of these treatises, see Stillman Drake, *The Controversy on the Comets of 1618* (Philadelphia: University of Pennsylvania Press, 1960).

[47] In his *Galileo eretico*, Pietro Redondi has established with his newly discovered Document G3 that shortly after its publication in 1623 someone denounced Galileo's *The Assayer* to the Holy Office as heretical since its teachings on atomism

One of the peculiarities in this complex exchange is that the very recent condemnation of Copernicanism goes almost unmentioned. In one place in the *Libra* where the use of Tycho's writings on comets is under discussion, Grassi asks rhetorically who else he should follow, and answers in part, "Or Copernicus? But he who is dutiful will rather call everyone away from him and will equally reject and spurn his recently condemned hypothesis."[48] On this sentence Galileo ironically comments, "As to the Copernican hypothesis, had not the most sovereign wisdom removed us Catholics from error for our own good and illuminated our blindness, I do not believe that this grace and benefit could have been derived from the reasons and experiences embraced by Tycho."[49] The merits of both Copernicanism and its condemnation were simply past the point of discussion.

A little later on at the beginning of the Third Part of the *Libra*, Grassi indicates that he has not forgotten Aquaviva's directives on

---

were thought to contradict the Dogma of the Holy Eucharist as defined by the Thirteenth Session (11 October 1551) of the Council of Trent. Redondi's thesis that the author of this denunciation was Orazio Grassi, S.J. is presented in great detail, but remains no more than an interesting conjecture (even if it be granted that this was a Jesuit plot, there were other plausible candidates, especially Christopher Scheiner, S.J.). Given the depth of detail about the Jesuit world at that time presented by Redondi, it is quite surprising that he makes no mention at all of the Jesuit tradition on obedience in general or of the Society's early specific rules on the teaching of Aristotelianism (which he could have used as more circumstantial evidence of the Jesuit authorship of the denunciation). Without any real direct supporting evidence at all, and therefore almost completely conjectural, is Redondi's additional and main thesis, i.e., Galileo's trial in 1633 for advocating Copernicanism in the *Dialogues* was a false front engineered by Pope Urban VIII, who was under severe political pressure from the Spanish and Jesuit bloc, to prevent the much more serious charge of Eucharistic heresy from being officially raised against Galileo. But if this dangerous heresy were truly contained in Galileo's published writings, which after all were available for anyone to read, then no amount of manipulation of the trial could have so successfully concealed the heresy that over 350 years could pass before anyone would have pointed it out as the real issue involved in Galileo's trial. Surely many other readers, past and present, would have seen what Grassi supposedly saw, thus revealing much sooner that the actual trial was a subterfuge. For an excellent review of Redondi's book, see V. Ferrone and M. Firpo, "From Inquisitors to Microhistorians: A Critique of Pietro Redondi's *Galileo eretico*," *Journal of Modern History* 58 (1986): 485–524.

[48] Drake, *Controversy on the Comets*, 71.
[49] Ibid., 184.

solid and uniform doctrine. "I wish to assert that here my whole desire is nothing less than to champion the conclusions of Aristotle. At present, I shall not delay over the question of whether the remarks of that great man are true or false."[50] Did Grassi personally reject some of these Aristotelian conclusions which he claims to defend? Although he says that he will play the role of Aristotle's champion, some of his own views about comets in these treatises, based on the work of Tycho, are quite anti-Aristotelian, e.g., he locates them far beyond the moon and moving in ways which would conflict with the spheres. As an informed astronomer he knows that the Aristotelian-Ptolemaic hypothesis is beset with serious difficulties; as a Jesuit he knows that the Church's condemnation of Copernicanism obliges him under religious obedience to accept the qualification that the Copernican hypothesis is erroneous. So just three years after the condemnation, Grassi turned to the Tychonic model as a compromise — a reaction which he shared with many other Jesuit astronomers at the time. How all of this can be squared with his announced support for Aristotle is simply left unclear — another common feature in Jesuit scientific treatises after 1616.

One may go a step further and ask whether Grassi may have actually been personally persuaded of the truth of Copernicanism. The question arises because there are a number of letters[51] by Guiducci and Galileo in September 1624 which indicate at least that Grassi was not close-minded on this critical point. Thus on 6 September Guiducci told Galileo, "Father [Grassi] said that when a demonstration of that motion [of the earth] has been found, then it would be necessary to interpret Sacred Scripture otherwise than has been done in those passages which speak of the stability of the earth and the motion of the heavens, and this is the opinion of Cardinal Bellarmine." And on the thirteenth he added, "It seems to me that he [Grassi] is not very opposed to the motion of the earth, if there are good reasons for this motion and if there are answers to the objections to the contrary." On the twenty-eighth he wrote, "It would be a

---

50 Ibid., 105.

51 Guiducci's Letters to Galileo (6, 13, and 28 September 1624) and Galileo's Letter to Cesi (23 September 1624). *Opere* XIII, 202–203, 205–206, 208–209, 210–211.

good thing if it were to happen that this man [Grassi] were to set his mind on the opinion of the motion of the earth, and then to remain tied and attached to it afterwards. I am not without hope for this." On the twenty-third Galileo wrote to Cesi, "Fr. Grassi has become quite friendly with Mario Guiducci, who wrote me that Grassi does not reject the motion of the earth, now that Mario has removed his major doubts. It seems to me that he is very much inclined to my opinions. . . ."

Was this "friendship" with Guiducci simply a devious device on Grassi's part to gain advantage in the ongoing dispute with Galileo, as some have suggested?[52] Or was Grassi's "Jesuit dilemma" behind these friendly overtures to Guiducci, i.e., as a scientist he was convinced of the truth of Copernicanism which his Church and Society had asked him to reject? The latter is at least not impossible. What we do know is that, although Grassi lived until 1654, he never wrote another treatise for publication on any topic, scientific or otherwise, after 1626 when he closed his debate with Galileo.

If Grassi's attitude toward Galileo was somewhat ambiguous, that of Christopher Scheiner, S.J. (1573–1650)[53] was perfectly clear: he thoroughly disliked Galileo. These mutually hostile feelings originated in about 1612 in a sharp dispute with Galileo over who first had observed sunspots.[54] Scheiner was a first-class observational astronomer, and became the leading authority in his day on the phenomena of sunspots. His *Rosa ursina* (1626–30) was the definitive study of this topic in the seventeenth century, and contributed to the eventual triumph of Copernicanism. Yet the work is marred by

---

[52] For example, see Redondi, *Galileo Heretic*, 186 ff.

[53] Scheiner was a German Jesuit who spent his entire career in various Jesuit universities north of the Alps, except for a critical ten-year period in Rome from 1624 to 1633. From the time of Galileo's trial in the latter year up to the present day the claim has sporadically been made that in some unspecified way either the Jesuits in general, or Scheiner in particular, were directly responsible for bringing Galileo to trial. However, there is no concrete evidence to establish whether this actually happened or how it might have happened. For an identification and evaluation of some of these claims, see Redondi, *Galileo Heretic*, 33–36.

[54] The futility of such priority disputes is underlined by the fact that Johann Fabricius was actually the first to make these observations, in Leiden in late 1610, which he published in 1611.

Scheiner's need to devote the first sixty-six pages to a bitter attack against Galileo for a long list of offenses, including plagiarism.

More interesting for our concerns, however, is the fact that the last hundred-fifty pages of the *Rosa ursina* contain an extensive justification of the view that the heavens are corruptible, fluid, composed of fiery material, and not different in nature from sublunary matter — all of which are themes which are actually opposed to the traditional teachings of Aristotle. On the other hand shortly after Galileo's trial, Scheiner wrote an attack on Galileo's *Dialogues* which bore the title *Prodromus pro sole mobile et terra stabili*,[55] which obviously was a defense of the traditional geocentric model of the universe. To make matters more complex there is good reason to believe that Scheiner actually was a Copernican in his personal convictions. The evidence for this is a direct statement to that effect by Scheiner's reliable fellow Jesuit and scientist, Athanasius Kircher (1601–1680).

> The good Father [Kircher], whom we saw when he traveled in haste through here, could not keep himself from admitting to us, in the presence of Fr. Ferrand, that Fr. Malapert and Fr. Calvius himself did not disapprove of the opinion of Copernicus, and were not very far from it, but they had been pressured and obliged to write in favor of the common views of Aristotle, which even Fr. Scheiner himself supported only because of force and obedience.[56]

If this statement can be taken at face value, no more evidence would be needed to establish the Jesuit dilemma: how could one reconcile religious obedience with intellectual honesty? How Scheiner could have ever tried to combine all of his views listed above into

---

[55] This treatise was not published, however, until 1651, one year after Scheiner's death. In a letter to Kircher (16 July 1633) written shortly before the completion of this treatise, Scheiner wrote, "When the *Prodromus* is finished, I will, with the help of God, defend the common astronomy against Galileo throughout the whole book, as has been recommended by the Pope, our General, and the Assistants, all in the pursuit of higher things" (*Opere* XV, 184). By his own direct admission Scheiner was acting out of religious obedience in this attack against Galileo.

[56] Niccolo Fabri di Peiresc's Letter to Pietro Gassendi (6–10 September 1633). *Opere* XV, 254.

one picture is impossible to say. His apologetics were inconsistent with his science.

The 1616 condemnation of Copernicanism also had a direct impact on biblical scholarship by converting exegesis into an instrument of doctrinal apologetics. An excellent example of this is the small book entitled *Tractatus syllepticus*[57] published by Melchior Inchofer, S.J. (1585?–1648) a few months after Galileo's trial. Inchofer was a German Jesuit based in Messina, Sicily, who had a general but undistinguished background in both theology and mathematics. He stands out as the only Jesuit who figured directly in the Galileo trial. His role was to serve as one of the three members of the Special Commission[58] which functioned something like a grand jury in September 1632 to determine whether there was a basis for a trial. This Special Commission uncovered the now-famous memorandum of injunction[59] of 26 February 1616 (which purported to summarize Bellarmine's meeting with Galileo) which was the basis of their recommendation to proceed. The next April the same group submitted their judgments[60] to the trial proceedings that Galileo's *Dialogues* had indeed violated the earlier injunction. This point was the central legal issue at the trial.

The ninety-three pages of the *Tractatus syllepticus* constitute a unified and sustained argument against Copernicanism on biblical grounds. All of the usually quoted passages from the Scriptures are discussed in detail in the context of their literal meaning, which is predictably taken to be the foundational sense of the Bible. The basic structure of Inchofer's argument consists in first identifying what we know from the biblical texts to be directly revealed *de fide* truth, i.e.,

---

[57] The full title is *Tractatus syllepticus, in quo, quid de terrae, solisque motu, vel statione, secundum S. Scripturam, et Sanctos Patres sentiendum, quave certitudinem alterutra sententia tenenda sit, breviter ostenditur* (Romae: Ludovicus Griganus, 1633).

[58] For a discussion of how Inchofer was selected as the Jesuit member of the Special Commission and of the role that he played at the trial, see Redondi, *Galileo Heretic*, 252–255, and William R. Shea, "Melchior Inchofer's 'Tractatus Syllepticus': A Consultor of the Holy Office Answers Galileo," in *Novità celesti e crisi del sapere*, ed. P. Galluzzi (Firènze:Giunti Barbèra, 1984), 283–292.

[59] *Opere* XIX, 321–322.

[60] Inchofer's judgment is printed in *Opere* XIX, 349–356.

as contained in the explicit deposit of faith and as requiring assent
from the religious believer. Second, further indirect *de fide* truths
of various types are established by deduction from the foregoing.
When all of this is put together, what emerges is an unmistakable
geocentric model of the universe, which is based on biblical authority
and which thereby requires religious assent from the true believer.

Some of the specifics are worth mentioning to capture the tone
of the argument. The following five propositions are listed by Inchofer as directly *de fide*: (1) God made the firmament in the middle
of the waters, to divide the waters from the waters; this firmament
is called the heavens; in that firmament he placed two large lights,
the larger one (the sun) to govern the day, and the smaller one (the
moon) to govern the night. (2) The heavens are up and the earth
is down. (3) God suspended the earth above the void. (4) When
Christ suffered, the sun underwent a miraculous disappearance, and
darkness endured above the whole earth for three hours, i.e., from
six to nine. (5) The sun moves, and in a circle.[61]

From the above Inchofer then argues that the following indirectly *de fide* truths logically follow: "the earth is eternally at rest"
in the sense that there is no local motion of the earth as a whole, in
the sense that there is no rotation of the earth on itself, and in the
sense of its unending duration; the earth is fixed in the center of the
world, and is in the lowest place; the whole heaven moves circularly
around the earth, and had a spherical shape.[62] The result is that the
traditional geocentric model of the universe now has the status of *de
fide* revealed truth, and Copernicanism is thereby a formal heresy.

Granting all this, Inchofer then discusses at length the question
of whether it is permissible even to argue about the earth being at
rest or in motion. His answer is an unequivocal "no." As a *de fide*
truth the stability of the earth is beyond dispute. This issue has been
permanently settled on the basis of the authority of the Bible and
without analysis of the new astronomical observations, which would
be irrelevant. He quotes from the Eighth Session of the Lateran
Council to sustain his view that, "When the principles or conclusions of the philosophers deviate from the true faith, the teachers

---

[61] *Tractatus syllepticus*, 30–34.
[62] Ibid., 44–47.

of philosophy are obliged to correct them with the manifest truth of the Christian religion."[63] Apparently all qualifying distinctions in the earlier discussions of this issue have been dropped. For the defensive mind the hegemony of theology over science has become total. Neither the 1616 condemnation of Copernicanism nor Bellarmine's earlier advice to Foscarini about treating it only as an hypothesis is overlooked.

> It is permitted to assume the motion of the earth hypothetically for the purposes of making mathematical calculations. For it is the clear mind of the Church that Copernicanism is permitted to make calculations even though the principles from which they are derived are absolutely condemned . . . by the judgment of the Congregation of the Index.[64]

This is truly a sad situation. The sophistication of theological discourse has considerably declined since the days of Bellarmine and Foscarini. The main thesis of Copernicanism, i.e., the double motion of the earth, has been declared to be formally heretical since it is contrary to what is claimed to be the *de fide* truth of the Bible. In addition the issue should not even be discussed, as it is too threatening to Christian belief. That is also how Galileo reacted to Inchofer's book.

> Recently a Jesuit priest has published a book in Rome in which he says that this opinion [the motion of the earth] is so horrible, dangerous, and scandalous that, if it were permitted in classrooms, in the public arena, in public disputes, and in publications, it would bring forth arguments contrary to the principal articles of the faith, for example, the immortality of the soul, creation, the incarnation, etc. Therefore arguments against the stability of the earth should not be allowed in public discussions. Indeed the stability of the earth should above all be maintained so firmly that nothing can stand against it in any way, either by way of argumentation or because of its own better evidence. The title of this book is *Tractatus syllepticus* by Melchior Inchofer, S.J.[65]

---

63 Ibid., 57.
64 Ibid., 48.
65 Galileo's Letter to Elia Diodati (25 July 1634). *Opere* XVI, 118.

Thus by the time of Galileo's trial the refutation of Copernicanism as an apologetic goal of Jesuit writers was well established. The
guilty verdict of the trial only accelerated this tendency beyond the
point of no return. By mid-century scriptural argumentation against
Copernicanism had even become a part of scientific treatises written
by Jesuits.

For example, by far the most significant Jesuit treatise on astronomy in the generation after Galileo was the *Almagestum
novum*,[66] written by Giovanni Battista Riccioli (1598–1671). This
massive study contains an extensive discussion of the hypothesis that
the sun lies motionless in the center of the universe with the earth
revolving around it. This is finally rejected as false on scientific and
religious grounds. Riccioli's argument is that although heliocentricism does save the appearances, it has not been proven as true
scientifically. Thus it may be entertained hypothetically for purposes
of calculation, but that is quite different from taking it absolutely,
a clear reminiscence of Bellarmine's advice to Foscarini. To deal
with the latter and main point, the issue becomes one of how to
interpret the Bible and who has the authority to do this. The familiar distinctions are applied. Scripture must be read literally unless
such a reading conflicts with (1) a truth found elsewhere in revelation or tradition, (2) a definition proclaimed by the pope, or (3) a
truth established by natural reason. The stability of the earth and
the motion of the sun involve no such conflicts, and are thus to
be taken literally in the Bible, as the Fathers always have done.
As such they are *de fide* truths. Even Tobias's dog wagging his tail
is mentioned as a parallel case. And all of this is discussed in a
scientific treatise.

In his justification of this argument Riccioli quotes extensively
from both the Scripture and Church documents, including the relevant texts of the Fourth Session of Trent and the profession of faith
prescribed by Pius IV, which in Riccioli's day was still used as an oath
taken by students and faculty at the opening of the academic year

---

[66] *Almagestum novum* (Bononiae: Typis Haeredis Victorii Benatii, 1651).
The arguments against heliocentricism on religious grounds are found in Part II,
pp. 479–500.

at the Jesuit colleges.[67] Also quoted *in toto* are the 1616 Decree against Copernicanism, the list of corrections ordered in 1620 for his *De revolutionibus*, and the full text of both the sentence and the abjuration statement from Galileo's trial. In the light of all this the condemnation of Copernicanism and of Galileo are said to have been proper and deserved.[68]

The same conclusion and the same apologetic use of religious argumentation in a scientific treatise are also found in the writings of the polymath Athanasius Kircher, the most prominent Jesuit scientist in the two generations after Galileo.

> We completely reject Copernicanism both for scientific reasons and because it seems to be contrary to Sacred Scripture which attributes rest to the earth and motion to the sun and stars. Therefore when affirmed absolutely and not as an hypothesis, Copernicanism has been rightly condemned by the Congregation of Rites in Rome, on 5 March 1616, by the mandate of Pope Paul V, and again on 22 June 1633, by the mandate of Pope Urban VIII.[69]

On the other hand Kircher was quite non-Aristotelian in his views about the structure of the world: the heavens, stars, and planets are composed of the same type of matter found in the terrestrial realm, and are thus corruptible; the heavens are fluid in nature and immobile as a whole, while the stars and planets move through it from east to west (another theme from Bellarmine), apparently driven by immaterial intelligences; the planets revolve around the sun which in turn revolves around an immobile earth at the center (in short, Tycho's model). By mid-century Kircher seems comfortable in departing from the solid and uniform doctrine of Aristotle

---

[67] Ibid., II, 479. This oath was published in the Papal Bull *Iniunctum nobis* (13 November 1564) at the end of the Council of Trent. See chapter 1 for a discussion of this oath.

[68] Riccioli's sincerity in his refutation of heliocentricism has been questioned by Rudolf Wolf in his *Geschichte der Astronomie* (Munich: R. Oldenbourg, 1877), 434.

[69] Athanasius Kircher, *Iter extaticum coeleste* . . . (Herbipoli: Sumptibus Joh. Andr. & Wolffg. Jun. Endterorum Haeredibus. Prostat Norimbergae apud eosdem, 1660), 39. The first sixty pages of this book summarize Kircher's cosmology and reply to heliocentricism.

in his cosmology but certainly not from the accepted biblical and ecclesiastical pronouncements against Copernicanism.

Also to be noted in the writings of all these Jesuit scientists is the pervasive influence of Bellarmine, both in regard to his biblically based cosmology with its changeable and fluid heavens, and in regard to his critically important advice to Foscarini to maintain Copernicanism only hypothetically and not absolutely. According to Grienberger's comments on Biancani's book mentioned earlier, Bellarmine's advice to Foscarini may well have been the central consideration in the deliberations of the Congregation of the Index as it decided on its Decree of condemnation.

The Jesuit dilemma remained intact. With the notable exception of some isolated Jesuit scientists of the first rank (e.g., Roger Boscovich and Girolamo Saccheri in the eighteenth century), Jesuit science in general was never to regain the promise it exhibited in the period from Clavius to Scheiner. It was one of the casualties of the condemnation of Copernicanism.

7

Reflections on Truth in Science and in Religion

Galileo once said that science is written in the book of nature, which always lies open in front of our eyes for our inspection.[1] To read it, we need only pay careful attention and know the language, primarily mathematics, in which it is written. The methods needed to read this book would constitute, in effect, the logic of science.

Galileo's use of this metaphor provided the delightful rhetorical implication, which he used pointedly, that some of his scientific opponents were reading instead merely books of fantasy and fiction. But the metaphor also had a more serious dimension. The book of nature motif was no doubt suggested to Galileo by the older notion of the Bible as the book of revelation. This book also is always open to be read, this time by the common man in whose language it was written. But in this case the language used needs additional interpretation to uncover the authentic content of God's revelation of the profound and marvelous story of salvation, since God has chosen to accommodate his words in the Scriptures to the understanding of the common man. The methods needed to read the book of revelation, which are primarily the principles of biblical exegesis, constitute in effect the logic of religious belief.

This metaphor of the two books, of which Galileo was fond, had significant consequences. For example, it provided an assurance that ultimately science and religion must be consistent, because an always

---

[1] From *The Assayer*, at *Opere* VI, 232. See Drake, *Discoveries and Opinions of Galileo*, 237–238.

truthful God is the author of both books. The ancient notion of the unity of all truth had always been based on this general concept. It also put a special emphasis on locating the comparison of science and religion on the terrain of truth. For any book is composed of sentences in a text, and the credibility of the story consists in the truth of these sentences. This propositional sense of the content of revelation as written down in the Bible by its scribes taking dictation from God was thrust into prominence by Counter-Reformation theologians, and was easily transferred to the book of nature in the sense that God wrote the laws of nature into the structure of the world at creation. In both cases one is asked to conceive a structure, whether it be the order of nature or God's plan for human salvation, as being expressed as a set of propositions in a text, and thus to be read off as true. This reinforced the tendency to compare science and religion in regard to their respective truth values.

In the course of human history there have been some religions which were not built upon a sacred text. In such cultures religion and science would interact in ways in which questions of comparative truth would be less likely to arise. But when a set of sacred texts is the essential foundation of religion, as is clearly the case in the Judeo-Christian tradition, then questions of comparative truth claims become central in the relations between science and religion. Galileo's metaphor of the two books highlights this basic point.

This topic of the nature and status of truth has been our constant companion as we have tried to trace in detail the role of the Bible in the Galileo affair. It provides an ideal theme to summarize and evaluate our findings in conclusion. As we have repeatedly emphasized along the way, the Galileo affair was a complex, multi-leveled set of developments. No one factor, including this one, caused or fully explains what happened. With this caveat in mind, let us reconstruct as best we can how the contrast between the truth of science and the truth of the Bible developed and how these two modes of truth interacted in the Galileo case.

SCIENCE AND THE BIBLE

When one compares the views of Bellarmine and Galileo on this topic, one is struck first by the enormous range of agreement between them. For example, both of them would reject a resolution of the science-religion controversy which claimed that the two never really come into contact, science being concerned with the physical world and religion with the transcendent, immaterial world. Although such a "two-world" solution would promise an inviting permanent peace through separation, it would strike both Galileo and Bellarmine as involving a naive understanding of Christianity. God's presence in the world, for example through creation, the Incarnation, and the eucharist, belies such a separation and an other-worldly conception of religion. As a result scientific accounts of the world which would cast doubt on such religious teachings cannot be so easily ignored.

Furthermore when conflicts do arise, neither Galileo nor Bellarmine would say that there is any easy way to resolve them. The unity of truth doctrine gives only a general assurance that reconciliation between science and religion is always possible in principle, but does not identify the specific locus for rethinking the issues. For the latter, one needs detailed principles of exegesis telling one how to read the two books.

On the side of science both Galileo and Bellarmine had a sense that a new era was getting under way, the former with great hope, the latter with hesitation, and both saw its emerging criterion of truth as a complex mix of sensory evidence and formal reasoning. Although neither was fully clear on how these two factors constitute scientific truth (the problems of inductive and verificational logic still remain unresolved by philosophers of science), they both believed that some scientific claims can be taken to be demonstratively proven, while others are not. In the former case the unity of truth principle requires one to reinterpret an apparently conflicting passage of the Bible or a theological dogma accordingly. In the latter case such a reinterpretation would be premature, even when the scientific view has been established as highly probable. As Galileo put it, "It is the highest prudence to believe that there is no demonstration of the mobility of the earth until such a proof has been given. And we do not ask any one to believe this point without a demonstration. . . . If the proponents were to have no more than ninety percent of the arguments on their side, they would be rebutted."[2]

So in the case of a proven scientific claim which appears to conflict with a religious teaching, both Galileo and Bellarmine agree with the Augustinian advice to reinterpret the latter to fit the former. The second case of a conflicting but unproven scientific claim is much more problematic.

On the topic of the principles of exegesis needed to read the book of revelation, Galileo and Bellarmine were again very much, although not fully, in agreement. We know from Dini[3] that Bellarmine read Galileo's *Letter to Castelli*, in an accurate copy, and that he did not find any objections to Galileo's discussion of the principles of biblical exegesis. Most of Galileo's views on this topic and on the relation of the Bible to science were already contained in the *Letter*. However, we do not know if Bellarmine read Galileo's later *Letter to the Grand Duchess Christina*, where these views are expanded. But it seems reasonable to conclude that Bellarmine would have agreed with Galileo on the following points.

The central purpose of the Scripture is for God to communicate to human beings what we need to know for salvation and for the spiritual life with God. Most of these matters transcend human reason (otherwise revelation would not be needed), and as such are not discussed in the natural sciences. In giving this revelation God has chosen to speak in the language of the common man. The result of this accommodation, i.e., the use of everyday language to express the sublimest mysteries, is a considerable amount of ambiguity in the Scriptures as to their true meaning. Hence the claim that every statement in the Bible is true must carry the important proviso that

---

[2] Galileo's Unpublished Notes on Bellarmine's Letter to Foscarini, paragraph 6. See Appendix IX A.

[3] Dini's letter to Galileo, 7 March 1615. See Appendix V. It should be noted that Galileo, suspecting foul play, had sent an accurate copy to Bellarmine through Dini. So Bellarmine's reactions were to the correct original text of the *Letter to Castelli*. But the copy submitted to the Inquisition, and later to the trial in 1633 where it was explicitly cited for heterodox views, was Lorini's adulterated copy. See the footnotes to Appendix IV for the critical changes which made the false copy objectionable while the true copy had not been criticized by Bellarmine.

we have first been able to grasp its correct meaning, that is, the meaning intended by the Holy Spirit in dictating the Scriptures.

There is little or no room for doubt that Galileo would have agreed with Bellarmine's methods for distinguishing the meanings of Scripture into (1) the literal meaning of the words (either simple or metaphorical), and (2) their spiritual meaning (allegorical, tropological, and anagogical). These, after all, were longstanding distinctions used by Catholic exegetes, and Bellarmine was merely reformulating that tradition. And certainly Galileo would never have challenged the pronouncement of the Council of Trent, repeated by Bellarmine, that it belongs to the Church alone, and not to individual believers, to interpret the Bible as to its true meaning in matters of faith and morals. That indeed was one of the main claims of the Catholics against the Protestants during the Reformation.

It is also rather evident that Galileo agreed with Bellarmine on the methodological principle of appealing to the Fathers of the Church, and specifically to their common agreement, to establish the meaning of a biblical text. As a principle, this was not in dispute. But Galileo correctly insisted on the further point that in applying this principle, one should also show that the Fathers had explicitly considered the matter at issue (i.e., heliocentricism), and were not just speaking in the unreflective common idiom of their day.

Thus there was a great deal of agreement between Galileo and Bellarmine on the principles of exegesis. But not total agreement. When Foscarini had objected in his *Defense*[4] that heliocentricism was not a "matter of faith and morals," and therefore was not covered by the Decree of the Fourth Session of the Council of Trent, Bellarmine countered with his critically important distinction that some things in the Bible are matters of faith because of their subject matter, while others are matters of faith because of the speaker of the words, i.e., because of the authority of the Holy Spirit. We have called this Bellarmine's principle of *de dicto* truth. Galileo objected vigorously (albeit prudently) in his unpublished private notes. If this be granted, and if the meaning of the geocentric language in the Bible is not to be taken as metaphorical, then Copernicanism has been defeated for theological reasons. Galileo's objection was that

---

[4] Appendix VII B.

it would follow from Bellarmine's principle that innumerable trivial matters of contingent fact (e.g., Tobias had a dog) become "matters of faith and morals," that is, things which must be accepted by the religious believer as necessary for salvation. But certainly the Council of Trent did not say, and did not intend to imply, that everything in the Bible is a matter of faith and morals.

Galileo's criticism of Bellarmine was very well taken. But Bellarmine had made a quite important point if his principle of *de dicto* truth is taken in another way, which indeed may have motivated his remarks to Foscarini. His more general claim is that the reason why *any* statement in the Scriptures is true is simply that God has said so. No other evidence, or proof, or justification, is needed or relevant. Galileo would have agreed with this! In the last analysis the acceptability of religious teachings in Catholicism is based on the notion that God is the author of both Scripture and tradition. At this bedrock level the truth value of what was revealed is due simply to the fact that God has said so. For Bellarmine that point was central in the defense of the entire religious edifice.

In effect Bellarmine's principle of *de dicto* truth can be taken as a general statement of the standard of truth to be used for the Bible. He extended this standard to also define "matters of faith and morals" in his reply to Foscarini, thus making everything in the Bible a matter of faith, to which Galileo rightly objected. But taken as a truth condition[5] for Scripture, Bellarmine's principle correctly identifies that standard as the mere fact that God has said so. This is quite different from the truth condition for natural human knowledge in general, and specifically for the natural sciences, i.e., empirical fact plus valid formal reasoning. This contrast is central to the interactions between science and religion.

In summary, Galileo and Bellarmine were very much in agreement on the level of the principles of biblical exegesis. The only

---

[5] Both Galileo and Bellarmine subscribed to the traditional commonsense definition of truth as the correspondence of what is said or thought to what exists in the real world, and applied that definition to both science and religion. On the other hand, by "truth conditions" we mean the criteria used to judge whether truth, as defined above, is actually present in a given case. These truth conditions are quite different for science and for religion.

substantial disagreement was on the latter's innovative *de dicto* principle as a standard for "matters of faith and morals." But when it came to the application of these principles to Copernicanism, the two parted company decisively. They both seemed to have presumed that the content of natural scientific knowledge is divided into three groups: Category I: propositions demonstrated to be true; Category II: propositions not demonstrated to date but which could be demonstrated in the future;[6] Category III: propositions which can never be conclusively proven to be true.[7]

Regarding Category I, if a conflict arises between the Bible and a proven scientific truth, then Galileo and Bellarmine agreed that the unity of truth requires us either to reinterpret the Scripture accordingly, or at least to say that we do not understand the meaning of the relevant passages. Regarding Category III, if a conflict arises between the Bible and a proposition which science cannot prove to be true, then Galileo concedes that the Bible takes precedence over science, and we should understand the scientific claim accordingly. The problematic area is Category II. What should be done when a demonstrable but not yet actually demonstrated proposition of science conflicts with the Scriptures? Unfortunately Galileo is not completely clear at this critical point. In a few passages he seems to accede, at least temporarily, to the authority of the Bible in such cases, but more commonly he argues that in such cases one should not fix the meaning of the Bible in any one definite way lest later scientific proof establish the opposite, and thus scandalize the Church. This was the ancient advice of Augustine, and Galileo was standing on firm ground.

What then was the status of heliocentricism in 1616? If this theory had belonged in Category I, then Copernicanism would not have been condemned, and Galileo and Bellarmine would have agreed on

---

[6] To apply this analysis to specific cases, one would need criteria to identify the demonstrable claims within the larger set of not-yet-demonstrated propositions. Galileo does not provide such criteria, although he clearly considers heliocentricism to be included in Category II.

[7] It is not clear how this impossibility is established, and whether it includes the practically impossible as well as the impossible in principle. Galileo's example, i.e., that the stars are animate bodies, is not very helpful.

the need to interpret the geocentric passages of Scripture metaphorically. Galileo's efforts to find a conclusive proof of heliocentricism
were designed to settle the issue permanently as a Category I case.

Short of this, he had to hope that the Category II solution
was available. Many scholars have argued that the main reason for
Galileo's trip to Rome in 1615–16 was to try to persuade Church
officials that Copernicanism belonged in Category II, and thus it
would be wise to take no action on the case. If he had succeeded,
then the process of temporizing could have gone on as long as necessary to establish a proof one way or the other. This is how the
dispute over the reconciliation of God's grace and human free will
had been handled by the same top officials in Rome less than ten
years earlier.

Why did this not happen? Why not simply temporize? There is
no way to answer this question definitively. Many hypotheses suggest
themselves, and no one of them gives a complete explanation for
this key issue of why condemnation was chosen over temporizing.
But if we can assume that the Church officials clearly perceived the
alternatives sketched above, then one main factor may have been that
they were convinced that heliocentricism is a Category III claim, that
is, impossible to prove! The reason simply is that what is false cannot
be proven to be true. And they were convinced that Copernicanism
is false because the Bible, and therefore God, asserts the opposite.
In such a Category III case science must give way to the Bible.

If this reasoning sounds strange and circular to the modern ear,
this is at least partially because our present culture assigns a superior
status to scientific truth over biblical truth, with the result that when
the two conflict, we almost automatically tend to think of adjusting
our understanding of the latter to fit the former, rather than *vice
versa*. This in itself is an interesting indication of the present state
of the science-religion relationship. But the situation was just the
reverse in 1616. In that culture biblical truth, understood to be the
word of God himself, was assigned a status superior to the truth of
science, an emerging new enterprise whose credibility was not well
understood. The result was that when the two conflicted, the Church
officials automatically tended to think of adjusting the science to fit
the Bible. For them, obviously, the word of God came first. As a
case in point, which we have examined in chapter 2, Bellarmine's

personal convictions on the topic were dominated by his lifelong belief in an elaborate biblical cosmology as the real truth of the matter, to which he gave preference over both Copernicanism and the Aristotelian-Ptolemaic model.

From all this it follows that, in sorting out the relations between science and religion, it is not enough to point out that science's truth condition is evidence plus reasoning while religion's truth condition is the authority of the word of God in the Bible. Granting this, the next question is which, if either, of these truth standards takes precedence in the case of a conflict, and why. That is the central issue, even after all the necessary qualifications are added to the truth conditions, e.g., the weakness of inductive and verificational logic for science, and the caveats on determining biblical meaning and the common agreement of the Church Fathers for religion. This, of course, does not solve the problem of relating science and religion, but merely attempts to define its location more precisely.

RELIGIOUS FAITH AND THE LOGIC OF AUTHORITY

All, or nearly all, of the participants in the Galileo affair were Roman Catholics. Many were high Church officials or professional theologians thoroughly acquainted with the dogma and history of their Church. They shared in common not only the credal content of their religion but also its very specific conception of the nature of religious faith. An analysis of this latter notion, as understood at that time, throws a very helpful light on some of the aspects of the condemnation of Copernicanism and Galileo's trial. Yet oddly enough this has received little or no attention by Galileo scholars.

Perhaps the clearest way to explain that conception of religious faith is to reflect for a moment on how we form common, everyday natural beliefs. Suppose I tell you that my wife's name is Rosemary and that I have two sons. If you do not, or for whatever reason cannot, directly check these claims for yourself, you can still choose either to believe or disbelieve what I have said. If you believe what I have said, then you do so because you accept my authority as a reliable source of that information. In so doing, you are not merely expressing confidence or trust in me as person, however, for you have come to know something which you did not know before you read this paragraph. Of course, you could be wrong in your new belief; I may want to deceive you, or I may be confused today, or I may be an habitual liar. But that does not change the general fact that natural belief or faith is an act of knowing something in which the reason for assenting to the information provided is the willingness to accept the authority of its source as reliable.

It takes only a moment's reflection to realize that a very large part, if not most, of natural human knowledge is of this type. What we learn from teachers, from reading the newspapers, from viewing the television news, from listening to our friends and neighbors, is all based on a willingness to accept the authority of a source of information. In some cases we can independently and directly check that information against empirical facts and in other cases we cannot. The other major type of natural human knowledge arises from direct experience of the object or event known. Science is contained in this latter category, as is implied by its truth condition of sense data plus argumentation. No one, of course, can directly experience all of the evidence and argumentation which justifies science, and so the individual scientist must also have faith, in the sense defined above, in what his peers tell him about their direct knowledge. But at bedrock level science is not based on this natural faith but on knowledge by direct acquaintance.

The extension of the above ideas to religious faith is quite straightforward and has had a long history. The traditional view was that religious faith is an act of human reason in which we assent to the truth of some information because we are willing to accept the authority of its source. In this case the source ultimately is God, who, unlike human sources, never deceives us. The assent is an act of the intellect, but its motivation is an act of the will, a choice to accept the authority as reliable. Thus the assent in religious faith is not motivated by evidence, proof, arguments, etc. The information relates to "things unseen" which we need to know for salvation and the spiritual life. As an act of reason, religious faith is an act of knowing something, and thus is not merely an expression of one's trust or confidence in God. Since it is a form of knowledge, faith is properly designated as "true" in the usual correspondence-to-reality sense of that word. Like natural faith, religious faith includes an act of the will in the acceptance of an authority. Unlike natural faith, it includes information about the transcendent world and its authority ultimately is God.

This rather specific notion of the psychology and epistemology of religious faith was common in Catholicism long before the seventeenth century. It is found, for example, more than three centuries earlier in Thomas Aquinas.[8] It was still widely accepted and used at the time of Galileo, as can be seen in the following account from Bellarmine.

> The definition of faith, given by the Apostle, attributes two characteristics to faith. First it causes things which are hoped for in the future to abide in the soul. Second it causes the intellect to assent to things which it does not understand. . . . Faith causes the intellect to give its complete assent. However this occurs not because of the evidence for a thing, nor because of an understanding of its causes or properties, but because one yields to the authority of the speaker. Hence in faith the object remains as obscure as it was before, but it is believed because of the authority of the speaker. Therefore, properly speaking, faith is not an understanding but an acceptance. . . .[9]
>
> There are two types of judgment or assent. The first is based on evidence and reason, the second on the authority of the speaker; the former is called understanding, properly speaking, the latter is called faith.[10]

This is the notion of religious faith shared by the participants in the Galileo affair, virtually all of whom were Catholics. If this notion be granted, several consequences follow. For example, religious faith cannot be acquired merely by human reason acting on its own; rather it is a gift from God. It is an act of knowledge, not merely an expression of trust or confidence in God. The knowledge must be true because its source is infallible. Religious faith always involves an act of the will, an act of choosing to accept the authority of God. The religious merit of faith is grounded in this submission of the will. Religious faith always includes, in other words, a non-cognitive or non-rational factor, i.e., free personal commitment, which is over and above any appeal to evidence or argumentation. This is the reason why religious faith is not the product of reason alone, and why

---

[8] *Summa Theologica* II–II, Questions 1–4.

[9] *De controversiis* IV, III, 5.

[10] *De controversiis* IV, III, 7.

religious disputes can so often be frustrating when evidence and argumentation prove to be of no avail.

This traditional Catholic notion of the psychology of religious belief is to be understood as applying to the level of the individual person. It was an attempt to account for what happens in the mind of the individual believer who accepts the Bible as the authoritative word of God. On the other hand the Church itself is the community of such believers. As an institution it has, in addition, its own distinctive organizational structure which evolves over time. Although the history of the Catholic Church from its founding in the days of Imperial Rome up through the Counter-Reformation is extremely complex, it is clear that during this period it evolved into an increasingly centralized form as an institution. This, in turn, became intimately interwoven with the scriptural authority upon which the religious culture was based.

In general when a religious community becomes structured through institutionalization, so does the authority on which personal religious faith is based. As a result a logic of authority begins to emerge, and the character of that logic is largely determined by how that authority is institutionalized. In the case of the highly centralized organization of the Catholic Church, the original authority in the sacred texts and traditions was extended into the persons, offices, and pronouncements of the institutional Church. Because this authority is so basic to the entire edifice of the religious institution, it tends to become a primary concern. In time the protection, strengthening, and exercise of that authority can overshadow other elements of religion, including specific teachings. For example, when an authoritative pronouncement has been made on an issue, the following years tend to focus on asserting the authority behind it and the regulations to implement it, while the previously discussed merits behind the pronouncement are no longer seriously considered. For a massive body of evidence in support of this claim, one need only recall the Jesuit dilemma of choosing between scientific truth and religious commitment.

In effect, centrally institutionalized authority tends to evolve into power. Human frailty being what it is, the potential for abuse increases. We begin to see an emphasis on obedience rather than rational evaluation, on tests of faith, on loyalty oaths, on intimidation, on secret proceedings, on unnamed accusers and unspecified allegations, on the use of the courts to suppress recalcitrants — and ultimately on the whole repertoire of the Inquisition.

This is not a fantasy scenario. Rather it is precisely what happened in the Galileo affair. Before 1616 the substantive questions about how science relates to the Bible were debated, and with some vigor. This debate was, in effect, the presentation of the case in the first trial. After the condemnation of Copernicanism such discussions ceased. Galileo's loyalty and obedience were tested by the injunction. Intimidation worked for a while. The publication of the *Dialogue* forced the Church to protect and assert its authority. Thus the second trial became necessary. However that trial was not about science and the Bible but about authority, power, and obedience. Concern for truth had evolved into concern for authority and power; critical debate was replaced by suppression of thought; astronomy and biblical exegesis gave way to legal injunctions and court judgments.

In chapter 5 we raised, but did not answer, the question of why the Church, through the explicit order of Pope Paul V, decided in 1616 to deal with Galileo by means of a personal injunction. That decision was the critical one, for without it there would have been much less likelihood of a later trial for Galileo. There were other alternatives. The Church could have simply allowed Galileo to infer for himself from the Decree of 1616 that future advocacy of Copernicanism would not be tolerated, or could have put the *Letters on Sunspots* on the *Index* "until corrected," or could have privately informed him of the decision on Copernicanism and asked for his acceptance without the heavy threat of a personal injunction. Why was the formal injunction route taken?

The hypothesis which suggests itself from our study is that the injunction was dictated by what we have called the logic of centralized authority. After the decision was made to condemn Copernicanism, the overriding issue became one of obedience to that decision, not the truth of astronomical theories. As a member of a religious order, Foscarini was already under an explicit vow of obedience, and thus could be controlled accordingly; the blanket condemnation of his *Lettera* in the Decree was more than enough pressure on him. The Jesuits, who were under an even stricter vow of obedience,

needed no further directives beyond the Decree not only to drop
any advocacy of Copernicanism by their members but also to attempt to oppose and refute that doctrine in the writings of others.
Religious obedience won out over scientific truth.

But Galileo, the most prominent and most likely and effective
spokesman for the condemned theory, was not a member of a religious order, and thus was not antecedently constrained by an explicit
vow of religious obedience but only by his general loyalty as an active
Catholic. That apparently was not enough. But the situation could
be remedied by imposing on him a special obligation in the form
of a legal injunction to accept and obey the Decree against Copernicanism. This was the explicit thrust of the pope's instructions to
Bellarmine for the meeting with Galileo. Refusal to agree was to result in an injunction; refusal to obey the injunction was to result in
imprisonment — strong orders which must have been motivated by
an equally strong concern to maintain authority. Henceforth Galileo
had to live under the equivalent of a formal vow of obedience on
this particular issue, at least in the eyes of the Church.

This thrust toward the use of obedience as a tool for the maintenance of power is a key element in the logic of centralized authority.
Its presence is evident in the struggles of the Jesuits in the aftermath
of the Decree of 1616. It is also suggested by the traditional Catholic
understanding of religious faith as consisting of an act of the will determining the judgment of reason because the authority of a speaker
is accepted. For influencing that act of the will in the direction of
the acceptance of religious authority was of primary importance for
the maintenance and flourishing of the religious culture.

In the last analysis the concern of science is to persuade human reason; the concern of religion is to win over the human will.
Science seeks understanding; religion seeks personal commitment.
Science focuses on truth; religion on morality. The rivalries between
science and religion often arise because these goals so easily overlap.

The disturbing question that remains is whether the pattern
of the logic of centralized authority described above was unique to
the Galileo case or whether it is more deeply rooted in the character of religious faith. If individual interpretation of Scripture and
personal moral conscience were major pleas from the reformers,
the Counter-Reformation was a surge in the opposite direction of

centralized authority in the Catholic Church. The Galileo case was another step in that direction. But is it necessary, is it even desirable, that the authority upon which a religious culture is based takes on a highly centralized structure as it is institutionalized? Or alternatively, is religious faith, as defined above, consistent with a democratization of its authority?

If we turn to the present day, the respective situations of science and Catholicism have changed considerably. The Catholic Church has established a further centralization of its religious authority in the proclamation of the infallibility of the pope in 1870. Simultaneously its social, political, and cultural power has lessened considerably. Meanwhile modern society has evolved more and more in the direction of the democratization of political authority and power. Also science has replaced religion as the dominant cultural force, and its power has increased tremendously through its marriage with technology. Is science itself subject to an analogous logic of authority and power, but one which exhibits a decentralized and more democratic structure? If so, science and Catholicism have been moving in opposite directions since the days of Galileo on the issue of how their respective authorities have become institutionalized. Furthermore, except for evolution, the issues which now dominate the science-religion interaction tend to be moral rather than cosmological in character.

Yet despite these massive changes since the age of Galileo, the Catholic conception of the nature of religious faith and the logic of centralized authority related to it seem to remain untouched. Could there be a second Galileo affair? What has been learned from the first one?

I

Decrees of the Council of Trent Session IV (8 April 1546)

DECREE ON TRADITION AND ON
THE CANON OF SACRED SCRIPTURE

The holy, ecumenical, and general Council of Trent, having been lawfully assembled in the Holy Spirit, with the same three legates of the Apostolic See presiding, constantly focuses its attention on preserving the purity of the Gospel in the Church, after errors have been removed. This Gospel, which was initially promised by the prophets in the Sacred Scriptures, was first promulgated by Our Lord Jesus Christ, Son of God, by his own mouth, who then commanded His Apostles to preach it to all creatures as the source both of all saving truth and of moral rules. The Council also clearly maintains that these truths and rules are contained in the written books and in the unwritten traditions which, received by the Apostles from the mouth of Christ Himself or from the Apostles themselves, the Holy Spirit dictating, have come down to us, transmitted as it were from hand to hand. Following then the examples of the orthodox Fathers, it receives and venerates with a feeling of equal piety and reverence both all the books of the Old and the New Testaments, since one God is the author of both, and also the traditions themselves, whether they relate to faith or to morals, as having been dictated either orally by Christ or by the Holy Spirit, and preserved in the Catholic Church in unbroken succession.

In addition the Council has resolved to write down a list of the sacred books in this Decree so that there can be no room for doubt as to what books are accepted by the Council. The true books are the following. In the Old Testament: the five books of Moses, i.e., Genesis, Exodus, Leviticus, Numbers, and Deuteronomy; Josue, Judges,

Ruth, the four books of Kings, two books of Paralipomemon, the first book of Esdras and the second which is called Nehemias, Tobias, Judith, Esther, Job, the Psalter of David containing 150 Psalms, Proverbs, Ecclesiastes, the Canticle of Canticles, Wisdom, Ecclesiasticus, Isaias, Jeremias with Baruch, Ezechiel, Daniel, the twelve minor prophets, i.e., Osee, Joel, Amos, Abdias, Jonas, Micheas, Nahum, Habacuc, Sophonias, Aggeus, Zacharias, and Malachias; and two books of the Machabees, the first and the second. In the New Testament: the four Gospels according to Matthew, Mark, Luke, and John; the Acts of the Apostles written by Luke the Evangelist, the fourteen Epistles of Paul the Apostle to the Romans, two to the Corinthians, to the Galatians, to the Ephesians, to the Philippians, to the Colossians, two to the Thessalonians, two to Timothy, to Titus, to Philemon, and to the Hebrews; two of Peter the Apostle, three of John the Apostle, one of James the Apostle, one of Jude the Apostle, and the Apocalypse of John the Apostle.

If there be anyone who will not accept these books as sacred and canonical, both as wholes and in all their parts, as they have been customarily read in the Catholic Church, and as contained in the old Latin Vulgate edition, and who knowingly and deliberately rejects the above-mentioned traditions, let him be anathema. Thereby let it be known to all what order and method this Council will follow, after having laid down the foundation of the confession of faith, and what testimonies and authorities it will primarily use in confirming dogmas and in restoring morals in the Church.

DECREE ON THE EDITION AND ON THE
INTERPRETATION OF THE SACRED SCRIPTURES

Moreover, since considerable benefit will accrue to the Church of God if it be made known which of all the Latin editions of the sacred books in circulation is to be taken as authentic, this same holy Council ordains and declares that the old Latin Vulgate edition, which has been approved for use in the Church for so many centuries, is to be taken as authentic in public lectures, disputations, sermons, and expositions, and that no one should dare or presume to reject it under any circumstances whatsoever.

Furthermore, to control petulant spirits, the Council decrees that, in matters of faith and morals pertaining to the edification of Christian doctrine, no one, relying on his own judgment and distorting the Sacred Scriptures according to his own conceptions, shall dare to interpret them contrary to that sense which Holy Mother Church, to whom it belongs to judge their true sense and meaning, has held and does hold, or even contrary to the unanimous agreement of the Fathers, even though such interpretations should never at any time be published. Those who do otherwise shall be identified by the ordinaries and punished in accordance with the penalties prescribed by the law.

The Council also properly wishes to impose limits in this area on publishers, who now without limits think that whatever pleases them is permissible, and who publish, without the license of ecclesiastical superiors, the books of the Sacred Scriptures and notes and commentaries on them by all authors indiscriminately, often with the name of the press omitted or falsified, and what is worse, without the name of the author, and who rashly sell such books which have been printed elsewhere. Hence the Council ordains and declares that henceforth the Sacred Scriptures, and especially the old Vulgate edition, will be printed as accurately as possible, and that no one is permitted to publish or to have published any books at all dealing with sacred matters without the name of the author, or to sell such books in the future, or even to possess them, unless these books have first been examined and approved by the ordinary, under the penalty of anathema and fines as stated in the canon of the most recent Lateran Council. If these persons be regulars, then in addition to this examination and approval, they must also obtain the permission of their superiors, who will examine the books in accordance with their own rules. Those who circulate or publicize such books in manuscript before they have been examined and approved are subject to the same penalties as the publishers. Those who possess or read such books will be taken to be the author if they do not identify the author. The approval of such books will be given in writing, and it will be authentically stated at the front of the book, whether it be printed or in manuscript. All of this, that is, the examination and the approval, shall occur without any fees, so that what should be approved will be approved and what should be condemned will be condemned.

Furthermore, the Council wishes to suppress that boldness which turns and twists the words and sentences of the Sacred Scriptures to all sorts of profane purposes; namely, to what is scurrilous, fabulous, vain, to flatteries, detractions, superstitions, to impious and diabolical incantations, divinations, prophesies, and defamatory libels. To remove such irreverence and contempt, so that henceforth no one would ever dare to misuse the words of Sacred Scripture in these or similar ways, it is ordained and commanded that all men of this kind, who are polluters and violators of the word of God, be restrained by the bishops with the penalties of the law and of their own choice.

APPENDIX
II

Diego de Zuñiga of Salamanca
[Didacus à Stunica Salmanticensis]
Commentary on Job (Toledo, 1584, pages 205 ff.)

On JOB 9:6: "He who moves the earth from its place,
and its pillars are shaken."

This passage states another effect of God to show his great
power and infinite wisdom. This passage seems to be a difficult one
indeed, but it is considerably clarified by means of the opinion of the
Pythagoreans, who think that the earth moves by its own nature and
that it is not otherwise possible to explain the motions of the stars
which vary a great deal in their speed and slowness. Philolaus held
this opinion, and so did Heraclides of Ponticus, as Plutarch says in
his *De placitis philosophorum*. Numa Pompilius agreed with them.
And what I find more astonishing, so did the divine Plato in his old
age who said that it would be a most absurd thing to think otherwise,
as Plutarch relates in his life of *Numa* XI. And Hippocrates in his
De flatibus says that the air is "tēs gēs ochēma," i.e., the chariot
of the earth. In our own day Copernicus explains the paths of the
planets by means of this opinion. There is no doubt that the locations
of the planets are much better and more certainly determined by
this doctrine than by what is found in Ptolemy's *Almagest* and in
the views of others. It is well known that Ptolemy was never able
to explain the motion of the equinoxes or to establish an exact and
fixed beginning of the year. He confesses this in his *Almagest* III, 2,
and leaves these matters for the discovery of later astronomers who

would be able to compare more observations over a longer period of time than he could. And although the Alphonsines and Thebit ben Core tried to explain this, they accomplished nothing. For the statements of the Alphonsines are internally inconsistent, as Ricius has shown. And although the argument of Thebit was more acute and established a fixed beginning of the year (which Ptolemy had sought), still it is now apparent that the progression of the equinoxes is longer than he thought was possible. Also the sun is known to be much closer to us than was formerly thought, by more than forty thousand stadia. Ptolemy and the other astronomers did not know the cause of the motion of the sun. But Copernicus determined and demonstrated the causes of all these things most clearly from the motion of the earth, with which all the remaining things agree more fittingly. And this opinion is not in the least refuted by what Solomon says in Ecclesiastes 1:4: "But the earth remains forever." For this only means that although there be many future ages and many human generations on the earth, still the earth itself remains one and the same and exists in the same way.

For the full passage is, "Generations will come, and generations will pass away, but the earth remains forever." As a result the context does not require one to say that the earth is immobile (as the philosophers maintain.) Although the Sacred Scriptures state that the sun moves in this chapter of Ecclesiastes and in many other places, while Copernicus claims that it stands immobile in the center of the universe, there is nothing which contradicts his view. For in their words both Copernicus and his followers assign the motion of the earth to the sun, for example, they often call the path of the earth the path of the sun. Finally there are no other passages in Sacred Scripture which more openly say that the earth does not move or which say, as in the present passage, that it does move. Therefore the present passage, which we have been discussing, is easily reconciled with Copernicus' opinion. And in order to show the marvelous power and wisdom of God, who initiates and maintains the motion of the whole earth, which is enormous by nature, the text adds, "and its pillars are shaken." This teaching means that it is moved from its foundations.

III

Robert Cardinal Bellarmine
Disputations on the Controversies Over Christian Faith Against the Heretics of the Day

Controversy I: On the Word of God
Book 3: On the Interpretation of the Word of God
Chapter 3: *The Question of the Judge of Controversies is Posed; also the Meanings of Scripture are Discussed.*

Now that it has been established that Scripture is obscure and needs interpretation, another question arises; namely, whether the interpretation of Scripture should be sought from some one visible and common judge, or should be left to the judgment of each individual person. This is indeed a most serious question, and all controversies depend, as it were, on it. Many have written on this question; but especially John Driedo in *De ecclesiasticis dogmatibus*, Book 2, Chapter 3; John Cochlaeus in his book *De scriptuarum et ecclesiae auctoritate*; the Cardinal of Warmia [Ermland] [Stanislaus Hosius] in *Contra prolegomena Brentii*, Books 2 and 3; Peter de Soto in defense of his *Methodus confessionis*, against the same *Prolegomena* of Brenz, Parts 2 and 3; Martin Perez de Ayala, in his book *De traditionibus*, assertions 2, 3, 4, and 5; Michael Medina in *De recta in deum fide*, Book 7; and Melchior Cano in *De locis theologicis*, Book 2, Chapters 6, 7, and 8.

Certain preliminaries must be noted in order to understand what is being asked. The first of these concerns the meanings of Scripture. For it is a peculiarity of Scripture, since it has God as its author, that it very often contains two meanings, the literal or historical, and the spiritual or mystical. The literal meaning is the meaning which the words immediately present; the spiritual meaning refers to something else other than that which the words immediately signify. This distinction is used by the Apostle in Corinthians 1:10, where he says that everything that happened to the Jews is an example for our improvement. What is said about the exodus of the Jews from Egypt, the crossing of the sea, the manna rained in the desert, and the water which flowed from the rock, he applies spiritually to Christians. Also Jerome in *In Ezechielem*, Chapter 2, where he deals with the Apocalypse and Ezekiel 2, teaches that these two meanings are signified internally and externally by the written book.

Philo in his book *De vita contemplativa* and Nazianzus in *Ad Nemesium* compare literal meaning to the body and spiritual meaning to the soul. Just as the generated Word of God has an invisible divine nature and a visible human nature, so also the written word of God has an external and an internal meaning. St. Gregory in *Moralia*, Book 21, Chapter 1, teaches that this is a characteristic only of divine Scripture.

Furthermore there are two types of literal meaning: simple, which consists of the proper meanings of words; and figurative, in which words are transferred from their natural signification to another. There are as many types of the latter as there are types of figures. When the Lord says in John 10, "I have other sheep which are not of this fold," the meaning is literal; but the figurative meaning is that other men besides the Jews must be gathered into the Church, which is said properly at John 11; namely, that he would gather together in unity the children of God who were scattered. Regarding figurative locutions, see St. Augustine, *De doctrina christiana*, Book 3.

More recent theologians distinguish three meanings of Scripture: the allegorical, the tropological, and the anagogical. In their allegorical meaning the words of Scripture, in addition to their literal meaning, signify something in the New Testament which pertains to Christ or the Church. For example Abraham, who indeed literally had two wives, one a free woman and the other a servant, and two sons, Isaac and Ismael, signifies God as the author of two testaments and as the father of two peoples, as the Apostle explains in Galatians 4. In their tropological meaning the words or events are used to signify something which pertains to morals. For example, the words, "Do not muzzle an ox treading corn," which are understood literally to be about a real ox, signify spiritually that orators should not be prohibited from accepting food from the people, as the Apostle explains in Corinthians 1:9. In their anagogical meaning the words or events are used to signify eternal life. For example, the words of Psalm 95, "And so, in anger, I swore that not one would reach the place of rest I had for them," which are understood literally to be about promises of land, also refer spiritually to eternal life, as the Apostle explains in Hebrews 4.

This distinction of spiritual meanings is not always observed by the ancient writers. For although they knew about all these meanings as they were relevant, still sometimes they call all of them allegorical, as does Basil in the beginning of his *Homiliae in Hexaemeron*, 9, and Augustine in his book *De utilitate credende*, Chapter 3. Also Jerome in his *Epistula ad Hedibiam*, question 12, included the allegorical under the name tropological, and contrariwise in *In Amos*, Chapter 4, included the tropological under the name allegorical.

Of these meanings the literal is found in every sentence of both the Old and the New Testament. And it is not improbable that now and then many literal meanings are found in the same sentence, as St. Augustine teaches in many places, and especially in *Confessiones*, Book 12, Chapter 26, in *De civitate Dei*, Book 11, Chapter 19, and in *De doctrina christiana*, Book 3, Chapter 27. Moreover all of the spiritual meanings are found in both testaments. For no one doubts that the Old Testament has allegorical, tropological, and anagogical meaning. And many think the same thing about the New Testament, and rightly so. For Augustine in *On John*, tractatus 122, explains allegorically the catch of fish when the net broke in Luke 5. But he explains it anagogically when the net did not break in John 21. Similarly in *On John*, tractatus 124, he explains allegorically what was said to Peter, "Follow me," and anagogically what was said of John, "If I want him to remain," John 21. And he explains tropologically, in John 13, the humility of God when he washed the feet of the disciples.

But however this may be, spiritual meaning is not found in every sentence of Scripture, in neither the Old nor in the New Testament. For the words, "Love the Lord your God with all your heart," in Deuteronomy 6, and in Matthew 22, and similar precepts, have only one meaning, that is, the literal meaning, as Cassiano rightly teaches in *Collationes* 8, Chapter 3. This being so, we and our adversaries agree that effective arguments ought to be sought in the literal meaning alone. For it is certain that that meaning, which is taken immediately from the words, is the meaning of the Holy Spirit. But there are various mystical and spiritual meanings, and although they are edifying when they are not contrary to faith and good morals, nevertheless it is not always clear whether they were intended by the Holy Spirit. As a result St. Augustine, in *Epistula 48 ad Vincentium*, rightly laughs at Donatistas who gave a mystical interpretation to the words, "Show me where you feed, where you lie down, in the south," and concluded that the Church of Christ was to continue only in Africa. Jerome also, in his commentary on Matthew 13, teaches that the dogmas of faith cannot be effectively established from the mystical senses.

Doubts regarding the literal meaning itself arise occasionally for two reasons. The first is the ambiguity of words, as is seen in Matthew 26, "Drink all of you from this." The words "all of you" are ambiguous, if only the words are examined. For it is not known whether this signifies all men absolutely, or only all the faithful, or all the apostles. The second and more serious case is the proper meaning of words. For since literal meaning is sometimes simple and sometimes figurative, as we said, it is doubtful in many places whether the true sense is simple or figurative. The words in Matthew 26, "This is my body," Catholics wish to be accepted simply according to the proper meaning of the words, but the followers of Zwingli take them in a metaphorical way. For this reason some have at times fallen into the gravest errors. An example is Origen who erred in this way by accepting figuratively what should have been taken simply, as Jerome teaches in his *Epistula ad Pammachium* concerning the error of John of Jerusalem, where he says that Origen so allegorized the terrestrial paradise that he lost the truth of history, interpreting trees as angels, rivers as celestial powers, and the human bodies of Adam and Eve as skin-like tunics, as if they had lived without a body before they sinned.

Others have fallen into the contrary error of taking as simple and proper, things which ought to be taken figuratively. An example is Papias, and those who followed him, Justinus, Irenaeus, Tertullian, Lactantius, and some others, who thought that what is said in Apocalypse 20, about the new Jerusalem and the thousand years in which the Saints will reign with Christ, is to happen here on earth. Their error was condemned by Jerome in the preface to his *In Isaiam*, Book 18, and in *In Ezechielem*, Chapter 36, and by Augustine in his *De civitate Dei*, Book 20, Chapter 7.

Our adversaries agree with us that the Scriptures ought to be understood in the spirit in which they were written, that is, in the Holy Spirit. The Apostle Peter teaches this in 2 Peter 1, when he says, "Understand this first, that no prophesies are due to individual interpretation. For the prophesies are never derived from human effort; rather the holy men of God spoke as inspired by the Holy Spirit." By this St. Peter proves that the Scriptures ought not to be explained by the individual mind but according to the dictates of the Holy Spirit, because they were not written by the human mind but by the inspiration of the Holy Spirit.

The whole question, therefore, comes down to this: Where is that spirit? We maintain that, although this Spirit is often absent in many individual persons, still it is certainly to be found in the Church, that is, in a council of bishops established by the highest pastor of the whole Church, or in the highest pastor with a council of the other pastors. We do not wish to enter into a discussion here about the highest pontiff and councils, as to whether the pontiff alone or a council alone can define something. We will deal with this in its own place. Rather here we say in general that the judge of the true meaning of Scripture and of all controversies is the Church, that is, the pontiff with a council, on which all Catholics agree and which was expressly stated by the Council of Trent, Session 4.

But all contemporary heretics teach that the Holy Spirit which interprets Scripture is not a group of bishops or of any other class of persons. Hence each individual ought to be the judge, either by following his own spirit if he has the gift of interpretation, or by committing himself to someone else whom he sees as having that

gift. In his preface to *Assertio omnium articulorum* Luther openly
refers us to the spirit which each person has when he diligently
reads the Scriptures. And in article 115 of the five hundred collected
by Cochlaeus from the books of Luther, the latter says, "Take this
advice: neither the Pope nor councils nor any other person has the
power to decide and establish what belongs to faith. Hence I should
say: Pope, you have decided with the councils; now I need to judge
whether or not I can accept it. Why? Because you will not stand for
me, and you will not answer for me, when I come to die. And only
a spiritual person can judge false doctrine. Thus it is madness to say
that councils can decide and establish what should be believed; for
often there is no one who has detected the ordinary divine spirit."
He says the same thing in Assertions 27, 28, and 29.

In his chapter on the Church in *In locis*, Philip seems to attribute something to the Church, but actually leaves all judgment
to each individual person. He asks, "Who will be the judge when
a disagreement arises about a sentence of Scripture, and there is
need of a word to settle the controversy? I respond that the word
of God is the judge, and the confession of the true Church accepts
this." However later he teaches that by "true Church" he does not
mean the prelates of the Church, nor the greater part of the faithful, but those few who agree with the word of God. Thus he covers
everything with darkness, and makes each person the judge. For
I cannot judge what is the true Church without first judging what
opinion agrees with the word of God. He says, "There is a difference
between judges of the Church and political judges. For in politics
either the monarch alone pronounces by his own authority or in a
senate the majority opinion prevails. But in the Church what prevails
is the opinion which agrees with the word of God; and the confession
of the pious, be they few or many, prevails over the impious." See
many places in his discussion of the characteristics of the Church.

Similarly, in the chapter on Sacred Scripture in his *Confessio
Wirtembergica* and extensively in his *Prolegomena*, Brenz teaches
against Peter de Soto on two points. First he says, "In the case of
eternal salvation it is not possible to hold a foreign opinion in such
a way as to embrace it without personally judging it." Secondly he
adds, "It pertains to each individual person to judge the doctrines
of religion and to distinguish the true from the false. But there is

a difference between the individual person and the prince; namely, the former has the private power, and the latter the public power, to judge and to decide the doctrines of religion," etc. In almost the whole book he tries to prove two things: that the secular prince can force his subjects, even under pain of death, to accept the faith which the prince judges to be true; and at the same time that the subjects are obligated to follow their own judgment whatever it is, and not another's. Brenz does not notice that it is absurd and contradictory to say that the prince commands but the subjects do not obey. Nor does he notice that if his opinion is true, then the Holy Roman Emperor and the other Catholic German princes would be acting rightly if they were to force all Lutherans under pain of death to accept the Catholic faith.

In his *Institutiones*, Book 4, Chapters 8, 9, 12, and 13, John Calvin orders an exact examination of the definitions of Scripture and especially of the general councils; then he makes individual persons the judges in matters of faith, not only of the Fathers but also of the councils. He leaves almost nothing to the common judgment of the Church. Finally Martin Chemnitz, in his examination of the Fourth Session of the Council of Trent, as well as all other contemporary heretics transfer the authority of interpreting Scripture from the bishops in councils to the spirit of individual persons.

APPENDIX

IV

Galileo's *Letter to Castelli*

To the Very Reverend Father and Most Worthy Gentleman:

Yesterday I met Sig. Niccolò Arrighetti, who gave me a report about you from which I derived the infinite pleasure of learning what I have never doubted; namely, the great satisfaction which you have given to the whole University, to its administrators as much as to its teachers and to every group of students. This applause has not increased the number of your competitors, as usually happens among men of similar accomplishments, but has restricted them to only a very few. Even these few will become quiet if they wish that this competition, which still usually merits the title of being a virtue at times, will not degenerate and change in character into a blameful affection which ultimately is more dangerous to those who clothe themselves in it than to anyone else. But what was most to my liking was to hear the account of the discussions which, thanks to the great kindness of the Grand Duchess, you had occasion to bring up at table and to continue later in the private chambers of the Grand Duchess, in the presence of the Grand Duke and the Archduchess, and the most illustrious and renowned Don Antonio and Don Paolo Giordano, and some well-known philosophers. What greater good fortune could one have than to see the Grand Duchess herself taking satisfaction from having this discussion with you, from raising doubts, from listening to solutions, and from remaining satisfied with your replies?

The particulars which you brought up, as reported by Sig. Arrighetti, have given me an occasion to return to some general considerations about natural conclusions, and in particular about the passage in Joshua which was mentioned by the Grand Duchess, with a few rejoinders from the Archduchess, as contradictory to the mobility of the earth and the stability of the sun.

In regard to the Grand Duchess' first general question,[1] I agree, as you most prudently proposed, conceded, and established, that it is not possible for Sacred Scripture ever to deceive or to err; rather its decrees have absolute and inviolable truth. Only I would have added that, although Scripture itself cannot err, nevertheless some of its interpreters and expositors can sometimes err, and in various ways.[2] The most serious and most frequent of these errors occurs when they wish to maintain always the direct meaning of the words, because from this there results not only various contradictions but even grave and blasphemous heresies. Accordingly it would be necessary to attribute to God feet and hands and eyes and even human and bodily feelings like anger, regret, hatred, and even occasional forgetfulness of the past and ignorance of the future. Many propositions are found in the Scriptures which, in respect to the bare meaning of the words, give an impression which is different from the truth, but they are stated in this way in order to be accommodated to the incapacities of the common man.[3] As a result, for those few who deserve to be distinguished from the common people, it is necessary that wise expositors provide the true meanings and indicate the particular reasons why the Scriptures are expressed in such words.

Granting then that in many passages the Scriptures not only can be, but necessarily must be, interpreted differently from the apparent meaning of the words, it seems to me that in cases of natural disputes Scripture ought to be put off to the last place. For both Sacred Scripture and nature are derived from the Divine Word, the former as dictated by the Holy Spirit and the latter as most carefully discovered in the laws of God. Moreover it is agreed that, to accommodate itself to the understanding of everyone, Scripture says many

---

[1] Lorini's adulterated copy of this letter begins with this sentence. In addition to several minor modifications, there are three major changes, plus an omission of any reference to the Tuscan royal family. See *Opere*, XIX, 299–301 for all the modifications in Lorini's text.

[2] In Lorini's copy, the words, "some of" and "sometimes" are omitted from this sentence.

[3] In Lorini's copy this sentence is changed to read: " . . . which, in respect to the bare meaning of the words, are false, but they are stated . . . "

things which are different from absolute truth in the impression it gives and in the meaning of its words. On the other hand nature is inexorable and immutable and cares not whether its hidden causes and modes of operation are or are not open to the capacities of humans, and hence it never violates the terms of its established laws. As a result it seems that natural effects, which either sense experience places before our eyes or necessary demonstrations reveal, should never be placed in doubt by passages of Scripture whose words give a different impression; and further not everything said in the Scriptures ought to be associated strictly with some effect in nature. Because of this characteristic alone, i.e., that Scripture accommodates itself to the capacity of uncouth and uneducated people, Scripture does not refrain from faintly sketching its most important dogmas, thus attributing to God himself conditions which are very far from, and contrary to, his essence.[4] So who would wish to maintain with certainty that Scripture abandons this characteristic when it speaks incidentally of the earth or the sun or other creatures, and has chosen to restrain itself completely within the limited and narrow meaning of the words? — and especially when it speaks about those created things which are very far from the primary purpose of the Scriptures? — or even when it speaks of things which, when stated and presented as bare and unadorned truths, would quickly damage its primary intention by making the common man more stubbornly resistant to be persuaded of the articles concerning his salvation?

Granting this, and also granting that it is even more obvious that two truths can never be contrary to each other, it is the task of wise expositors to try to find the true meanings of sacred passages in accordance with natural conclusions which previously have been rendered certain and secure by manifest sensation or by necessary demonstrations. Furthermore, as I have said, although Scripture has been dictated by the Holy Spirit, for the reasons mentioned above it is open in many passages to interpretations far removed from the literal meaning; and moreover we cannot determine with certitude that all the interpreters speak with divine inspiration. As a result I believe that it would be prudent to agree that no one should fix

---

[4] In Lorini's copy this sentence is changed to read: " . . . Scripture does not refrain from perverting its most important dogmas . . . "

the meaning of passages of Scripture and oblige us to maintain as
true any natural conclusions which later sensation or necessary and
demonstrative proofs might show to be contrary to truth. Who would
wish to place limits on human understanding? Who would wish to
assert that everything which is knowable about the world is already
known? And therefore, except for the articles concerning salvation
and the foundations of the faith, against the strength of which there
is no danger that any valid and forceful doctrine could ever arise,
it would be perhaps the best advice not to add anything without
necessity. Granting this, what greater confusion could arise than from
the increase of questions from people who, besides our not knowing
whether they speak with inspiration by heavenly power, we do know
are totally barren of the intelligence needed not only to challenge
but even to understand the demonstrations used by the most exact
sciences to confirm their conclusions?

I believe that the authority of Sacred Scripture has the sole
aim of persuading men of those articles and propositions which,
being necessary for salvation but being beyond all human discourse,
cannot come to be believed by any science or by any means other
than by the mouth of the Holy Spirit himself. I do not think that
it is necessary to have belief in cases in which God himself, who is
the source of meaning, of discourse, and of intellect, has put the use
of revelation to one side and has decided to give to us in another
way the knowledge which we can obtain through science. This is
especially true of those sciences of which only a very small part, and
then as projected in conclusions, is to be found in the Scriptures.
Such is precisely the case with astronomy, of which there is such a
small part in the Scriptures that the planets are not even mentioned.
However if the sacred writers had intended to teach us about the
arrangements and movements of the celestial bodies, they would not
have said so little, almost nothing, in comparison with the infinite,
highest, and admirable conclusions contained in this science.

Let me show you, Father, if I am not mistaken, how those who
immediately quote passages of Scripture in natural disputes which
are not directly related to the faith, proceed in a disorderly way, and
are even often harmful to their own interests. Such people really
believe that they know the true meaning of a particular passage in
Scripture, and consequently they firmly think that they already have

in hand the absolute truth about the question they intend to dispute. Then let them tell me quite frankly whether they think that he who maintains what is true in a natural dispute has a great advantage over someone else who maintains what is false. I know that they would answer "yes," and that one who maintains the true side will have a thousand experiences and a thousand necessary demonstrations on his side, while the other can have only sophisms, fallacies, and paralogisms. But if one knows that he has such an advantage over his adversary when he stays within the limits of nature and uses only philosophical weapons, then why, when he comes later to a debate, would he quickly use dreadful and irresistible weapons, which alone would terrify any more skillful and expert defender? To tell the truth, I believe that he is the terrified one, and that, sensing his inability to stand firm against the assaults of his adversary, he will shake in his boots to find a way of not allowing himself to draw near. As I have already said, he who has truth on his side has a great advantage, indeed the greatest advantage, over an adversary. And it is impossible for two truths to conflict. As a result we should not fear the assaults which come against us, whatever they be, as long as we still have room to speak and to be heard by people who are experts and who are not excessively affected by their own interests and feelings.

To confirm this, I come now to a consideration of the particular passage from Joshua which occasioned three comments to the Grand Duchess. And I will seize upon the third, which was presented as mine, as indeed it truly is. But I will add for you some further considerations which I do not believe have been put in writing previously.

Let it be granted and conceded to an adversary for now that the sacred text should be taken in its exact literal meaning; namely, that God was asked by Joshua to make the sun stand still and to prolong the day so that he could obtain the victory. And I also ask my adversary to observe the same rule that I observe, that is, that he not bind me but free himself in regard to altering or changing the meaning of the words. I say, then, that this passage most clearly shows the falsity and impossibility of the Aristotelian and Ptolemaic world system, and is also very well accommodated to the Copernican system.

First I ask my adversary if he knows by what motions the sun is moved. If he knows, he must reply that the sun has two motions; namely, an annual motion towards the east and a daily motion towards the west.

Next I ask him whether both of these motions, which are different and contrary to each other, belong to the sun and are both proper to it. He must reply "no," for the only proper and special motion of the sun is its annual motion. The other motion is not proper to it, but belongs to the highest heaven, that is, the first sphere, which in its rotation carries along the sun and the other planets and the stellar sphere and which is ordained to give a rotation around the earth in twenty-four hours by means of a motion, as I have said, which is contrary to the sun's natural and proper motion.

I come then to the third question, and I ask him which of these two motions of the sun causes day and night; namely, its own proper and real motion, or the motion of the first sphere. He must reply that day and night are caused by the motion of the first sphere, and that the proper motion of the sun does not produce day and night but rather the various seasons and the year itself.

Now if the day depends not on the motion of the sun but on the motion of the first sphere, who does not see that, in order to lengthen the day, one needs to make the first sphere stop, and not the sun? Thus if someone understands these first elements of astronomy, does he not also recognize that if God had stopped the motion of the sun, then instead of lengthening the day, he would have shortened it and made it briefer? For since the motion of the sun is contrary to the daily rotation, then to the degree that the sun moves towards the east, to the same degree it will be slowed down in its motion towards the west. And if the motion of the sun is decreased or annulled, it will move to the west in a proportionally shorter time. This is observable if one looks at the moon, whose daily rotation is slower than that of the sun in proportion to its own proper motion being faster than that of the sun. Therefore it is absolutely impossible in the system of Ptolemy and Aristotle to stop the motion of the sun and thereby to lengthen the day, as the Scripture states to have happened. Hence either one must say that the motions are not arranged as Ptolemy said, or one must alter the meaning of the words, and say that, when the Scripture says that God stopped the sun, he really wished to say that he stopped the first sphere. But in order to accommodate himself to the capacity of those who are hardly able to understand the rising and setting of the sun, he said the contrary of what he ought to have said as he spoke to humans steeped in the senses.

Let me add that it is not credible that God would have stopped the sun without paying attention to the other spheres. For without any reason he would have changed all the laws, relations, and dispositions of the other stars in respect to the sun, and would have greatly disturbed the whole course of nature. But it is credible that he stopped the whole system of celestial spheres which, after an intervening period of rest, he returned consistently to their functions without any confusion or alteration.

But since we have already agreed not to alter the meaning of the words of the text, we must have recourse to another arrangement of the parts of the world, and then see if it agrees with the bare meaning of the words, taken straightforwardly and without hesitation, as to what actually happened.

Now I have discovered and have proven with necessity that the globe of the sun rotates on itself, making one full revolution in about one lunar month, in exactly the same way that all the other celestial rotations occur. Moreover it is quite probable and reasonable that the sun, as the instrument and highest minister of nature, as if it were the heart of the world, gives not only light, as it clearly does, but also motion to all the planets which revolve around it. Therefore, if in agreement with the position of Copernicus we attribute the daily rotation primarily to the earth, then who does not see that, in order to stop the whole system without any alteration in the remaining mutual relation of the planets but only to prolong the space and time of the daylight, it is sufficient to make the sun stop, exactly as the literal meaning of the sacred text says? Behold then that in this second way it is possible to lengthen the day on earth by stopping the sun, without introducing any confusion among the parts of the world and without altering the words of Scripture.

I have written much more than my indisposition allows. So I will end, offering my services and kissing your hands, petitioning Our Lord for a good holiday and every happiness.

Florence, 21 December 1613

V

The Galileo-Dini Correspondence

A: GALILEO'S LETTER TO DINI, 16 FEBRUARY 1615:

To the Very Illustrious and My Most Respected Reverend Father:

Since I know that you, Very Illustrious and Most Reverend Father, were immediately notified of the repeated invectives which were made from the pulpit a few weeks ago against the teaching of Copernicus and his followers, and even against mathematicians and mathematics itself, I will not repeat the particulars which you have already heard from others. But I wish very much for you to know that, although neither I nor others have made any commotion or expressed any resentment over their insults which we, with great care, have not aggravated, still their enflamed anger has not been put to rest. On the contrary that same priest [Lorini] who made complaints last year in private conversations has returned from Pisa and has again raised his hand against me. From somewhere or other he has acquired a copy of a letter which I wrote last year to the Father Mathematician at Pisa [Castelli], and which deals with the import of sacred authority in natural disputes and with the explication of a passage in Joshua. He has then complained loudly about that letter and has claimed, from what I hear, to have found many heresies in it; in short he has opened up a new field of attack against me. Now since no one else who has read that letter has mentioned the slightest degree of scruple to me, I have come to wonder whether whoever transcribed it may have inadvertently changed some words, which, together with a disposition toward censorship, may make things appear quite differently from what I had intended. And since I understand that some of these Fathers, including in particular the same one who gave the sermon [Caccini], have gone there to cause some mischief with their copy of that letter of mine, it seemed to me to be worthwhile to send to you, Reverend Father, an exact copy of what I wrote. I request that you do me the favor of reading the letter with the Jesuit Father Grienberger, a famous mathematician and my great friend and patron; also if the opportunity presents itself, would you please take advantage of it to present a copy to the Illustrious Cardinal Bellarmine. These Dominican Fathers intend to use my letter to try to bring about, or at least they hope to bring about, the condemnation of Copernicus' book and of his opinion and teaching.

I wrote my letter "with a fast pen." But these recent controversies and the motives which these Fathers adduce to show the lack of merit in this opinion, which thereby ought to be condemned, have led me to look into what more has been written on similar topics. Indeed I have found not only that everything I have written has already been stated by others; but also this has revealed what great circumspection is needed in dealing with natural conclusions which are not matters of faith and which can be arrived at from experience and necessary demonstration, and what a pernicious thing it would be to assert, as a doctrine settled in Sacred Scripture, a proposition the contrary of which could be demonstrated at some time in the future. On these topics I have drafted a very extensive treatise, but I do not yet have it in a finished enough form to be able to send you a copy; I will do so as soon as I can. Whatever be the value of my arguments and discussions in that treatise, I am at least sure that one will find more zeal in it for the Church and the dignity of the Sacred Scripture than is found in my persecutors, who are trying to prohibit a book admitted for many years by the Church without having ever seen, read, or understood it. I merely ask that its teachings be examined and its arguments be evaluated by the most Catholic and most expert persons, that its propositions be confronted with sense experience, and that it not be condemned before it is found to be false, it being granted as true that a proposition cannot be both true and false. Since there is no shortage in Christendom of men who are most expert in this profession, it would seem that the truth or falsity of this doctrine ought not to be deferred to the judgment of those who are uninformed and who are clearly known to be affected by feelings of bias. This is quite well known to be a fact by many people, who see all the maneuvering, and who are at least partially informed of the machinations and schemings.

Nicholas Copernicus was not only a Catholic but also a religious and a canon. He was called to Rome under Leo X when the reform of the ecclesiastical calendar was taken up at the Lateran Council, and he was treated as a great astronomer. This reform of the calendar remained undecided then for the sole reason that the length of the years and months, and the motions of the sun and the moon, were not sufficiently established. Therefore by order of the Bishop of Sempronia, who was in charge of this matter at that time, Copernicus set himself to work on these periods with new observations and most accurate investigations. From this followed, in short, a knowledge which not only accounted for all the motions of the celestial bodies but which also won for him the title of being the greatest astronomer, whose teaching was later adopted by everyone and which was used ultimately for the correction of the calendar. His work on the paths and arrangements of the heavenly bodies was reduced to six books which were published at the request of Nicholas Schoenberg, Cardinal of Capua, and which were dedicated to Pope Paul III. Since that time they have been read publicly without any scruples. But now these good Fathers, motivated only by a sinister feeling against me and knowing that I highly esteem this author, boast that they will give the proper award to his work by declaring it to be heretical.

But what is even more worthy of consideration is that the first move against this opinion by some of my enemies was to allow the impression to be given that this book was really mine, without mentioning that it was published seventy years ago. Other persons have come to adopt this same style, as they attempt to establish a sinister image of me. They have succeeded to such a degree that when Monsignor Gherardini, Bishop of Fiesole, arrived a few days ago, in full view of many people where some of my friends were present, he burst out with the very greatest vehemence against me, showing very strong emotions, and said that he would inform Their Serene Highnesses in detail because my extravagant and erroneous opinion had caused so much talk in Rome. Perhaps he has already done this, if he has not yet been restrained by having been correctly advised that the author of this teaching is not a living Florentine but a dead

German, who published it seventy years ago and who dedicated the book to the Supreme Pontiff.

I continue to write, not reminding myself that I am speaking to one who is quite informed about these matters, perhaps even better than myself, since you live in the place where the greatest noises have been made. Excuse my prolixity, and if you find any merit in my cause, please give me your support, for which I will always be obligated. With this I kiss your hands with reverence; remember me as your most devoted servant, and I pray for the greatest happiness for you from our God.

Galileo Galilei

Florence, 16 February 1615.

P.S.: Although it is difficult for me to believe that there is a movement getting under way to try to destroy this author, nevertheless, knowing by other means how great is the power of my bad luck, and adding to this the ill-will and ignorance of my enemies, I seem to have good reason not to be assured completely by the great prudence and sanctity of those who will make the final decision, since even they cannot be completely unaffected by this fraud which goes about under the guise of zeal and charity. In order to avoid as best I can any deficiency in myself and in what I have written, you will soon see, Reverend Father, true and pure zeal, as I desire that my writings at least be first seen, and then later let us accept whatever resolution is pleasing to God. (For as far as I am concerned, I am quite prepared and inclined "to tear my eye out lest it scandalize me," before I would contravene my superiors when I cannot do otherwise, and before I would take what I now seem to believe and understand to be a prejudice of my mind.) I believe that the quickest remedy would be to call upon the Jesuit Fathers, who are so much better educated than these Fathers. Therefore you can give them a copy of the letter [to Castelli] and also, if you wish, read to them this present letter to you; and afterwards, with your usual kindness, please keep me informed of what you have learned. I do not know whether you might have an opportunity to meet with Sig. Luca Valerio and to give him a copy of the letter; he is on the staff of Cardinal Aldobrandino and might be able to intervene with him. On this and on all other matters I submit myself to your kindness and prudence, and I entrust my reputation to you. Again I kiss your hands.

B: DINI'S LETTER TO GALILEO, 7 MARCH 1615:

To my Very Illustrious and Most Worthy Gentleman:

These days of carnivals, and the many theater performances and other celebrations which have occurred, have hindered me from contacting the persons whom you seek. So instead in the meantime I have made many copies of your letter to Father Mathematician [Castelli]. I then gave one copy to Father Grienberger, along with the letter which you wrote to me. I have done the same for many others, including the Illustrious Bellarmine, with whom I spoke at length about the things which you have written. On these matters he has assured me that I should not hesitate in any way to speak about what he said orally. In respect to Copernicus the Cardinal said that he could not believe that he would be prohibited; rather he believes that the worst thing that could happen to Copernicus would be that some marginal notes might be added to the effect that his doctrine was introduced to save the appearances, or some such thing, similar to those who have introduced epicycles but do not believe in them. He also said that with similar caution you could speak on any occasion of these things as if they were structured according to the new constitution, and that it does not appear at present that there is anything in the Scriptures which is more contrary than the passage, "He exulted like a hero to run his course . . . " etc. [Psalm 18:5–6], which all the commentators up to the present have interpreted as attributing a motion to the sun. When I replied that this indeed could be said to be our sole way of understanding the matter, he replied that the issue was not of current concern and that thus there was no occasion to raise a fuss or to condemn anything concerning these opinions. And if you have included in your writings some interpretations which would bring cause, the Cardinal will be glad to point this out. And since he knows that you have said that you submit yourself to the determinations of the Holy Church, as has been stated to me and to others, this will be of very great benefit. Since the Cardinal told me that he would summon Grienberger to discuss the matter with him, I went this morning to visit with Fr. Grienberger to learn if there was anything new. I did not find anything of substance other than that he said that he would have preferred that you would first establish your own demonstrations and then only later begin to speak of Scripture. I replied to him that, even if you had acted in this way, you would have believed it to be wrong to first establish one's own results and then later to think of Scripture. In regard to the arguments which you have developed, Father Grienberger doubts whether they may not be more probable than true, since some other passages of Scripture make him apprehensive.

This morning I sent a copy of the letter to Sig. Luca Valerio, with whom I have still not had a private conversation. I also went to see Cardinal Del Monte to inform him, but I discussed only other things with him since I found there some people who do not please me. But I will return there since he has a great affection for you. I will also meet with Cardinal Barberini to give him a copy, which he already expects since I have already hurriedly given him a partial account. But by now he has perhaps already been fully informed by Sig. Ciampoli, with whom I have already met for that purpose. I will continue on the same business whenever I see that I can help the cause, of which I speak confusedly, as you see. For everyone should be on their guard in negotiations of such importance, although mathematicians do not experience as much doubt as do the professors of the other sciences. This is as much as I can say now. So without more I kiss your hands, praying to God for what you desire.

P. Dini

Rome: 7 March 1615

C: GALILEO'S LETTER TO DINI, 23 MARCH 1615:

To the Very Illustrious and My Most Respected Reverend Father:

I will respond briefly to your kind letter, My Very Illustrious and Most Reverend Father, because the poor state of my health does not permit me to do otherwise.

The first point which touches me is that the worst judgment that could fall upon Copernicus' book would be that some marginal notes would be added to the effect that his doctrine was introduced to save the appearances, in the same way that others have introduced eccentrics and epicycles without believing that they exist in nature. To this I reply (always submitting myself to those who are wiser than I, and always acting out of zeal that what happens is done with very great caution) that in regard to saving the appearances, Copernicus himself has already undertaken this task, and he has satisfied some of the astronomers who follow the customary and traditional method of Ptolemy. But then after this, he put on the garb of a philosopher and considered whether the Ptolemaic constitution of the parts of the world could actually exist in nature. He saw that it could not. And realizing that the problem of the true constitution of the world was worth investigating, he directed his work to studying this constitution, recognizing that if the one arrangement of the parts of the world had failed and could not be true to the appearances, this other one would have acquired a much greater degree of truth and reality, and at the same time philosophy might have acquired a very excellent piece of knowledge, namely, the knowledge of the true arrangement of the parts of the world. He has discovered a very great number of specific events observed in the stars as a result of many years of observation and study, without which even a mind of the very greatest learning and of the quickest attention cannot come to a knowledge of the constitution of the world. With repeated studies and very long labors he arrived at those things which he later explained admirably for all who study him carefully and who have the ability to follow him. As a result anyone who tries to argue that Copernicus did not think that the mobility of the earth is true will, in my opinion, be unable to persuade anyone, except perhaps those who have not read all of his six books which are full of teachings which depend on the mobility of the earth, which he explains and confirms. And although in his Dedication he clearly states and confesses that the idea of the motion of the earth will be thought to be foolish by the common man, whose judgment he says he does not heed, it would be much more foolish to try to claim that this is an opinion which he introduced but did not fully and truly believe.

A little further on it is said that the principal authors who introduced eccentrics and epicycles did not consider them to be true. I will never believe this, at least in regard to our own age when astronomers need to accept them with absolute necessity, as the senses themselves show us. For since an epicycle is simply a circle described by the motion of a star whose revolution does not include the terrestial globe, do we not see that four such circles are described by the motion of the four stars around Jupiter? And is it not clearer than the sun that Venus describes a circle around the sun without including the earth, and thus it forms an epicycle? And the same is true of Mercury. On the other hand an eccentric is a circle which includes the earth, but the earth is not located in its center but is off to one side. Hence there is no doubt that the path of Mars is eccentric to the earth, for we see that it is sometimes closer and sometimes further away because its surface appears very small at one time and is sixty times greater at another time. As a result, in regard to its own rotation, Mars encircles the earth and is eight times closer to the earth from one time to another. All these things, and a great many other similar things, have recently been discovered from sense experience. As a result to wish to admit the mobility of the earth only with the same concessions and probability attributed to epicycles and eccentrics is to admit it most securely, truly, and irrefutably.

There are two groups of people who have denied eccentrics and epicycles. The first are those who, being totally ignorant of the observations of the motions of the stars and of what needs to be saved, deny without any foundation what they do not understand. Unlike the others they are not worthy of consideration. The others, being more reasonable, do not deny that the circular motions described by the bodies of the stars go around centers other than the earth, which is obvious; indeed, to the contrary it is clear that none of the planets makes a rotation which is concentric with the earth. Rather, thinking that celestial bodies are located in spheres which are solid and separated from each other, they only deny that these spheres carry the bodies of the planets because they would grind and scrape on each other. I believe that these people speak more properly. But this is not to deny that the stars move in circles eccentric to the earth or in epicycles, which are the true and simple assumptions of Ptolemy and the great astronomers. Rather it is a denial of the distinct and solid material spheres introduced by the founders of the theory to help beginners to understand it and to assist in making calculations. These spheres are fictitious and unreal, and the issue is left open of how God makes the stars move through the immense space of the heavens, within fixed and certain paths, without their being forced or tied down.

Thus in regard to Copernicus it is my opinion that the mobility of the earth and the stability of the sun are not open to compromise, since these are the principal points and universal foundation of his whole doctrine. Therefore it is necessary either to condemn it all or to leave it be by itself, speaking of course always within the limits of my capacities. But in such a decision it would be well to consider most carefully, ponder, and examine what he has written. I have done my best to show this in one of my writings, in so far as Holy God has permitted me, not having any other aim than the dignity of the Holy Church and not directing my weak labors to any other end. This very earnest and pure affection is indeed the value which will be perceived in that writing, which otherwise might be full of error and of matters of little importance. It would have already been sent to you, Reverend Father, except that, in addition to my numerous and grave indispositions, I have recently experienced an attack of colic pain which has greatly distressed me. I will send it soon. Nevertheless, after having gathered together all the arguments of Copernicus, having reduced them to a clarity understandable to many when before they were so difficult, and having added many, many other considerations based always on celestial observations, on sense experience, and on the confrontation of natural effects, I now wish with the same zeal to offer them next at the feet of the Highest Pastor and to the infallible determination of the Holy Church, which will decide in its great prudence what value they may appear to have.

Regarding Father Grienberger's opinion, I truly praise him, and freely leave the work of interpretation to those who know infinitely more than I. That brief letter which I sent you, Reverend Father, is, as you see, a private letter written more than a year ago to my friend for him alone to read. But he allowed copies to be made without my knowledge. I know that the letter has come into the hands of that same man who attacked me so bitterly from the pulpit. And I know that the letter has been taken there [Rome]. So I thought it would be wise to make another copy to be used for very close comparisons, especially since that man and his theological followers are spreading the rumor here that my letter is full of heresy. Thus it is not my intention to undertake a task which is so far beyond my abilities. Yet one should not lose confidence that the Divine Goodness sometimes decides to instill a beam of its immense wisdom in humble minds, especially when they are adorned with sincerity and holy zeal. On the other hand, when the issue at hand is the reconciliation of sacred passages with new and uncommon natural teachings, it is necessary to have a complete understanding of that teaching, for one cannot compare two chords if one hears only one of them. If I knew that I could make a contribution out of the weakness of my talents, I would venture to say that between some passages of the Sacred Writings and this structure of the world many agreements are to be found which are not recognized, it seems to me, by the common philosophy. You have pointed out to me, Most Reverend Father, that the text of Psalm 18 is reputed to be quite contrary to that opinion. But I have made some new reflections on it, which I send to you with little hesitation since you have said that the Most Illustrious and Most Reverend Cardinal Bellarmine would gladly welcome whatever comments I have on these passages. Thus in giving satisfaction to his direct wish, and in knowing that he has received my contemplations, such as they are, I do this as the highest prudence dictates. My only intention is to honor and respect such sublime knowledge, to be obedient to the wishes of my superiors, and to submit all my work to their decision.

Whatever might be the truth of the matter in reality, I would not claim that others could not provide a much better interpretation of the meaning of the Prophet; indeed, I am inferior to all and place myself below all wise men. But it seems to me that there is to be found in nature a most spiritual, tenuous, and fast-moving substance which is diffused throughout the universe, which penetrates everything without resistance, and which warms, vivifies, and fecundates all living creatures. It seems that the senses themselves show that the main recipient of this spirit is the body of the sun, from which an immense light is radiated throughout the universe, accompanied by that caloric spirit which penetrates all vegetable bodies, making them alive and fruitful. It is reasonable to conclude that this spirit is something different than light, for it penetrates and is diffused through all corporeal substances, even the most dense, while light does not penetrate through many of them. Just as we see and feel that fire emits both light and heat, and that the latter passes through all bodies, even the most solid and opaque ones, while the former is blocked by solidity and opacity; likewise emanations from the sun are both lucid and caloric, and the caloric part is more penetrating. As I have said, the body of the sun is a recipient of this spirit and this light, and thus it preserves what it has received from outside of itself and is not the principle and first source from which the spirit and light were originally derived. It seems to me that there is certain evidence of this in the Sacred Scriptures where we read that, before the sun was created, the spirit with its caloric and fecund powers "warmed the waters or watched over the waters" for future generations. Also light was created on the first day, while the body of the sun was created on the fourth day. From this we can conclude with great probability that this fecund spirit and this light diffused throughout the whole world came together and were united and strengthened in the body of the sun. Thus the sun was located in the center of the universe, and later, having been made more splendid and vigorous, it diffuses itself again.

This first-born light, which was not very brilliant prior to its encounter and union with the body of the sun, is attested to by the prophet in Psalm 73:16, "You are the day and you are the night; You have made the dawn and the sun." This passage is usually taken to mean that before God made the sun, he made a light similar to that of the dawn. Moreover the Hebrew text has "light" in place of "dawn," which suggests that the light which was created prior to the sun was very much weaker than that same light after it had been received, strengthened, and emitted again from the body of the sun. This view seems to be alluded to in the opinion of some of the ancient philosophers who believed that the brilliance of the sun is due to the encounter in the center of the world of the light of the stars which, located spherically around that center, send their rays there, where they meet and intersect at one point, and increase and redouble their light a thousand times. Afterwards this strengthened

light is reflected and is emitted about very vigorously, full as it were
of masculine and vivifying heat, and is diffused to vivify all the bodies which rotate around that center. To make a comparison, just as
the heart of an animal continually regenerates the vital spirits which
sustain and vivify all the members of the body, while at the same
time the heart also receives from elsewhere the food and nutrients
without which it would perish; likewise, while the sun receives its
food from outside of itself, it also conserves the source which continually emits that light and prolific heat which vivifies all the members
which rotate around it. In regard to this marvelous force and energy
of that spirit and light of the sun, which is diffused throughout the
universe, I could produce many testimonials from philosophers and
important writers. But I will content myself with only one passage
from Blessed Dionysius the Areopagite, who says in his book *De di-
vinis nominibus*, "This light collects and gathers to itself everything
which is seen, is moved, is illuminated, is warmed, and in a word everything which is contained in its light. Thus the sun is called 'Ilios'
because it holds everything together and unites what has been dis-
persed." And a little further on below he writes, "Although the sun
which we see illuminates whatever comes under our senses, no matter how numerous and different their essences and properties might
be, nevertheless that sun is one, and equally illuminates, renovates,
nourishes, protects, perfects, divides, joins, warms, makes fruitful,
increases, changes, strengthens, produces, moves, and vitalizes all
things; and each thing in this universe participates for its own benefit in one and the same sun; and the sun has equally in itself the
anticipations and causes of the many things which participate in it;
indeed with a greater reason. . . . "

Given this philosophical position, it is perhaps one of the main
avenues to enter into the contemplation of nature. And I speak
always with that humility and reverence which I owe to the Holy
Church and to all its most learned Fathers, whom I revere and obey
and to whose judgment I submit myself and all my thoughts. Now I
believe that the passage of the Psalms which says that, "God placed
his tabernacle in the sun," ought to be taken to mean that he put
it in the most noble place in the entire sensible world. A little later
on it is said that, "He proceeded as a bridegroom from his chamber
and he exalted as a hero in running his course." I would understand

this to be said of the radiating sun, that is, of its light and the above-mentioned spirit which warms and fecundates all material substances and which is most quickly diffused throughout the whole world as soon as it leaves the body of the sun. Every word of the text fits this interpretation exactly. In the word "bridegroom" we have the power to reproduce and make fruitful. "Exalts" refers to the emanations of the sun's rays, which in a way occur by fits and starts, as the meaning clearly shows. "As a hero" or "as a strong man" denotes the efficacious power and activity of penetrating all bodies, together with the highest velocity of motion through immense spaces, for light emanates as though it were instantaneous. The words, "he proceeds from his chamber," confirm that his emanation and motion should be attributed to the light of the sun and not to the body of the sun itself. For the body and globe of the sun is the recipient and "like a chamber" for that light, and it would not be good to say that "the chamber proceeds from a chamber." In what follows, "his progress is from the highest heavens," we have the first derivation and separation of that spirit and light from the highest parts of the heavens, that is, from the stars of the firmament or perhaps from the seats of the most sublime. "And its path goes up to its highest point" refers to the reflection and, as it were, the re-emanation of that light up to that same summit of the world. What follows, "Nor is there any thing which escapes its heat," refers to the vivifying and fecundating heat, which is distinct from the light, and which is much more penetrating through all material substances, even the most dense. For there are many things which fend off and recover from the penetration of light, but from this other power "there is nothing which escapes its heat." I ought not remain silent about another of my considerations which touches on this issue. I have previously discovered the continuous path of some dark materials on the body of the sun, where they appear to our senses as very dark spots, and which later become consumed and dissolved there. And I have indicated how these perhaps can be taken to be parts of the food, or maybe the excrement of food, which some ancient philosophers thought the sun needed to sustain itself. I have also demonstrated, by continuous observations of this dark material, that the body of the sun must revolve upon itself. And furthermore I have pointed out that it would be reasonable to believe that the motion of the planets around the sun depends on this rotation of the sun. Moreover we know that the purpose of this Psalm is to praise the laws of God, which the prophet compares to the celestial body, which is the most beautiful, most useful, and most powerful of all material things. Thus having sung encomia to the sun, and not being ignorant of the fact that all the moving bodies of the world are made to revolve around it, the prophet passes on to the greatest perogative of the divine law, and wishing to make it superior to the sun, he adds, "The law of God is immaculate, turning souls. . . ." It is as if he wished to say that this law is so much more excellent than the sun; that it is spotless, it has the power to turn souls around itself, its condition is too excellent to be covered with spots, as is the sun, and it makes the bodily globes of this world rotate.

Not being an expert on Sacred Scripture, I recognize and confess my excessive boldness in attempting to speak about the explication of the meanings of such lofty matters. But since I submit myself totally to the judgment of my superiors, I can be excused in accordance with the established interpretation of the verse, "The testimony of God is for the faithful, as it gives wisdom to children." I have the hope that in his infinite wisdom God can direct some small ray of his grace to the purity of my mind to give me some illumination about the hidden meanings of his words. What I have written, dear Father, is only a small off-spring which needs to be recast in a better form, and which needs to be washed and licked clean with affection and patience. For it is only a sketch, and although its components are capable of being formed into a very proportional figure, they are for now disorganized and in a rough condition. If I have the opportunity, I will recast it into a better form. Meanwhile I ask that you do not permit this letter to come into the hands of anyone who, instead of the delicacy of a mother's tongue, makes use of the coarseness and sharpness of a step-mother's teeth, and thus instead of cleaning it up, tears it apart and shreds it all to pieces. With this I reverently kiss your hands, together with Sig. Buonarroti, Guiducci, Soldani, and Giraldi, who are present at the sealing of this letter.

Galileo Galilei

Florence, 23 March 1615

APPENDIX

VI

Paolo Antonio Foscarini

A Letter To Fr. Sebastiano Fantone, General of the Order, Concerning the Opinion of the Pythagoreans and Copernicus About the Mobility of the Earth and the Stability of the Sun and the New Pythagorean System of the World

in which it is shown that that opinion agrees
with, and is reconciled with, the passages of
Sacred Scripture and theological propositions
which are commonly adduced against it.

In response to a request from Vincenzo Caraffa of Naples, a Knight of the Order of St. John of Jerusalem (and a man of such rare quality that in him, if I may state the truth, nobility, kindness, universal knowledge of much learning, courage, religion, goodness, and every virtue, all rival each other for preeminence), I have decided to write a defense of a new opinion, or rather of a revived opinion which has recently been brought back to light in our day from the darkness of oblivion where it was buried; namely, the mobility of the earth and the stability of the sun. In ancient times this opinion was maintained by Pythagoras, and later is to be found in the writings of Copernicus, who derived from this hypothesis the system and constitution of the world and the location of its parts.

I have previously written to you about this, Most Reverend Father, as you know. At present I am soon to make a trip, at your command, and come to preach at Rome. Indeed this opinion ought to be located in its proper place in a treatise on cosmography, which I have yet to write and which should be published together with my *Compendio dell'arti liberali*, which is now completed. For these reasons I have decided to send to you, Most Reverend Father (to whom I owe all my actions and my very self), this brief report of my entire project and to describe the foundations on which this opinion can be, and ought to be, based. I do this lest this opinion (which otherwise seems reasonable and probable) is taken to be quite repugnant and contrary, as it appears to be, not only to physical arguments and to principles commonly accepted by all (which would be less harmful), but also to the greater authority of Sacred Scripture (which is more serious).

To anyone who has just encountered this opinion, it will without doubt appear to be one of the oddest and most monstrous paradoxes he has yet heard. This is caused completely by old habits, strengthened over many centuries. Once a habit is established and men are hardened into opinions which are trite and plausible, and which are part of everyone's common sense, then both the educated and the uneducated embrace them and are hardly able to be dislodged from them. The force of habit is so great that it is said to be another nature. Thus it happens that something with which one is familiar, even if it be an evil, becomes more loved and desired than a good which is unfamiliar. These latter may even be things which would be helpful and very appropriate to one's nature and inclinations.

The very same thing is also true of opinions. As soon as they have firmly established their roots in the soul, any opinion which is different from the customary one seems as a result to be like disharmony to hearing, as darkness to vision, as a stench to smell, as bitterness to taste, and as roughness to touch. For ordinarily we do not weigh and judge a thing according to what it is itself, but according to the decree of an authority which remains unmentioned. However, since this authority is only human, it should not be held in such importance that it causes us to condemn, to reject, or to put aside what is evidently true to the contrary, whether this be shown accidently by some better proof not previously noticed or occasionally by sensation itself. The road to the future should not be closed so that our descendants are neither able nor venturesome enough to discover more and better things than the ancients handed on to us.

The cleverness of the ancients in making discoveries was not much superior to that of our own times. The moderns seem to be their equals in the making of discoveries; indeed advances have occurred more quickly, if we take the large, long view backwards. Nevertheless knowledge and the arts, both liberal and mechanical, always continue to improve. Many examples of this could be presented, but will not be here, since in a case which is so clear, the attempt to accumulate evidence and proof would only be tedious and would also decrease the clarity of what is publicly known to be true.

But I will not pass over this in complete silence. Could it not be said, at any rate, that the experiments of the moderns have on some particular issues closed the venerable mouths of the ancients and have established that some of their most important and solemn teachings are empty and false? The mobility of the earth is no more paradoxical and strange than the notion of the antipodes or the notion that the torrid zone is inhabitable, views discussed by many ancients of great and respected authority. The former notion was thought by many of them, and the latter by all of common sense, to be impossible, and was flatly denied. Nevertheless by their considerable diligence and courage, rather than by authority, the moderns have shown (to their great good fortune and eternal glory) that both of these notions are quite true. Thus the majestic white beards of the ancients were wrong; they have been believed too easily and their false imaginations have been solemnized.

For the sake of brevity I will omit the many dreams of Aristotle and other ancient philosophers which have recently been discovered to be simply dreams. I will only say that, if they could have seen and observed what the moderns have seen and observed, and if they would have understood their arguments, then without doubt they would have changed their minds and would have believed these most evident truths. As a result there is no need to respect the ancients so much that everything which they have stated is believed to be established, and to hold it to be most certain, as though it were revealed and descended from heaven.

What is central in this matter is that if something is found to be contrary to divine authority, and to the sacred words dictated by the Holy Spirit, and to its inspired interpretation by the Sacred Doctors, then in that case one ought to abandon not only human reason but also sense itself. If all the best conditions and best possible circumstances are given, and if something contrary to divine authority is presented to us (even if it is so clear that one cannot evade it), one still ought to reject it, and judge with certainty that what is presented is a deception and that it is not true. For knowledge through faith is more certain than any other knowledge which we have from any source or means. This indeed has been confirmed by St. Peter. Although in the transfiguration he saw and perceived the glory of God with his own senses, and understood the words which praised Him, still in comparing all this with the light of faith, he added, "We have firmer knowledge of what was said in the prophecies" (2 Peter 1:19).

When the opinion of Pythagoras and of Copernicus appeared on the world stage, it wore such a strange costume that at first sight it immediately seemed to be contrary (among other things) to various passages of Sacred Scripture. As a result (and rightly so, given this presupposition) it was judged by all to be sheer madness, to put it in one phrase. But because the common system of the world proclaimed by Ptolemy had not been completely satisfactory to the learned, there was always a suspicion, even among its advocates, that there is some other truer system. For although all the phenomena and appearances relating to the heavenly bodies are saved by this common system, they are saved with innumerable difficulties and by a patchwork of spheres (of various forms and shapes), epicycles, equants, deferents, eccentrics, and a thousand other fantasies and chimeras, which are more like beings of reason than real things.

Among these fantasies is the notion of swift motion. I have not found anything less well grounded, and more controversial, and easier to argue against and reject than this; namely, a real sphere without stars which moves the lower spheres. All these spheres were introduced to account for the variety of motions in the celestial bodies, and no other account seemed able to save them and to reduce them to a certain and definite rule. As a result the advocates of the common opinion have confessed in their writings on the system of the world that they cannot guess or teach the true system, but can only study the one which is more probable and which, with good reason, can save the celestial appearances more conveniently.

After this the telescope was invented, and by its reliable sensory evidence many beautiful and very curious things were discovered in the heavens, which were unknown prior to this century. For example, the moon has mountains; both Venus and Saturn are composed of three bodies, and Jupiter of four bodies; within the vicinity of the Milky Way, the Pleiades, and the nebulae there are many very large stars. And thus new fixed stars, new planets, and new worlds have appeared to us. Furthermore this same instrument has shown that it is very probable that Venus and Mercury do not really revolve around the earth, but more likely around the sun, and that only the moon revolves around the earth. Should it not next be inferred that the sun stands firmly in the center and that the earth and the other celestial orbs revolve around it?

Hence from this and many other arguments it becomes apparent that the opinion of Pythagoras and Copernicus is not contrary to the principles of astronomy and cosmography, but rather it has no small degree of probability and likelihood. It is much better than the many other opinions which challenge the common system, but are only delirious searchings; for example, those which have come from the imaginations of Plato, Callipus, Eudoxus, and later Averroes, Cardanus, Fracastorius, and other ancients and moderns. The Pythagorean opinion surpasses all of these as easier, more accommodated to all the phenomena, and more useful in calculating the motions of the celestial bodies with a fixed rule and without any epicycles, eccentrics, deferents, or swift motions. This opinion was defended as the true system not only by Pythagoras first, and later by Copernicus, but also by many other famous and courageous men; for example, Heraclitus, the Pythagorean Ecphantus and the whole Pythagorean school, Nicetas of Syracuse, Martinus Capella, and many others.

Those whom we have described above as searching for new systems cannot be counted as defenders of this opinion (because they rejected the view of Pythagoras). However, because of them

this opinion was rendered probable and was at least indirectly confirmed, because they claimed that the common system was defective
and not completely free of difficulties and contradictions. Included
among these people is the Jesuit Father Clavius, a most learned
man, who sees the weak foundation of the common opinion, but on
the other hand he rejects the Pythagorean opinion. Nevertheless he
concedes that, in order to alleviate the many difficulties which the
common system does not fully resolve, astronomers are forced to
try to provide some other system, which he exhorts them to do with
strong encouragement.

But what other opinion can be found which is better than that
of Copernicus? As a result many moderns have been attracted to
it and finally persuaded to accept it, although with some degree
of anxiety and regret. For it appears to them that it is so contrary
to Sacred Scripture that it cannot be reconciled with the passages
which contradict it. Because of this that opinion has more or less
retreated into the background, and for some time now has appeared
with its face covered and with considerable embarrassment. Indeed
it seems to be held in check by the following moral maxim:

> Judicium populi nunquam contempseris unus,
> Ne nullis placeas dum vis contemnere multos.
> [Never be one to scorn the popular judgment,
> You will please no one if you condemn the majority.]
> [*Disticha Catonis* II, 29]

In giving further consideration to these issues (I am motivated
by the desire to increase, illuminate, and perfect the received doctrine as much as possible and to remove all errors so that it glistens
with pure truth), I have come to reason with myself as follows. The
Pythagorean opinion is either true or false. If it is false, it is not
worthwhile to speak of it or to take it into consideration. If it is true,
then it is of little importance if all philosophers and astronomers
in the world deny it; rather there would be, as a result, a need to
formulate a new philosophy and astronomy based on the new principles and hypotheses which that opinion requires. Also that opinion
would not be opposed to Sacred Scripture, because one truth is not
contrary to another.

Hence, if the Pythagorean opinion is true, then without doubt
God has dictated the words of Sacred Scripture in such a way that

they can be given a meaning which agrees with, and is reconciled with, that opinion. This is the motive which has led me (given that that opinion already is clearly probable) to look and search for ways and means to accommodate many passages of Sacred Scripture to it, and to interpret these passages, with the aid of theological and physical principles, in such a way that they are not openly contradictory. As a result, if by chance this opinion should in the future become explicitly established as a certain truth (although now it is taken as only probable), no obstacles would arise which would worry or hinder anyone, and thus unfortunately deprive the world of that venerable and sacred association with truth which is desired by all good people.

As far as I know, and may it be pleasing to God, I am without doubt the first one to undertake this project. I believe that considerable appreciation will be expressed by those who are studying this issue, and especially by the most learned Galileo Galilei, Mathematician to the Most Serene Grand Duke of Tuscany, by the most learned Johannes Kepler, Mathematician to the Sacred and Invincible Majesty of the Empire, and by all the illustrious and most virtuous members of the Academy of the Lynx, who universally accept this opinion (if I am not mistaken). And indeed I have no doubt that these and other learned men could easily find similar reconciliations with the passages of Scripture. But speaking for the profession of which I am a member, and as a sign and proof of my great love of truth, for as the poet says,

> Nullius addictus jurare in verba magistri,
> [I am not bound to swear as any master dictates]
> [Horace, *Epistles* I, 1, 14]

I wish to offer these thoughts of mine, such as they are and having nothing better, to the service of these men and to all men of letters and virtue, secure in the knowledge that they will be received with the same candor of mind with which they are given.

Coming thus to the matter at hand, I say that all the passages of Sacred Scripture which seem to be contrary to this opinion fall, in my judgment, into six groups.

The first group consists of passages which state that the earth is stationary and does not move. For example, Psalm 93:1, "You have made firm the orb of the earth, which will not move;" Psalm 104:5,

"You fixed the earth on its foundations, it will not change forever and ever;" Ecclesiastes 1:4, "The earth stands firm forever;" and similar passages.

The second group consists of passages which say that the sun is moved and rotates around the earth. For example, Psalm 19:4–6, "He pitched a tent for the sun, who comes out of his pavilion like a bridegroom, exulting like a giant to run his race, departing from the beginning of the heavens, and going up to its furthest edge, and nothing can escape his heat." Also in Ecclesiastes 1:5–6, "The sun rises, and sets, and returns to its place; reborn there, it rotates through the south and is curved toward the north." As a result the retrograde motion of the sun is said to be a miracle in Isaiah 38:8, "The sun went back ten lines," and in Ecclesiasticus 48:23, 26, "In his days the sun moved back, and added to the life of the king." In the book of Joshua 10:12 the miracle is related as to how Joshua commanded the sun to stop by saying, "Sun, stand still over Gibeon." But if the sun actually were stationary and the earth revolved around it, then this would not have been miraculous. And in order to preserve the light of the day, Joshua should not have said, "Sun, stand still," but rather, "Earth, stand still."

The third group consists of passages which say that the heavens are at the top and the earth is at the bottom. For example, the passage of Joel 3:3, as quoted by St. Peter in The Acts of the Apostles 2:19, "I will display portents in heaven above and signs on earth below," and other similar passages. Thus it is said that Christ descended from heaven in the incarnation, and ascended into heaven after the resurrection. But if the earth were to revolve around the sun, the earth would be in the heavens, and thus would be better described as "above" rather than "below." This is confirmed by the opinion in question which places the sun in the center, Mercury above the sun, Venus above Mercury, and the earth, together with the moon which revolves around it, above Venus. Thus the earth together with the moon is said to be in the third heaven.

The fourth group consists of passages describing hell as in the center of the world, which is the common opinion of theologians. This is also confirmed by the following argument. Since hell, taken in the strict sense of the word [inferno], ought to be in the lowest part of the world, and since in a sphere no part is lower than the center, it follows that hell is in the center of the world. Now since the world has a spherical shape, then one must say either that hell is in the sun (if the sun were to be in the center of the world), or that hell is in the center of the earth, as one truly ought to hold. If the earth actually were to revolve around the sun, it would necessarily follow that hell together with the earth would be in the heavens, and that hell also revolves with the earth around the sun in the third heaven. But there is nothing more monstrous or extravagant than that.

The fifth group consists of passages which always contrast heaven to earth, and also earth to heaven, as having a relation like a circumference to its center and a center to its circumference. But if the earth were in the third heaven, it would be on one side and not in the middle. Consequently the earth and the heavens would not exist in that same, continuous relationship in which they always seem to be contrasted and to be joined together, according to both Sacred Scripture and common reason. Thus it is said in Genesis 1:1, "In the beginning God created heaven and earth;" in Psalm 115:16, "Heaven belongs to God, he gave the earth to the sons of men," and in a thousand other places he is called, "He who made heaven and earth." In Matthew 6:10 the Lord teaches us to pray, "Your will be done, on earth as in heaven." And St. Paul says in 1 Corinthians 15:47–48, "The first man, being from earth, is earthly; the second man, being from heaven, is celestial;" in Colossians 1:16, "In him were created all things in heaven and on earth;" and later on at 1:20, "Everything in heaven and everything on earth, he reconciled with the blood of his cross;" and at Colossians 3:2, "Let your thoughts be on heavenly things, not on the things that are on the earth;" and innumerable similar passages. Therefore, since these two bodies are always placed in contrast to each other, and since the heavens without doubt are located toward the circumference, the earth clearly is located at the center of the world.

The sixth and last group consists of passages (taken from the Fathers and the theologians rather than from Sacred Scripture) which say that after the day of judgment the sun will become stationary in the east and the moon in the west. But if the Pythagorean opinion were true, this stationary state ought to be attributed to the earth and not the sun. For if it is the earth which is now moved around the sun, then on that day it would be the earth which stops. Further, if the earth were to become stationary, there is no reason why it should stop in one place rather than another; or why one side of its surface should face the sun rather than another; or why whatever side is deprived of the light of the sun would be more horrible, and more gloomy, and worse in every way than the other side. There are many other absurdities which would also arise.

These are the groups of opposing passages which contain and assemble all the weapons and arguments which present the gravest opposition and test to the Pythagorean opinion. Nevertheless it is possible to defend that opinion easily (in my judgment) by means of six principles, which I will now formulate, which are like the firmest bastions made of impregnable material, and which are the antitheses of the six groups of passages already mentioned.

Before I present these principles, I profess first, with all the modesty proper to a Christian and to a member of a religious order, that everything I am about to say is reverently submitted, now and always, to the judgment of the Holy Church, prostrating myself at the feet of the Highest Pastor. The motive which has caused me to write is neither boldness, nor ambition, nor vainglory, but the love and desire to help my fellow man in the study and discussion of truth. On the issue at hand I have no particular inclination to the one opinion or to the other. Rather I favor whatever opinion will be shown to me by clear arguments to be more probable and likely by the advocates of that doctrine. Thus I stand indifferent and neutral, and I look to those to whom it properly belongs to resolve this controversy.

The first and most important principle is the following. When Sacred Scripture attributes something to God or to any creature which would otherwise be improper and incommensurate, then it should be interpreted and explained in one or more of the following ways. First, it is said to pertain metaphorically and proportionally, or by similitude. Second, it is said (as it is usually put in Latin) "secundum nostrum modum considerandi, apprehendendi, concipiendi, intelligendi, cognoscendi, etc." [according to our mode of consideration, apprehension, conception, understanding, knowing, etc.]. Thirdly, it is said according to the vulgar opinion and the common way of speaking; the Holy Spirit frequently and deliberately adopts the vulgar and common way of speaking. Fourthly, it is said under the guise of some human aspect.

I will give examples of these explications. God does not walk, because he is infinite and immobile; he has no bodily members, because he is pure act; and for the same reason there are no passions in his mind. Yet one finds in Sacred Scripture, in Genesis 3:8, "He walked in the garden after midday," and in Job 22:14, "He walked around the poles of the heavens." Elsewhere in a thousand places he is said to walk, to depart, to look at, to rush; also to have bodily organs, eyes, ears, lips, a face, a voice, a countenance, hands, feet, a stomach, clothes, arms; and also to have many passions, like anger, sorrow, regret, etc. What ought to be said about this? Without doubt such attributes are said of God (to speak like the scholastics) metaphorically, proportionally, and by similitude.

The passions can also be interpreted as revealing God under the guise of some human trait. Thus "God is angry" reveals him under the guise of anger; "God is sorrowful" reveals him under the guise of sorrow; "God regrets that he made man" reveals him under the guise of regret, etc. Thus God is said to be in the heavens, to move in time, to reveal or conceal himself, to notice and count our steps, to search out, to stand in the doorway, and to knock on the door. But this does not mean that he occupies any physical place, or that he is in motion and in time, or that he performs any human action or behavior; all this refers rather to our human mode of understanding. The latter distinguishes in him attributes which are one and the same thing in him and in relation to each other; it divides his actions in time although they occur in one and the same indivisible instant; and it represents something which is most perfect in God as though it always has some degree of imperfection.

Thus, following the common opinion, Scripture attributes to the earth a foundation and limits, which it does not have; to the sea an endless depth; and to death, which is a privation (and thus is not an existing thing), it attributes actions, motions, passions, and other properties which it does not have, and also epithets and other characteristics which are quite unsuitable. For example, "Is not bitter death removed? He prepared the instruments of death. Death came upon them. You raise me from the gates of death. In the midst of the shadow of death, death will devour them. Love is as strong as death. Death is the first-born. Death and damnation say . . . etc."

And who does not know that the story of the rich glutton is full of such common phrases? Also it is said in Ecclesiasticus 27:12, "The holy man is stable in wisdom, like the sun, while the fool changes, like the moon." But the moon never changes, as has been truly demonstrated by the astronomers. For always one half of it is illuminated and the other half is in the dark. This property never varies in it, but only in relation to us and according to the common opinion. Hence it is clear that the Sacred Scripture speaks in accordance with the common language of popular reason and of ordinary people; and thus according to the appearances and not according to actual reality.

Also in the description of the creation of all things in Genesis 1, light is said to have been created before everything else, and then the text adds, "Evening came and morning came: the first day." And immediately afterwards, in distinguishing and comparing different acts of creation by assigning them to different days, the text says, "Evening came and morning came: the second day," and still later, "the third day," "the fourth day," etc. As a result many doubts arise. And I will examine all of them in accordance with the common system. Thus it will be realized that, even if that system is granted, there is still sometimes a need, in order to avoid many difficulties, to understand Sacred Scripture according to the common meaning and language, and as related to us, and not according to the nature of things themselves. Even Aristotle recognized this distinction when he said in *Physics* I, 1, "The same things are not 'knowable relatively to us' and 'knowable' without qualification" [184a18].

First, then, if light was created before the heavens, it would have rotated by itself and without the heavens in the first time that it generated the distinction between day and night. But this is quite contrary to those who say that celestial bodies are moved only accidentally by the motion of the heavens, "as a knot in a board is moved by the motion of the board."

Next, if light was created together with the heavens and is moved with it, another doubt arises which is also found in the previous case. For light is said to generate day and night, morning and evening, either in respect to the universe or only in respect to the earth and to us who inhabit it. But this cannot occur in respect to the universe. For the rotating sun (granting the assumption of the common opinion) does not generate day and night unless there be opaque bodies having no light other than that of the sun. These bodies are illuminated in one of their halves and no more (i.e., in a hemisphere); namely, in that half of their globe which faces the sun (for the sun can never illuminate more than half, or really a little more in smaller bodies), while the other half remains obscure and dark in a shadow caused by the body itself.

Thus the distinctions of the various days by the light of the heavens, as described in Sacred Scripture, ought not to be understood absolutely as in itself and as in nature, but only in respect to the earth and to us who inhabit it, and thus in respect to us. Hence there is nothing new or unusual in saying that Sacred Scripture speaks of things in respect to us, in relation only to us, and according to appearances, and not according to things themselves and according to nature, i.e., absolutely and simply.

Let us assume that someone wishes to interpret these days of the Scriptures not just according to us but according to nature. He might say that each rotation of the light of the heavens always returns to the same point from which it started. Hence it is not necessary to refer to any shadow or darkness, which is the only thing which constrains one to interpret the Scriptures in relation to us.

In opposition to this interpretation, I would argue as follows. If the Scriptures had intended to speak of the rotation of the light absolutely, and not in respect to us, then it would not have used the words "evening" and "morning," which naturally connote the relation of the sun to us and to the earth. For "morning" is the time in which the sun first begins to appear and reveal itself in the east above our horizon and in our hemisphere. And "evening" is the time in which that same sun begins to reveal itself in the west and begins to illuminate that other horizon and hemisphere which comes after ours.

And the word "day" is the correlative of the word "night." Thus it is clear that these three words, "evening," "morning," and "day," without doubt are not intended to refer to the rotation of the light in itself and absolutely, but only in relation to us and in respect to us. And this is the way that morning and evening, night and day, are actually caused. And in Genesis 1:16 it is said, "God made two great lights: the greater light to govern the day, the smaller light to govern the night and the stars." Thus both in this proposition and in the specific details things are said which disagree with the real being of the celestial bodies.

Hence it is necessary to interpret the words of Scripture according to the above-mentioned rules, and especially according to the fourth rule that words are to be interpreted "according to the vulgar meaning and the common mode of speaking," which is the same as saying, "according to appearances and in relation to us or in respect to us." For first in the proposition it is said, "God made two great lights," referring to the sun and the moon. But as a matter of true fact, both of these lights are not "great." Although the sun is one of the great lights, this is not true of the moon, if we are speaking according to the truth of the matter and not in respect to us. Furthermore Saturn is one of the truly great lights; it is a little smaller than, or perhaps equal to, the sun and much larger than the moon. The same is true of some of the stars of the first magnitude; for example, Canopus, sometimes called Arcanar, in the end of the river; Sirius in the mouth of the Great Dog; Rigel in the foot of Orion; Orion's right shoulder; and other such stars. Hence "two great lights" is to be understood in relation to us and according to the vulgar opinion, and not according to the true and real being which these bodies have.

Secondly in the specific details it is said that "the greater light governs the day," referring to the sun. Here the literal sense of the Scripture fits well with the reality of the facts, for the sun is the greatest light and the largest globe of all. But what immediately follows, "the smaller light governs the night," which refers to the moon, cannot be understood as true of its real being. For the moon is not really a smaller light; rather this is true of Mercury, which is much smaller than the moon, and of many stars.

Someone might still wish to maintain that the text does not speak of the stars but of the lights, for immediately it next specifies "the stars;" and thus what we have said applies to a comparison of the stars to each other, but not of the lights, i.e., the sun and the moon. Certainly those who would wish to say this would show that they do not have the slightest taste of mathematical science, not even with the tip of the lips, for they have a quite erroneous understanding of celestial bodies. For the sun and the moon, considered in themselves and as they would appear at a much greater distance than they actually are, would be no different than the stars, and thus are called greater lights only in respect to us. Likewise the stars in themselves are not different from the sun and the moon, but are only more distant; and because of that interval they reasonably appear to be much smaller and to have less splendor. Thus, other things being equal, the greater or smaller distance is what makes the celestial bodies appear to be larger or smaller, both in respect to their light and in respect to their size.

Granting this, then what is said next in Genesis, i.e., "and the stars," should be interpreted as distinguishing the stars from the sun and the moon in the same sense as indicated; namely, according to the vulgar sense and the common mode of speaking. For according to reality and the facts, all the shining globes of the celestial bodies are indeed very large; and if we were as close to them as we are to the moon, they would appear as big as the moon or even larger. And if we were very far away from the sun and the moon, they would appear to be stars.

However without doubt the brightness of the sun would be greater in intensity than the brightness of any star. The reason for this is the following. It must be conceded that some stars (for example, the fixed stars which twinkle) are luminous in themselves and by their proper nature (which is controversial and not certain), and shine without receiving their light from the sun, which also does not derive its light from another. However, since the brightness of no star can be compared to that of the sun, which was created by God first and as the greatest of all lights, it clearly follows that if any similar star were as close to us as is the sun, thus appearing to have the same size, it would still not be as bright as the sun. On the other hand, if the sun were as far away as one of these stars, appearing thus to be as small as that star, it would not display the same small amount of brightness as that star, but would be much brighter.

Finally the earth also is just another moon or star. This is exactly how it would appear if it were seen from afar at the proper distance;

one would be able to see in it from there (in the changes of brightness and darkness caused there by the sun as it brings on night and
day) the very same changes of aspect which are seen in the moon
from here. This same thing has been observed in the triple body
of Venus, and it is not unreasonable to say that this also occurs in
the other planets, which are not luminous of themselves but receive
their light from the sun. Since we know that these things occur otherwise in reality and in fact, then when they are found to be written
in the Sacred Scriptures or are found in ordinary human judgment,
they ought always to be understood according to the vulgar sense
and the common mode and style of speaking and thinking.

Coming thus to our main point, and using the same argument,
if the Pythagorean opinion were true, it would be easy to reconcile
it with those passages of Sacred Scripture which are contrary to it,
and especially with those passages of our first and second groups, by
using our principle; that is, by saying that in those places Scripture
speaks according to our mode of understanding, and according to
appearances, and in respect to us. For thus it is that these bodies
appear to be related to us and are described by the common and
vulgar mode of human thinking; namely, the earth seems to stand
still and to be immobile, and the sun seems to rotate around it.

Hence Scripture serves us by speaking in the vulgar and common manner; for from our point of view it does seem that the earth
stands firmly in the center and that the sun revolves around it, rather
than the contrary. The same thing happens when people are carried
in a small boat on the sea near the shore; to them it seems that the
shore moves and is carried backwards, rather than that they move
forwards, which is the truth. The professors of optics have explained
the reason for this fallacy in our vision and senses in this case, but
there is no need to wander beyond my purpose into that issue. As
Virgil makes Aeneas say,

> Provehimur portu, terraeque, urbesque rededunt.
> [We left port, and the earth and towns receded.]
> [*Aeneid* III, 72]

But why is it that the Sacred Scriptures are so often adapted to
the common and vulgar opinion, and do not instruct us in the truths
of the secrets of nature? That is a question worth considering, and

it is not right for us to pass over it in silence since it is a part of our first principle.

I say briefly that this happens because of the exquisite distribution of divine wisdom, which adjusts itself to each person according to his nature and capacity; for the natural and necessary scientists, naturally and necessarily; for the liberal arts, freely; for mighty people, nobly; for common people, humbly; for the educated, learnedly; for the simple, vulgarly; and thus for all, it adapts itself to each one's style.

Secondly it is not God's intention to instruct us in this life in curiosities which overcome the mind with doubt, with uncertainty as to what is permitted, with commitments which plunge the world into disputes, litigation, and controversy, and with a tendency to uncertainty in all things. As is said in Ecclesiastes 3:11, "He handed the world over to their disputation, but man could not grasp the work which God made from the beginning up to the end." And he will not pronounce judgment before the end, when "He will light up all that is hidden in the dark," as St. Paul says in 1 Corinthians 4:5.

Thus God's only intention is to teach us the true road to eternal life. Once this has been attained, "then we shall see him face to face" (1 Corinthians 13:12), and "we shall be like him because we shall see him as he is," (1 John 3:2). There he will reveal to us, *a priori*, easily, and perfectly, the truth of all these curiosities and doctrines, which we can now know only *a posteriori*, imperfectly, and with great effort and fatigue in this life in which "we now look through a mirror into an enigma" (1 Corinthians 13:12).

And this is why, in Ecclesiastes 15:3, the wisdom of God revealed to us in the Sacred Scriptures is called "saving wisdom" and not "absolute wisdom." This wisdom is associated with salvation, which is a gift, because the Scriptures have no other purpose than the attainment of salvation. Thus when St. Paul went to Corinth to preach, he focused attention only on Christ Crucified, with these words, "I have not claimed to know anything among you, except Jesus Christ, as Christ crucified" (1 Corinthians 2:3). Although he was otherwise most learned, he did not pretend to teach anything other than the way to heaven.

Thus God, speaking through Isaiah, says, "I, God, teach you what is useful" (Isaiah 48:17). To which the gloss ought to be added, "but not subtle things." For God does not teach us whether the heavens and the elements have the same kind of primary matter; whether a continuum is composed of indivisibles or is divisible to infinity; whether the elements are mixed formally; how many celestial spheres and globes exist; whether there are epicycles and eccentrics; what is the power of plants or of stones; what is the nature of animals; whether the planets all have the same path; what is the order of the universe; or what are the marvels of minerals and of the whole of nature.

Rather he teaches only what is useful; that is, his holy law, whose purpose is to enable us to come in the Word to a perfect knowledge and vision of the entire order, marvelous proportion, and the harmony and disharmony of the universe and its parts. We are not able to know anything distinctly "until we have entered into the Sanctuary." Then we will see distinctly and clearly, and will understand without difficulty, direct or indirect, the truth of all these curiosities which in this life have been left to the industry of human inquiry and investigation (as best it can do). Since these matters have little or no usefulness, in some cases it would perhaps be harmful to know; and on the other side, to avoid harm, in some cases it would perhaps be useful not to know. And thus with marvelous wisdom God has determined that only his holy faith is most certain, and everything else in this world is doubtful, uncertain, vacillating, ambiguous, and two-sided.

Although in the Church there are various opinions on philosophical and scholarly matters, nevertheless there is only one truth of faith and salvation. Hence I say that God determined that the faith, which is necessary for salvation, is without doubt and is unshakable, certain, immutable, and known to all. He has also established one, infallible ruler, i.e., the Holy Church which is washed in his blood. *The Church together with its visible head, the Supreme Pontiff* (assisted by the Holy Spirit whose primary intention is our sanctification) *cannot err, in matters of faith and our salvation only. But the Church can err in practical judgments, in philosophical speculations, and in other doctrines which do not involve and pertain to salvation.**

This then is the reason why God has not settled in the Sacred Scriptures questions of speculation and curiosity, which do not contribute to our edification and are not useful for salvation; and why the Holy Spirit so often adapts to the vulgar and common opinion and does not teach anything new, unusual, and concealed. Consequently it is clear how and why one should not use the above-mentioned passages to derive anything certain in the resolution of such questions. Also with our first principle one can easily ward off and avoid the force of passages of the first and second groups, and any other allegations taken from Sacred Scripture, as contrary to the opinion of Pythagoras and Copernicus, if indeed that opinion is already known to be true by other means.

More particularly, passages of the second group can be avoided and interpreted in another way with the same principle mentioned earlier; namely, in terms of common speech and of the ordinary way of apprehending things as they appear to us. For we frequently, commonly, and properly say that an agent, which remains fixed, moves, not because it itself moves, but by extrinsic denomination; namely, it is said to move because of the motion of a subject which receives its influence, action, and a quality which is induced in the subject by the agent.

For example, a fire burning in a fireplace is a stationary agent. A man who is cold stands in front of the fire to warm himself. First he warms one part of his body; then he turns another part of his body toward the fire to warm it; turning thus in a circle, he warms his whole body. It is clear that the fire does not move. Yet by the motion of the subject, that is, the man who received the heat and the action of the fire, the form and quality of its heat moves from part to part around the man's body and always takes up a new place. And thus, although the fire is motionless, still because of its effects, the fire is said to move around all the parts of the man's body and to warm him; not by a motion which moves the fire, which was taken to

---

*The words in italics in these two sentences were omitted from seventeenth-century Latin and English translations of Foscarini's *Letter* published in Northern Europe.

be motionless, but by a motion which moves the body which receives the heat of the fire part by part. The same account applies to the successive illumination of the parts of an apple which moves in a circle facing the light of the burning candle which is stationary.

In the same way one can say that the sun rises and sets and moves around the earth, although there is no motion or mutation in it. For its light, which is the effect, form, and quality introduced by it as an agent into the earth as a subject, moves forward because of the motion of the earth and always takes up a new place above its surface.

Thus it is truly said (according to common parlance) that the sun moves above and rotates around the earth. This is not because the sun moves (for the earth is what is properly supposed to move and to receive the sun part by part); rather it is because when the earth moves in the opposite direction, there is also a motion of the quality emitted and sent by the sun to the earth, which is the light of day, which rises in one part of the earth and sets in another according to the condition of its motion. Consequently the sun itself (which does not move except by supposition) is said to rise and set only by extrinsic denomination.

With this one can interpret the command of Joshua, "Sun, stand still," in Joshua 10:12, and the miracle of the sun not moving, by saying that what is properly said to have stopped was not the body of the sun, but the light of the sun on the earth. This was caused not by the stopping of the sun, which is always motionless, but by the stopping of the earth which receives the light of the sun. The earth, which usually and ordinarily rotates toward the east, followed the light of the sun and moved toward the west; thus the stopping of the earth caused the light to stop.

Proportionally in the same way one could explain the passage of Isaiah 38:8, concerning the miracle of the sun turning backwards ten lines in Ahaz's timepiece. As another example, if the hand is rotated around the light of a burning candle which is at rest, the light moves on the hand without the candle being moved, illuminating the hand part by part. From this one can say that the light rises and sets on the hand, coming to one place and leaving another, by extrinsic denomination from the motion of the hand, without the candle being moved at all.

This is sufficient to explain my first principle; to establish it there was a need to be somewhat prolix because of the difficulty and importance of what it contains.

The second principle is this. All things, be they spiritual or corporeal, perpetual or corruptible, unchangeable or changeable, have been given by God a perpetual, immutable, and inviolable law of their being and nature, as is said in Psalm [148:6], "He established things for eternity, and for all ages he has decreed a law which will not pass away." By this law things always maintain a perpetual structure in their being and actions, and come to acquire a fixed name, and are most stable in their condition. Thus it is said that chance (which is the most unstable and variable thing in the world) is constant and invariable in its continuous volubility, inconstancy, vicissitude, and variation, as the verse says:

> Et semper constans in levitate sua est.
> [It is always constant in its lightness.]
> [Ovid, *Tristia* 5, 8, 18]

Now since the motions of the heavens have been determined by the ordinary law never to cease, the heavens are said to be immobile and immutable. Thus the heavens move with constancy, and terrestrial things change immutably; for the former never vary in their motion, nor the latter in their mutation.

With this principle one can interpret all the passages of Sacred Scripture which belong to the first group, which say that the earth is stable and immobile. For in its own nature the earth contains a triple local motion, according to the opinion of Copernicus (namely, a diurnal motion, by which it revolves on itself; an annual motion, by which it revolves through the twelve signs of the zodiac; and a motion of inclination, by which its axis is always pointed to the same part of the world, and which causes the inequality of the days and the nights), plus still other different species of mutations; namely, generation and corruption, increase and decrease, and alterations of various types. Nevertheless in all this the earth is always stable and from the beginning has never varied from the pattern given by God, always moving constantly and immutably in all three species of motion just mentioned.

The third principle is this. If a thing moves in one of its parts but not as a whole, it cannot be said to be moved simply and absolutely but only accidentally, for "simply" refers rather to its stability. For example, if a glass of water, or some other portable measure, were taken from the sea and carried from one place to another, it cannot be said that the sea absolutely and simply was moved from one place to another, but only accidentally and relatively, that is, in respect to one of its parts. Indeed it would be better, simply speaking, to say that the sea is unmovable in its own place, but is movable insofar as one of its parts is moved or carried off.

This principle is evident in itself; and with it one can resolve and explain those passages which seem to conclude that the earth is immobile. For it can be maintained that the earth in itself and absolutely, that is, taken as a whole, does not change, that is, it is not generated or corrupted or increased or decreased or altered as a whole, but only in respect to its parts. This is the true sense of the text of Ecclesiastes 1:4, which says this very thing, "A generation goes, a generation comes, yet the earth stands firm forever." It is as if one wished to say that, although the earth in its parts is generated and corrupted, and on it occur the vicissitudes of the generation and corruption of things, nevertheless as a whole it is never generated or corrupted but remains perpetually immutable.

This is exactly like a ship which at one time has a plank removed and replaced with another, then its lateen-yard is changed, then a piece of the rudder, then another part, and another; yet it is always the same ship. And thus the passages of Scripture do not speak of local motion but of the other types of change; namely, in the substance, quantity, and quality of the earth. If one wishes to say that the Scripture speaks of local motion, then one would have to interpret it with the following principle, that is, in relation to the natural place which the earth has in the universe, as I will now explain.

The fourth principle is that every material thing, whether it be mobile or immobile, from the beginning of creation has its own proper, natural, and proportionate place. If it leaves that place, it is moved violently; if it goes to that place, it is moved naturally. Nothing as a whole can be moved from its natural place, for that would cause a very great disturbance and horrible disorder in the universe. Therefore neither the whole earth, nor the whole of water, nor the whole of the air, can be pulled and lifted as a whole from its designated place and site, or from the true system and constitution, which it has in the universe, in relation to the order and disposition of the other bodies of the world. No star, not even errant ones, or globe or sphere can leave its place, even though it moves with other motions. Thus everything, even though it moves, can still be said to be immobile and stable in its proper place in the sense indicated above, that is, as a whole. But it is not improper to say that it experiences motion in its parts, which then are violent and not natural motions.

Thus although the earth is mobile, it can be said to be stable and immobile in the sense indicated. For it does not move in a straight line outside the orbit assigned at its creation; rather, it always moves circularly in that orbit. It is found to be located in what is called the great orbit, above Venus and below Mars, between them in the heaven in which the common opinion ordinarily places the sun. In this place it moves around the sun and around the two interior planets, that is, Venus and Mercury. Around it revolves the moon, which is another but ethereal earth, which Macrobius says is the opinion of the ancient philosophers. Thus it does not change in structure nor vary in content. Therefore, because of this uniformity the earth always has the same fixed orbit which it never leaves, and so it can be said to be stable and immobile, in the same way in which the heavens and all the elements can be said to be immobile in their own species.

The fifth principle, which differs little from the preceding one, is this. Some things were created by God such that their parts are separable from each other and from the whole, while other things do not have such parts, at least when considered collectively. The first are contingent, the second are perpetual.

Now since the earth is a perpetual creature, its parts are not separable nor able to be disjoined collectively from itself and from its center (which determines its true place) and from the whole. For as a whole the earth is always stable in itself, rolled up into a globe, united and coherent; its parts are not distinguished or separated from the center, nor among themselves, except accidentally or by violence, after which they immediately and naturally return to their proper place. In this way then the earth is said to be immobile and immutable.

In this same way not only the earth, but also the sea, the air, the heavens, and anything else (though otherwise mobile) can be said to be immobile, provided that its parts are not separable, at least when considered collectively. This principle differs from the preceding one only insofar as that one considers the parts in relation to place, while this one considers the parts in relation to the whole.

This speculation also uncovers another secret. For it reveals the proper nature of the heaviness and lightness of things, a problem which the common philosophy of Aristotle does not easily avoid or explain without considerable controversy. According to the principles of this new opinion, heaviness properly speaking is simply a certain natural appetite and inclination of parts to reunite with their whole. This was established by divine providence not only for the earth and the bodies on it, but also for celestial bodies (as is credible) and for the sun, the moon, and the stars. Because of this inclination the parts of all these bodies gather together and are joined so firmly that no one of them could find any place of rest other than the center of the body of which it is a part. The striving of all the parts from every direction toward the center, and their consequent compression, causes the spherical and round figure of the celestial bodies and preserves them always in this shape and in their being.

Lightness, on the other hand, is the expulsion of thinner and rarer bodies from association with more solid and dense bodies (to which they are heterogeneous), and this is caused by the power of heat. Thus the motion of heavy things is compressive, while the motion of light things is expulsive, for heat has the property of expanding and rarefying anything to which it is applied, joined, and communicated.

As a result heaviness and lightness are found not only in our terrestrial globe and in the bodies on it, but also in the bodies which are said to be in the heavens. For those parts which have a proclivity to move to the center are heavy; those which tend towards the circumference are light. Therefore both heavy and light parts exist in the sun, the moon, and the stars. Consequently the heavens are not a noble body composed of the fifth essence. They are not constituted of a matter which is different from the elements. Nor are they immutable in every species of mutation, i.e., in their substance, quantity, and quality. Nor are they of such a marvelous and unusual condition as Aristotle insistently portrays them to be. Nor are they as solid, impermeable, and impenetrably and stubbornly dense as everyone commonly believes them to be. On the contrary comets can be generated in the heavens (according to this opinion); and the sun exhales (as is suspected), or maybe attracts, various vapors to the surface of its body, which perhaps causes the sunspots which are observed as varied anomalies on its surface. Mr. Galileo has written about them so well that there is no need for me to say anything more about them.

And if some passage to the contrary were to be found in Sacred Scripture, it is excluded by the principles given above, proportionally applied. Thus solidity can be understood as "not admitting a void, or any break or penetration in which a void might occur." As a void is impossible in all bodily creatures, it is particularly repugnant to the heavens, a body which by its nature is the most rare of all and whose thinness is beyond all human comprehension. Perhaps the heavens have the same proportion of rarity and thinness in relation to air, as air has in relation to water, or even greater.

Another consequence from these same principles is the recognition of how wrong Aristotle was when he said:

> For one simple body there is one simple motion. The latter has two species; circular and straight. Straight motion is twofold: from the center and to the center. The former is the motion of light things: air and fire. The latter is the motion of heavy things: water and earth. Circular motion, which is around the center, belongs to the heavens, which are neither heavy nor light. [De caelo I, 3, 270b27–31]

This whole philosophy has disintegrated and fallen into ruin. On the other hand in the new opinion it is agreed that, although it is true that one simple body has only one simple motion, this motion is always a circular motion. For only by a circular motion can any simple body remain in its natural place, be united with itself, and have a motion properly "in a place." This happens because what is moved still remains united with itself, and although it is in motion, it still remains at rest in the same place.

But straight line motion, which is properly said to be motion "to a place," belongs only to things which are outside of their natural place, and which are found at a distance from each other and from union with the whole from which they are separated and divided. Such things are contrary to the order of nature and to the form of the universe. It follows that straight line motion belongs only to things which do not have in themselves the perfection and completeness which they should have by their proper nature. Thus by means of straight line motion they try to be reintegrated with their own whole, and to reunite with their own unity, and to reach their natural place, which is the only place where they can finally stop and experience rest andrepose.

As a result straight line motions are not truly uniform and simple, for they vary according to the irregularity of lightness or weight and heaviness of their bodies. Thus they do not equally preserve the same velocity and slowness from beginning to end. Hence things which fall downwards because of their weight have a slow motion at first, but later, as they fall, their velocity increases, and to the degree that they approach closer to the center, their velocity increases accordingly.

On the other hand things which rise because of their lightness (for example, terrestrial fire which is simply burning smoke) do not ascend to a very great height before they suddenly vanish and disappear and are lost from view, because of the rapid expansion and rarefication which they acquire by moving upwards as they are freed from the force and violence which held them in a downward place against their nature.

For this reason it is quite clear that no straight line motion can be said to be simple. This can be concluded either from the argument already given, i.e., that it is not equal and uniform, or from the fact that it is always mixed with a circular motion, which arises in the straight line motion because of the hidden tendency, due to the identity of nature, for parts always to seek their whole. Hence if a whole moves circularly, then even though the parts may move accidentally in a straight line motion, they must seek their own whole, and thus also have a circular motion (which is not evident or clear) which conforms to the motion of the whole. Therefore it is firmly established that only circular motion is simple and uniform and equal and the same in structure, for it itself is the cause why it never is less.

Furthermore straight line motion, which is found in both heavy and light things, is itself the cause of its deficiency and imperfection; namely, it always tends towards and aspires to an end and to its own termination. For as soon as heavy and light things have reached their proper and natural place, they immediately cease the motion which was caused in them by their heaviness and lightness. Although circular motion relates to the whole, and straight line motion to the parts, this difference does not make them opposite motions, such that the one is called straight and the other circular, and that the one could not exist together with the other. For both can exist together and reside naturally in one body, just as it is natural for man to be both sensory and rational because these different properties are not opposed to each other. Thus only rest and immobility are opposed to motion, and one species of motion is not opposed to another.

Other differences in motions, i.e., from the center, to the center, and around the center, are not really but only formally distinct, like a point, a line, and a surface. These things cannot exist without each other, and none of them exist without a body. Hence it is seen that this philosophy is as far removed from Aristotle's as the new cosmographical system is removed from the one commonly held up to now. But I say this in the context of my fifth principle, since it is in no way my present intention to determine the truth or falsity of this position, although I would maintain that it is most probable.

The sixth and last principle is this. A thing is said to be something simply when it is related to, and compared with, a whole class, or at least to many things and to a large part of that class, but not to a few things representing a small part of the class. For example, a jar cannot be said to be absolutely large because it is large in comparison with two or three or a few other jars; but it will be absolutely large if it is larger than all other jars or the greater part of them. A man will not be absolutely tall because he is taller than a pygmy; nor is he absolutely short because he is shorter than a giant; but he will be called absolutely tall or short in comparison with the ordinary stature of the greater part of the human race.

Likewise one ought not say that the earth is simply high or low because it is such in comparison with a few other parts of the universe. Consequently one ought not say that it is absolutely high because it is such only in comparison with the center of the world or with a few parts of the universe which stand closer to the center, as do the sun, Mercury, and Venus. Rather such names should be assigned when the earth is compared with the greater number of spheres and bodies in the universe. Therefore the earth, in comparison with the whole circuit of the eighth sphere which includes all material creatures, and in comparison with Mars, Jupiter, Saturn, and the moon, and much more in comparison with other bodies (if there are any) above the eighth sphere, and in particular the empyrean heaven, can be truly said to be in the lowest place in the world, as if it were in the middle or center. And it cannot be said to be above any of them except the sun, Mercury, and Venus. Hence absolutely and simply the earth can be said to be a low body, and not a high or middle body.

And so to come to the earth from heaven, especially if one is talking about the highest or empyrean heaven (as is understood in the descent of Christ in his most holy incarnation), and to go from earth to heaven (as is understood of the ascent of Christ into heaven in his glorious ascension), are properly said to be a true descent from the circumference to the center and a true ascent from the parts closest to the center of the world to its furthest circumference. In this way theological propositions can be quite properly justified.

And our principle is supported much more by the fact (which I have observed) that almost all the passages of Sacred Scripture which contrast heaven, in the singular, with the earth are much more properly and appropriately understood and interpreted as referring in particular to the empyrean heaven (which is above everything and is spiritual in its purpose), and not to the lower and intermediate heavens which are corporeal and which were made for material creatures. Thus when one speaks of the heavens, in the plural, one refers to everything without distinction, i.e., both the empyrean and the other lower heavens together. Anyone (who carefully examines the matter) will find that this explanation is quite true. And the third heaven, into which St. Paul was swept up, is understood by this principle to be the empyrean heaven.

The "first heaven" refers to the entire immense space of moving and wandering bodies illuminated by the sun, in which are located the planets and the moving earth together with the immobile sun in the center of all the spheres. The sun is like a king who sits majestically and observantly on his throne, eternally constant and steady, ruling and governing all existing celestial bodies, rotating on itself, needing nothing from them who need everything from him, like an immortal and eternal lamp lit in the center of the theater of the world, illuminating all of its parts with its unspeakable worth and dignity.

The "second heaven" refers to the starry heaven, which is commonly call the eighth sphere or the firmament, which contains all the fixed stars. This heaven (according to the opinion under discussion), like the sun and the center, is totally deprived of all motion and is completely immobile; the center and its furthest circumference are both immobile.

The "third heaven" or empyrean heaven is the home of the blessed. This also explains and justifies the marvelous secret and profound mystery revealed enigmatically by Plato to Dionysius of Syracuse, "All things are around the king of all; second things around the second; and third things around the third."* For God is the center of spiritual things, the sun of corporeal things, and Christ of mixed things. Without doubt each of these centers supports the things corresponding to them; it is always their center, and the center is the more noble place. Hence in the center and middle of animals is located the heart, and in the center of plants is located the fruit, which contains the seeds which perpetuate them and which virtually contain the whole plant. This is enough to note, since we are not able to write more for now about these matters. With this sixth principle the passages and arguments of the third, fourth, and fifth groups are specifically resolved.

We might add that the sun, Mercury, and Venus (in relation to the earth) ought to be said to be above and not below the earth, even though they are below the earth in relation to the whole system of the universe and absolutely speaking. The reason is that in relation to the earth they always appear above its surface. Although they do not rotate around the earth, nevertheless because of the motion of the earth, they are always in opposition to one part or another of

---

*Plato, *Epistle II*, 312e, as quoted in Theodoretus of Cyrrhus, *Graecarun affectionum curatio* II, 78.

the earth's circumference. Now a part of a spherical body which is
closer to the circumference and more distant from the center is said
to be above; and a part which is closer to the center is said to be
below. Now since the sun, Mercury, and Venus are not only above
the surface and circumference of the earth but are outside of it by
a great distance, they successively face every part of the earth, and
they are far removed from its center. Hence it clearly follows that
they are above in relation to the earth. So the earth is below in
relation to them, although on the contrary in relation to the whole
universe, the earth is much higher than them.

The sixth group of passages contains a difficulty which is shared
by both the common opinion and the Copernican opinion, and thus
is not an important problem to solve. But insofar as it is opposed to
the Copernican view in particular, it is quickly resolved by our first
principle. The problem, which was mentioned in our discussion of
the fourth group of passages, is that hell, which is inside the earth,
would rotate around the sun and would be in the heavens. To me
this seems to arise from ignorance, or slander, or a wish out of envy
to do violence with evil-sounding words, rather than to provide any
argument based on the nature of things. For "heaven" here does not
mean paradise, nor is it used in its usual sense. Rather (in accordance
with the Copernican opinion) it means that type of air, which is most
subtle and pure (as was said above), and which is far more tenuous
and rare than our air. For through it pass (as they rotate in their
paths) the solid bodies of the stars, moon, and earth (for the sphere
of fire is denied and eliminated by this opinion.)

Now it is not a drawback in the common opinion that hell
stands in the center of the earth and of the world, having heaven
and paradise above, below, and on all sides of it, and that it is located
in the middle of all the celestial bodies, as if in a very noble place.
So likewise this is not a drawback in the new opinion which is not
very different from the other system, mentioned above, in respect to
the same or similar consequences. For in both the common opinion
and the Copernican opinion, hell is the scum of the elements, and
it is located in the center of the earth to imprison and punish the
damned. Hence there is no need to flee from the sound of evil
words because of a lack of effective arguments. For there is no
doubt what the meaning is. For anyone who holds this opinion, who

has a well-ordered mind, and who is well instructed in the liberal arts, especially in mathematics, it will be quite clear that there is not much difference between the two opinions on this matter.

From these principles and their delineation it is very clear that the opinion of Pythagoras and Copernicus is so probable that it is perhaps more likely than the common opinion of Ptolemy. For from it one can derive the most precise system, and the hidden constitution, of the world in a way which is much more solidly based on reason and experience than is the common opinion. It is also quite clear that the new opinion can be explained in such a way that there is no longer any need to be concerned whether it is contrary to passages of Sacred Scripture or to the justification of theological propositions. On the contrary it not only saves the phenomena and appearances of the celestial bodies with ease, but it also reveals many natural reasons which otherwise would be difficult to find. In effect it simplifies both astronomy and philosophy by eliminating all those superfluous and imaginary things which were previously used to reduce the great variety of celestial motions to reason and rules.

And could it not be that, in the marvelous structure of the candlestick placed in the Tabernacle of God, out most loving God wished to represent secretly to us the system of the universe, and in particular of the planets? The text says, "You will construct a candlestick made of pure gold, having a shaft, branches, cups, small globes, and lilies" (Exodus 25:31). This passage describes five things: the shaft of the candlestick in the middle, reeds or branches on the sides, cups, small globes, and lilies. Since there can be only one shaft, the branches are then immediately described as follows. "Six branches are to extend from the sides of it, three from one side, three from the other."

It could be that these branches signify the six heavens which rotate around the sun as follows. Saturn, which is the slowest and furthest away, completes its path around the sun through all twelve signs of the zodiac in thirty years; Jupiter, which is closer, in twelve years; Mars, which is still closer, in two years. The earth, which is closer than that, moves through its path together with the orb of the moon in one year, i.e., in twelve months. Venus, which is still closer than all of these, in nine months. Finally Mercury, which is the closest of all to the sun, in less than three months, i.e., in eighty days, in which it completes its whole revolution around the sun.

Having described the six branches, the Sacred Text goes on to discuss the cups, the small globes, and the flowers as follows. "Let there be three cups shaped like nuts for the first branch, together with its small globes and lilies; and likewise three cups shaped like nuts for the next branch, together with its small globes and lilies; and the same for all six branches extending from the shaft. On the candlestick itself there will be four cups shaped like nuts, with small globes and lilies for each. The small globes are located under two branches extending from one shaft, for a total of six."

The weakness of my mind prevents me from penetrating into everything contained in this most wise arrangement of things; yet astonished and amazed in my admiration, let me add this. Could it be that these three cups, in the shape of nuts located on each branch of the candlestick, are intended to signify globes (like our own earth) which are more fit to receive influences than to give them? More precisely could it be that they signify those globes discovered by the telescope which are associated with Saturn, Jupiter, Venus, and perhaps other planets? Could it be that the Sacred Scripture insinuates that there is some hidden proportion between those globes and the small globes and the mysterious flowers? But let us restrain our human boldness, and wait with Harpocratic silence for what time, the father of truth, will reveal and show to us. Solomon made ten candlesticks of the same type which Moses constructed, and he placed them, five on each side, in the temple which he built to the Highest God. All this has the most profound and recondite significance.

There is also some mystery about the apple of the knowledge of good and evil, which was forbidden to our first parents, and which some say was really an Indian fig. In that fruit there are many seed particles, each of which has a center which in itself is solid and hard, while around the circumference its matter is more rare and soft. This is similar to the earth which in its center and neighboring parts is stony, metallic, and solid, while as one goes closer to the circumference, its parts are more rare and soft; and above it is water, and above that is air, which is the rarest and softest of all bodies.

These same features of the Indian fig are found in the pomegranate, which has many seeds with separate centers, in each of which, in the parts more removed from the center up to the circumference, there is a material which is so soft that a slight squeeze produces a very thin liquid or juice. The Divine Wisdom has seen fit to make mention of this when speaking of the embroidery on the priestly vestment of Aaron. God said, "Around the bottom of this tunic make pomegranates colored violet and purple and scarlet, and place bells in between so that there is a golden bell and a pomegranate and than another bell and a pomegranate" [Exodus 28:33–35; 39:24–26]. Solomon acknowledges that this is a symbolic portrait of the world when he says, "For the whole orb of the earth was marked on his robe, the glorious names of the ancestors in four rows of stones, and your majesty on the diadem of his head" (Wisdom 18:24).

The same thing is symbolized by the grape, and all other fruits, but especially by the fig, the grape, and the pomegranate, as we have already shown. Hence these three things almost always go together in the Sacred Scriptures. For example, in Numbers 20:5 the people of Israel complain to Moses and Aaron, "Why did you lead us out of Egypt, and bring us to this wretched place? It is unfit for sowing; it brings forth no figs, no vines, no pomegranates." This shows they preferred these fruits above all others. And in Joel 1:12, "The vine has withered, the fig tree wilts away; pomegranate, and palm, and apple, every tree in the field has dried up because gladness has faded among the sons of men." And in Haggai 2:19, "No seed is sprouting, and the vine and fig tree, pomegranate and olive, still have not flowered." In Deuteronomy 8:8 the promised land is praised as, "A land of wheat and barley, of vines, of figs, of pomegranates, and of olives." In building the temple under divine inspiration, Solomon put many rows of pomegranates for decoration at the tops of the columns, as Sacred Scripture mentions in not one but many places [1 Kings 7:20; 2 Kings 25:17; 2 Chronicles 3:16; Jeremiah 52:22].

Finally Sacred Scripture on various occasions presents other notable passages, which are worthy of long and mature consideration, dealing with the issue of the order of the heavens and the system and arrangement of both material and spiritual creatures. The Holy Spirit has presented all this enigmatically in symbols, parables, and images, lest he completely dazzle us with the immense splendor of such excellent things.

From this I conclude that in this same way we can philosophize (on doctrinal matters which are ambiguous) by means of the Sacred Scriptures, especially if we try to understand the prophesies, which otherwise are most obscure. They will be fully understood and grasped only when they have already been fulfilled, and not before. Likewise when the true system of the universe has come to be known and to be established as true, only then will the meaning of these images and enigmas be understood.

Before the coming of the Son of God revealed the mystery of the Most Holy Trinity, no one could understand, or even guess, the meaning of these words: "In the beginning God [Elohim] created heaven and earth." For since the word "Elohim" is plural (as if the text said "Gods"), it could not be seen how that word could agree with the singular verb "created" [creavit]. But once the mystery of the unity of the essence and Trinity of persons in God was revealed, it was immediately realized that the singular "created" refers to the unity of essence (for the external works of the Trinity are undivided), and the plural "Elohim" refers to the persons. Who could have ever guessed this secret previously?

Again the name of God is repeated three times when David says, "God bless us, our God, God bless us" (Psalm 67:6). At first this seems to be a pleonasm and an excess of redundant repetition. But later it became clear that this text presents the blessings of different persons, i.e., the Father, the Son, and the Holy Spirit. Sacred Scripture contains innumerable examples similar to this. So in conclusion I will say with David, "How magnificent are your works, Lord. Your thoughts are too profound; the unwise man does not know them, and the fool does not understand them" (Psalm 92:5–6).

This is as much as I now need to say theologically about the not improbable opinion of the motion of the earth and the stability of the sun. I wish to render this account to you, Most Reverend Father, knowing that all are most thankful for your great love for sound doctrine and the truth.

Further (as a report on my other studies) I hope to send you, as soon as published, the first and second volumes of my *Institutionum omnium doctrinarum*, which will contain the liberal arts, as I have indicated in my *Syntaxi*, which has already been published under its own name. The five other volumes to follow, which I have already promised (containing philosophy and theology), will be somewhat delayed because they are still being written. In the meantime I hope to publish my book *De oraculis*, which is already completed, together with my treatise *De divinatione artificiosa*. As my pledge I am now sending you, along with this letter, my treatise *De divinatione naturali cosmologica*, which deals with natural predictions and forecasts of changes in the weather and other things pertaining to nature.

Finally I pray for every true blessing from God, whose most sacred hands I humbly kiss.

From the Carmelite convent in Naples, 6 January 1615.

Your most humble servant,
Father Paolo Antonio Foscarini

VIIA

An Unidentified Theologian's Censure of Foscarini's *Letter*

This treatise excessively favors the rash opinion of the motion of the earth and the immobility of the sun, as is clear on pages 8 to 11.[1] On page 9[2] the author not only refutes but also ridicules many things which are taught by the authors of the opposite opinion. On page 13[3] he openly says, "The indicated opinion has a clear probability." But what is clearly contrary to Sacred Scripture obviously cannot be probable.

On page 24[4] he says that the words of *Genesis*, "Evening came and morning came: the first day," should not be understood literally and as referring to nature, but only in relation to the earth and to us. But this cannot be said. For although day or night never occurs in the universe as a whole but only in one or the other of its hemispheres, nevertheless when it is day or night in one hemisphere, that day exists as a real thing in nature and not merely in relation to us or only as an appearance.

The objection which the author states in the same place against this truth only shows that day and night and morning and evening occur in a series in relation to us and to the earth, but it does not prove that they do not exist in nature.

From page 29 to the end of the treatise[5] the author tries to defend the indicated opinion by showing that Sacred Scripture can be

---

[1] In Appendix VI, p. 219, line 7 to p. 222, line 18.
[2] P. 219, line 19 to p. 220, line 2.
[3] P. 221, line 22.
[4] P. 228, lines 14–28.
[5] P. 232, line 12 ff.

253

reconciled with it, and thus anyone can embrace it without any fear of contradicting the sacred teachings. But his reconciliation contorts the Sacred Scriptures, and explains them contrary to the common explication of the Holy Fathers, which agrees with the more common, indeed the most common, and most true opinion of almost all astronomers.

On page 29[6] he says that the words of Psalm 92, "For he has made firm the orb of the earth which will not move," and those of Psalm 103, "He established the earth on its own foundation which will not move forever," are to be understood according to appearances. But this explication cannot be accepted. For when a real reason or cause of some effect is assigned, it cannot be understood as only an appearance. And in those texts the Holy Spirit assigns the reason for the immobility of the earth, when he says that it is established on its own foundation.

On pages 38 and 39[7] the author explains the above passages in a different way when he says that the earth is immobile in the sense that it is constant and stable in its own motions. Against this stands the fact that the same thing could be said of the moon and of the other celestial orbs and stars. Furthermore Sacred Scripture says nothing specifically about the immobility of the earth.

On page 41[8] he explains the immobility of the earth in a third way, namely, that it moves in such a way that it does not leave the place which is natural to it. Against this likewise stands the fact that the author says nothing specifically about the earth which is not also found in the other elements and the celestial orbs.

On page 45[9] he says that the heavens are very thin and tenuous, not solid and dense. This is clearly contrary to Tobit 37, "Together with this you have created the heavens which are most solid and spread out like the air." This cannot be explained as an appearance (as the author indicates) because the solidity of the heavens is not apparent to us.

---

[6] P. 232, lines 15–21.
[7] P. 237, lines 4–21.
[8] P. 238, line 33 to p. 239, line 26.
[9] P. 240, line 31 to p. 241, line 20.

APPENDIX
VIIʙ
Foscarini's *Defense* of His *Letter*

[N.B.: The words *in italics* in this translation are omitted from the shorter version of the *Defense*. See footnote 29 in chapter 4.]

It is not easy for me to accept the characterization of rashness with which the opinion that the earth moves has been branded, an opinion which has been confirmed by weighty arguments by many of the most learned astronomers of our day. But in order to deal with this matter briefly (since I am pressed by the heavy burden of conducting forty public meetings), the testimony of only one most learned man will have to suffice; namely, Melchior Cano, O.P., Bishop of the Canary Islands, who is not the least among the best of theologians. In his *De locis theologicis*, Book 12, Chapter 10, he distinguishes three types of rashness. First he says that those things are rash which, when they occur, are the result not of deliberation but of chance; thus those things are rash which are blurted out turbulently and without consideration. As examples he mentions things which are imagined rather than carefully grounded in the life of a pious man or in the activities of Christ the Lord. Secondly he says that what is asserted with insolence and excessive impudence is asserted rashly. His example is saying that the Blessed Virgin was not assumed bodily into heaven. In this group are all propositions which exclude anything from the universal law of faith and the Scriptures without proper testimony or probable reason. Thirdly he says that a proposition is rash if on a doctrine of faith it opposes a common decree and definition of the universal Church. His example is the Articles of Paris. If one were bold enough to maintain something opposed to those Articles in matters pertaining to faith and religion, he would without doubt be thought to be rash. Thus says Cano.

Granting this, I argue as follows. The assertion that the earth moves does not belong to the first type of rashness. For it is not pronounced without consideration or by chance or without foundations derived from the proper principles of the natural and mathematical sciences. Nor does it belong to the second type, for it is not one of those propositions which would exclude anything from the universal law of faith and the Scriptures without proper testimony or probable reason. Rather it agrees most fittingly with the Scriptures according to the methods and arguments used most commonly by the Holy Fathers, if one follows exactly the rules of the Holy Fathers and scholastic theologians which they themselves used most frequently in interpreting the Scriptures. Finally it does not belong to the third type of rashness, for it is not opposed on a doctrine of faith to any common decree of the universal Church. Therefore the proposition that the earth moves is in no way rash.

No one should object that this proposition seems to disagree with a notion held by the Holy Fathers in philosophical matters, for in Book 7, Chapter 3, Cano carefully establishes this point. I will present his words faithfully lest it seem that I wish to create a deception to defend my *Letter*. Cano says that when the authority of the Holy Fathers, whether few or many, is applied to the faculties which are contained in the natural light of reason, that authority does not supply certain arguments, but is only as strong as the convictions of reason in agreement with nature. The primary reason for this is that the Holy Fathers were not concerned with the examination of the teachings of philosophy. They either bade farewell to the books of the philosophers (to dedicate themselves completely to divine wisdom), or they occasionally said hello at the borderline. Indeed for thirteen years Gregory Nazianzus and Basil put aside all secular books and directed their work only to the volumes of Sacred Scripture, as is related by Rufinus Tyrannius in *Historia ecclesiastica*, Book 2, Chapter 9 (of his part), and by Jerome in the Preface to Book 3 of his *Commentaria . . . in Galatos*. Cano says that for more than fifteen years he picked up in his hands no author of secular writings, and that if perchance something should come up in a conversation, we should remember it like an old dream in a fog. A little later he says about our studies: How often does anyone now say that he has read Aristotle? How many bring up the name or the books of Plato? The living hardly remember the ancients at a distance. Our whole world speaks of farmers and fishermen; they are the whole world. So says Cano. I do not look for more examples since this is so obvious that we do not need more. The fact is that some of the ancient holy men did not know, or were only slightly acquainted with, the physicists and the metaphysicians. Others for the most part were Platonists before their conversion to the faith. As a result when they encountered philosophical questions, they either followed common and rhetorical opinions or they turned to whatever was accepted from the Platonists in the Christian schools. Hence learned men sometimes detect errors (which happen in human philosophy) in the ancient holy men. It would be quite easy to give examples of this, but it is not fitting to point this out in our ancestors in these small matters. So says Cano.

Hence it does not seem absurd for learned theologians to depart from the understanding of the Fathers (while preserving the reverence due to them) in matters which are philosophical and which pertain to the human sciences, which are acquired by diligence, experience, long observation, and the investigation of human discourse. *However this is not the case in matters pertaining to faith, religion, and morals, where the older dogmas are truer and more valuable, and where innovators and those who abandon the common interpretation of the old Fathers are justly condemned as heretics.* Thus Vincent of Lérins, a most learned and zealous defender of the dogmas of the Church, in his golden booklet against the profane novelties of heretics, says that we should investigate and follow with great care the consensus of the Holy Fathers, not in every little question of the divine law, but only or especially in the rules of faith. In *Contra Faustum*, Book 2, Chapter 13, St. Augustine says that the Holy Fathers and all the authors who fall outside of the canonical Scriptures sometimes perhaps say things which do not agree with truths that are rather hidden and difficult to know. Therefore he says that to prevent later writers from being excluded from the most wholesome work of treating and examining difficult questions of language and style, one should separate the excellence of the canonical authors of the old and new testament from the books of later writers. Therefore if in the latter books something should perhaps seem to depart from the truth, because it is not understood as was said, in this case the reader has the freedom to judge his approval of what pleases him and his rejection of what offends him. So says Augustine.

This same conclusion has been derived from Augustine by Thomas Stapleton, an outstanding person who deals with theological controversies, in his *Principiorum fidei doctrinalium demonstratio*, Book 7, Chapter 12. First he shows that the authority of the Holy Fathers prevails when (on matters of faith and of what it is necessary to believe) all or at least a large number of them say the same thing. He immediately adds that the case is different regarding matters which can be ignored without loss to the faith or which are more subtle and need to be investigated by the reason and art of learned men. In these latter cases, while the connection to the faith is preserved, the best and most learned defenders of the Catholic rules sometimes disagree, as Augustine says in *Contra Julianum*, Book 1. Likewise some of the Fathers can occasionally teach something contrary to truth. So says Augustine, and Stapleton who refers to him.

Hence it is not rash to depart from the common interpretation of the Fathers in matters not pertaining to the faith, especially if this occurs because of a pressing and persuasive reason. Cajetan, a Dominican, a Cardinal of sacrosanct dignity, and a man of conspicuous talent and great learning, explicitly teaches the same thing at the beginning of his *Commentaria in Genesim*. The same is maintained by Pererius (a Jesuit whose piety is equal to his extensive learning), and by Cano in the work mentioned above, Book 7, Chapter 3, except that he sometimes seems more freely to extend this view even to things which pertain to faith and to the edification of morals. But this latter restriction is most correctly stated by the Council of Trent, Session IV, and before that by the Lateran Council, Art. 11, under Leo X, and by many other councils, with the urging and assistance of the Holy Spirit. For all the councils declare that the very words which I introduced above should be understood as referring to matters which pertain to faith and morals.

However in matters which pertain to the natural sciences and which are discovered and are open to investigation by human reason, the Sacred Scripture ought not to be interpreted otherwise

than according to what human reason itself establishes from natural experience and according to what is clear from innumerable
data. Benedict Pererius, whom I cited just above (whose authority
is more than of the greatest weight, the testimony of the Holy Fathers being nonetheless still maintained), says the following in his
Commentaria in Genesim, Book 1, Chapter 1. In dealing with the
teaching of Moses, we must carefully and completely avoid thinking and saying anything positively and assertively which is contrary
to manifest experience and to the arguments of philosophy or the
other disciplines. For since every truth agrees with every other truth,
it is not possible for the truth or the sacred writings to be contrary to
the true arguments and experiences of the human sciences. So says
Pererius. From this it is clear that if the arguments of philosophy and
mathematics will have established a system contrary to the Ptolemaic
system, which has been accepted up to the present, we ought not
to affirm emphatically that the sacred writings favor the Ptolemaic
system *or the Aristotelian opinion*, and thus create a crisis for the
inviolable and most august sacred writings themselves. Rather we
ought to interpret those writings in such a way as to make it clear
to all that their truth is in no way contrary to the arguments and
experiences of the human sciences (as Pererius says). And Pererius
is not the only authority to say this. St. Augustine proves the same
point in his *De Genesi ad litteram*, Book I, Chapter 21, where he
writes that we should undoubtedly maintain that, when the wise men
of this world are able to truly demonstrate something about the nature of things, then we should show that this is not contrary to the
sacred writings. He makes the same point in Chapter 18 where he
says that, in matters which are obscure and far removed from our
senses, if we should read something in the divine writings which is
open to multiple opinions, the faith which nourishes us being preserved, then we should not precipitously commit ourselves to any
one of these opinions lest we be later defeated when perchance a
more carefully examined truth will have destroyed that opinion.

Many authorities have shown that the Sacred Scriptures most
wisely speak to the hearing of the common man, and in matters pertaining to the human sciences, it does not much care what opinion
anyone holds; it accommodates itself to any opinion and to the common manner of speaking. Thus in his commentary on Jeremiah 28,

St. Jerome says that many things are said in the Scriptures according to the opinion of the time in which the events occurred, and not according to the truth of the matter. Also in *Adversus Helvidium* Jerome says that the Scriptures often express the opinion of the common man, as a law of history. In his commentary on Matthew 4, Jerome says that it is customary in the Scriptures for the historian to narrate the opinion of the people according to their common belief at the time. Chrysostom says the same thing about the passage in John 1, where Jesus is called the son of Joseph. The same is found in St. Thomas, *Summa Theologica*, I–II, 98, 3, ad 2, and in Jerome's commentary on Osee 5, where it is said that the Scriptures frequently speak according to the opinion of the common man. In his *Thesaurus*, Book 5, Chapter 6, St. Cyril says that sometimes Scripture uses words wrongly. And in *Contra Celsum*, Book 4, Origen says that Sacred Scripture proportions what it says to the hearing and use of its listeners.

Furthermore the wisest scholastic theologians and the Fathers use this method of interpreting Scripture, and they present glosses of the same kind that we have given. This is evident in St. Thomas' *Summa Theologica* I, 70, 1, ad 5, where in interpreting the two great lights in Genesis 1, he says that the moon appears to be greater to the senses. In his *Commentaria in Genesim*, Book 1, Pererius departs, as he openly declares, from the interpretation of Augustine, which he refers to and rejects in that passage, as contrary to mathematical proof. He glosses and interprets that passage in the same way, saying among other things that the moon is thought to be larger than the other celestial bodies according to common opinion and the judgment of vision. The same interpretation is given by Juvilius, according to Aloysius Lippomano's *Catenae in Genesim* 1, 6. Cajetan says the same thing about Genesis. Lippomano also gives the same gloss in the place mentioned above, saying that Scripture speaks in human terms. Ambrosius Catharinum [Lancelot Politi] says the same things about the first chapter of Genesis; namely, when Scripture says things which do not agree with the science of astronomy, it should be interpreted as speaking according to appearances. I could offer innumerable interpretations of this kind, *for example, the inconsistencies and absurdities which have resulted when some of the Fathers have interpreted passages differently, which has introduced certain errors into astronomy.* But I will omit them for the sake of brevity.

Furthermore this method of interpretation does not abandon the literal sense. For as Paul of Sancta Maria, the Bishop of Burgos, says in his additions to the *Postilla* of Nicholas of Lyra, when we interpret Scripture metaphorically or as speaking in human terms or according to the common opinion (regarding its subject matter), we do not thereby reject the literal sense, for this is the literal sense. St. Thomas also says this in his *Summa Theologica* I, 1, 10, ad 3. As the Bishop of Burgos says, what is contrary to right reason cannot be taken for the literal sense, for that is not intended by its author, God, who is the first truth from whom all truth is derived. Hence in his *De Genesi ad litteram* St. Augustine says that, since Sacred Scripture can be interpreted in many ways, one should not adopt any one interpretation so absolutely that one would continue to assert that this is the meaning of Scripture even after certain proof has shown that it is false. This would cause infidels to mock the Scriptures and would block them from the path of belief. So says the Bishop of Burgos. His words are worthy of careful consideration. They say something which should be held up before the eyes of all interpreters; namely, in matters pertaining to the sciences acquired by human effort, no one ought to be so addicted to a philosophical sect, or to defend some philosophical opinion with such tenacity, that he thinks that the whole of Sacred Scripture should henceforth be understood accordingly. For otherwise, since something new is always being added to the human sciences, and since many things are seen with the passage of time to be false which previously were thought to be true, it could happen that, when the falsity of a philosophical opinion has been detected, the authority of the Scriptures would be destroyed since that authority has been based on an interpretation which we had thought was true and correct (but nevertheless it was not). Therefore we should not be so tenaciously committed to the philosophy of Aristotle or to Ptolemy's world system that we seem to wish to defend them as we would home and hearth. *Nor should the passages of Sacred Scripture be so rigidly interpreted according to the opinion of Aristotle and Ptolemy.* Nor should the passages of Scripture be interpreted according to the meaning of these philosophers only. For otherwise, if it becomes evident that the teachings of these philosophers are false or hardly probable because of some argument or new observation or experience or proof (as clearly often happens), and if we have grounded our understanding of the dogmas of Scripture on such teachings, then we could destroy our faith in the Scriptures because of our own imprudence.

The Bishop of Burgos, mentioned above, uses the following argument to prove that there is no danger of destroying the literal sense when we use a method of interpretation which says that sometimes the Scriptures speak in human terms and in the common sense. He says that when the words signify both properly and figuratively, the literal sense is not the figure itself but rather that which is figured. Thus when Scripture speaks of God's arm, the literal sense is not that he actually has such a bodily part, but rather what the bodily part signifies; namely, his operative power. Likewise, when it is said that God descends, and so forth, it must be said that the literal sense is not that God moves in some way, but that he acts like one descending when he applies his providence to inferior things. Thus it is clear that there can never be any falsity in the literal sense of Sacred Scripture because of such locutions. So says the Bishop of Burgos.

Let us apply this doctrine (which is also held by St. Thomas and other theologians) to our proposition; namely, that the earth moves. When the Scriptures say that the earth is at rest and the sun moves, using the opinion of the common man and the common opinion of some of the ancient wise men, who did not perceive this as clearly as their successors (*who have come to understand this by their own efforts and as a special gift from God*), it does not say anything false because it describes them in this way. For the earth truly has a certain state of rest of its own, but in a different sense than is commonly thought. And the sun truly has a motion of its own, for it rotates on itself around its own center in thirty days (as is seen from sunspots.) Therefore the earth is at rest and the sun moves, but not in the ways that the common man thinks nor as the common opinion of philosophers has held up to now, but in a more subtle way. But the ancient sages up to the present have not known this because they did not observe or grasp (they were unable, not possessing the instruments recently invented by human ingenuity) those things which were reserved for the observation and apprehension of the present age by the singular and marvelous providence of God.

Finally let us conclude with Chrysostom's *Homily* 39 on John. Anyone who tries to mine metals, but is ignorant of the art, will not find a vein of gold, but will undertake only a useless and confused effort. Likewise those who do not understand the order of the Sacred Scriptures and have not studied their properties and laws, but rather take everything at the sound of the words, confusing gold with earth, will never discover their hidden treasure. So says Chrysostom. Although I could add much more about this complex issue, I will end my discourse lest I be too prolix, having presented the above arguments in defense of my letter. In all things I submit myself to the Holy Roman Church, and if the occasion arises in the future, I will provide more and better arguments, with the help of God.

Fr. Paolo Antonio Foscarini of Venice, Theologian of the Carmelite Order, and Provincial of Calabria. Manu propria.

VIII

Bellarmine's *Letter To Foscarini*

To the Very Reverend Father Paolo Antonio Foscarini,
Provincial of the Carmelite Order of the Province of Calabria:

My Very Reverend Father,

I was pleased to read the letter in Italian [see Appendix VI] and the treatise in Latin [see Appendix VII B] which Your Reverence sent to me. I thank you for both of them, which indeed are quite full of ingenuity and learning. And since you have asked for my reactions, I will state them very briefly, for you now have little time to read and I have little time to write.

Firstly I say that it appears to me that Your Reverence and Sig. Galileo have acted prudently in being satisfied with speaking in terms of assumptions [*ex suppositione*] and not absolutely, as I have always believed Copernicus also spoke. For to say that the assumption that the earth moves and the sun stands still saves all the appearances better than do eccentrics and epicycles is to speak well, and contains nothing dangerous. But to wish to assert that the sun is really located in the center of the world and revolves only on itself without moving from east to west, and that the earth is located in the third heaven and revolves with great speed around the sun, is a very dangerous thing, not only because it irritates all the philosophers and scholastic theologians, but also because it is damaging to the Holy Faith by making the Holy Scriptures false. Although Your Reverence has clearly exhibited the many ways of interpreting the Holy Scriptures, still you have not applied them to particular cases, and without doubt you would have encountered the

very greatest difficulties if you had tried to interpret all the passages
which you yourself have cited.

Secondly I say that, as you know, the Council [of Trent] has
prohibited the interpretation of Scripture contrary to the common
agreement of the Holy Fathers. And if Your Reverence will read
not only the Holy Fathers but also the modern commentators on
Genesis, the Psalms, Ecclesiastes, and Joshua, you will find that they
all agree on the literal interpretation that the sun is in the heavens
and rotates around the earth with a great speed, and that the earth
is very far from the heavens and stands immobile in the center of
the world. Ask yourself then how could the Church, in its prudence,
support an interpretation of Scripture which is contrary to all the
Holy Fathers and to all the Greek and Latin commentators. Nor
can one reply that this is not a matter of faith, because even if it is
not a matter of faith because of the subject matter [*ex parte objecti*],
it is still a matter of faith because of the speaker [*ex parte dicentis*].
Thus anyone who would say that Abraham did not have two sons
and Jacob twelve would be just as much of a heretic as someone who
would say that Christ was not born of a virgin, for the Holy Spirit
has said both of these things through the mouths of the Prophets
and the Apostles.

Thirdly I say that whenever a true demonstration would be
produced that the sun stands in the center of the world and the
earth in the third heaven, and that the sun does not rotate around
the earth but the earth around the sun, then at that time it would be
necessary to procede with great caution in interpreting the Scriptures
which seem to be contrary, and it would be better to say that we do
not understand them than to say that what has been demonstrated is
false. But I do not believe that there is such a demonstration, for it
has not been shown to me. To demonstrate that the assumption that
the sun is located in the center and the earth in the heavens saves the
appearances is not the same thing as to demonstrate that in truth the
sun is located in the center and the earth in the heavens. The first
demonstration, I believe, can be given; but I have the greatest doubts
about the second. And in case of doubt one should not abandon the
Sacred Scriptures as interpreted by the Holy Fathers. Let me add
that the words, "The sun rises and sets, and returns to its place . . . "
[Ecclesiastes 1:5] were written by Solomon, who not only spoke as

inspired by God, but who also was a man more wise and learned than all others in the human sciences and in the knowledge of created things, and all this wisdom he had from God. Thus it is not likely that he would assert something which was contrary to demonstrated truth or to what could be demonstrated. You might tell me that Solomon spoke according to appearances, since it appears to us that the sun rotates when the earth turns, just as it appears to one on a ship who departs from the shore that the shore departs from the ship. To this I respond that, although to him who departs from the shore it does seem that the shore departs from him, nevertheless he knows that this is an error and he corrects it, seeing clearly that the ship moves and not the shore. But in respect to the sun and the earth, there has never been any wise person who felt a need to correct such an error, because one clearly experiences that the earth stands still, and the eye is not mistaken when it judges that the sun moves, just as it is not mistaken when it judges that the moon and the stars move. And this is enough for now.

With cordial greetings, Reverend Father, and I pray for every blessing from God.

Cardinal Bellarmine

12 April 1615

IX

Galileo's
Unpublished Notes (1615)
A: ON BELLARMINE'S "LETTER TO FOSCARINI"

1. Copernicus assumes eccentrics and epicycles; these are not his reason for rejecting the Ptolemaic system (since they undoubtedly exist in the heavens), but rather other difficulties are.

2. In regard to the philosophers, if they be true philosophers, i.e., lovers of the truth, they should not be irritated. Rather, if they realize that they have held a false belief, they should thank those who have shown them the truth; and if their opinion stands firm, they will have reason to boast rather than be angered. The theologians also should not be irritated. For if they find that this opinion is false, then they would be free to condemn it; and if they discover that it is true, they ought to thank those who have opened the way to finding the true sense of the Scriptures and who have prevented them from falling into the grave scandal of condemning a true proposition.

In regard to falsifying Scripture, this is not and never will be the intention of Catholic astronomers, such as myself. On the contrary our opinion is that the Scriptures agree perfectly with demonstrated natural truth. However theologians who are not astronomers should guard against falsifying Scripture by trying to interpret it contrary to propositions which could be true and proven about nature.

3. It could be that we would have difficulty in explaining the Scriptures, etc. But this is because of our ignorance, and certainly not because there really is, or could be, an insuperable problem in reconciling the Scriptures with demonstrated truth.

4. The Council [of Trent] speaks "of matters of faith and morals," etc. It is then said that if the disputed proposition is not a

"matter of faith because of its subject matter" [*de fide ratione ob-jecti*], it is still a "matter of faith because of who said it" [*de fide ratione dicentis*], and that therefore it would be included in the de-cree of the council. It is replied that then everything which is in Scripture is a "matter of faith because of who said it," and thus in this respect ought to be included in the regulations of the coun-cil. But this is clearly not the case, because then the council ought to have said, "The interpretations of the Fathers must be followed for every word in the Scriptures," rather than "in matters of faith and morals." Thus having said "in matters of faith," it seems that the council's intention was to mean "in matters of faith because of the subject matter." It would be much more a "matter of faith" to hold that Abraham had sons, and that Tobias had a dog, because the Scriptures say so, than to hold that the earth does not move, granting that the latter is found in the Scriptures themselves. The reason why the denial of the former, but not of the latter, would be a heresy is the following. Since there are always men in the world who have two, four, six, or even no sons, and likewise since some-one might or might not have dogs, it would be equally credible that someone has sons or dogs and that someone else does not. Hence there would be no reason or cause for the Holy Spirit to state in such propositions anything other than the truth, since the affirmative and the negative would be equally credible to all men. But this is not the case concerning the mobility of the earth and the stability of the sun, which are propositions far removed from the apprehension of the common man. As a result it has pleased the Holy Spirit to accommodate the words of Sacred Scripture to the capacities of the common man in such matters which do not concern his salvation, even though in nature the fact be otherwise.

5. In regard to the location of the sun in the heavens and of the earth outside the heavens, as Scripture seems to say, etc. This truly seems to me to be simply a way of speaking in accordance with our understanding and apprehension. For indeed everything which is contained by the heavens is in the heavens, as everything which is contained by the walls of a city are in the city. Or if there be any advantage to be gained, something is more in the heavens or in a city if it is in the middle, and as is said, in the heart of the city and of the heavens. The qualification "in relation to us" arises

because we inhabit the realm of the elements which surround the earth and which are very different from the celestial realm. But this qualification will always be there no matter what the elements are. And it will always be true that "in relation to us" the earth is down and the heavens are up. For all the inhabitants of the earth have the heavens above their heads, which is up for us, and the center of the earth is under their feet, which is down for us. Thus in relation to us the center of the earth and the surface of the heavens are the most distant places; namely, the end points of up and down for us, and they are diametrically opposed points.

6. It is the highest prudence to believe that there is no demonstration of the mobility of the earth until such a proof has been given. And we do not ask anyone to believe this point without a demonstration. Rather we ask, for the good of the Holy Church, that what the followers of this doctrine know and can offer be examined with the greatest care, and that nothing be admitted unless it has a force which is greatly superior to the reasons on the other side. If the proponents were to have no more than ninety percent of the arguments on their side, they would be rebutted. But when everything offered by the philosophers and astronomers on the other side is proven to be for the most part false and without any importance, then the position of the proponents should not be scorned and be considered to be a paradox because of the fact that it cannot be demonstrated conclusively. And indeed this can be a great advantage. For it is clear that those who are on the false side cannot have any argument or evidence of value; while on the side of truth, there is the advantage that everything agrees and is consistent.

7. It is true that to show that the appearances are saved by the mobility of the earth and the stability of the sun is not the same thing as to demonstrate that this hypothesis is really true in nature. But it is equally and even more true that the other commonly accepted system is not able to give reasons for these appearances. The latter is undoubtedly false, just as it is clear that the former, which corresponds to the appearances perfectly, could be true. No greater truth can be, or ought to be, sought for in a position than that it corresponds to all the particular appearances.

8. It is not asked that the interpretations of the Fathers be abandoned in a case of doubt, but only that one try to arrive at

certitude about what is in doubt. And therefore one should not scorn what is, and has been, concluded by the greatest philosophers and astronomers, after having taken all necessary care to understand their conclusions.

9. We believe that Solomon and Moses and the other sacred writers knew the constitution of the world perfectly; as they also knew that God does not have hands or feet or anger or forgetfulness or regret; nor would we ever cast doubt on this. But we would repeat what St. Peter and especially St. Augustine have said about this; namely, that the Holy Spirit has chosen to speak in this way for the reasons which they give, etc.

10. We come to recognize the error of the apparent mobility of the beach and the stability of the boat after we have stood many times on a beach as we observe the motion of a boat and many times in a boat as we observe the beach. Thus if we could stand at one time on the earth and at another time on the sun or on another star, perhaps we could in each case come to a secure sensory recognition of which of them was moving. But if we could observe only these two bodies, it could always seem to us that the one on which we stand is motionless; just as for someone who can observe only the water and the boat, it will always seem that the water is moving and the boat is motionless. There is a great disparity between a small boat which is isolated from all its surroundings and an immense beach known by us to be immobile from thousands and thousands of experiences, immobile, that is, in relation to the water and to the boat. And this is quite different from the comparison of two bodies, both of which are solid and equally disposed to motion and to rest. Hence it would be more proper to make a comparison of two boats to each other: in this case it would always appear that the boat on which we were located was absolutely at rest, as long as all the time we could not establish any relations except between the two boats.

There is then a great need to correct the error regarding appearances as to whether the earth or the sun moves, it being clear that to someone who is on the moon or any other planet, it would always seem that that star is fixed and the other stars move. But this and many other more superficial arguments of the followers of the common opinion need to be unraveled with very great clarity, so that when they demand a hearing, they are not approved. But it is far from our concerns now to give such a detailed consideration of what has been brought against them. Furthermore neither Copernicus nor his followers have ever used these appearances concerning the beach and the boat to prove that the earth is in motion and the sun is at rest. Rather they use this only as an example, not to demonstrate the truth of their position, but to show that no repugnance would arise, in respect to one simple appearance of the senses, between a stable earth and a mobile sun, if the contrary were truly the case. If this were Copernicus' demonstration, and if his other proofs did not conclude with greater force, then I truly believe that no one would applaud him.

B: ON TRUTH IN SCIENCE AND IN SCRIPTURE

The mobility of the earth and the stability of the sun could never be contrary to the faith or to Scripture, if this were ever actually proven to be true in nature by philosophers, astronomers, and mathematicians by means of sense experience, exact observations, and necessary demonstrations. In such a case, if any passages of Scripture seem to say the opposite, we should say that this is due to the weakness of our intellect, which has not been able to penetrate into the true meaning of Scripture on this point. For it is a common and most correct teaching to say that one truth cannot be contrary to another truth. Therefore those who would juridically condemn something need first to prove that it is false in nature by challenging the arguments to the contrary.

Now as a protection against error, let us ask from what starting point should one begin; that is, from the authority of the Scriptures or from the refutation of the demonstrations and evidence of the philosophers and astronomers. I answer that we ought to begin from the place which is more secure and far removed from any occasion of scandal; and this is the starting point of natural and mathematical arguments. I claim that if the arguments to prove the mobility of the earth are found to be fallacious and demonstrative of the contrary, then we will have firmly established the falsity of that proposition and the truth of the contrary, which we now say is in agreement with the meaning of the Scriptures. Indeed one could freely and without danger condemn that proposition as false.

On the other hand, if these arguments are found to be true and necessary, there will not be any occasion of prejudice against the authority of Scripture. For this will cause us to remain cautious that in our ignorance we have not penetrated into the true meaning of the Scripture, which we can then pursue aided by the newly discovered natural truth. Thus the starting point of reason is secure in every way. But on the contrary, if we stand solely on what seems to us to be the true and most certain sense of Scripture, and if we proceed to condemn such a proposition without examining the force of the demonstrations, then how great a scandal will follow when sense experience and arguments prove the contrary? And who will have plunged the Holy Church into confusion: those who have given the highest importance to demonstrations, or those who have neglected them? Thus we see which path is more secure.

We maintain that a natural proposition which is proven to be true by natural and mathematical demonstrations can never be contrary to the Scriptures; rather in such a case it is the weakness of our intellect which prevents us from penetrating into the true meaning of the Scriptures themselves. On the other hand, those who try to refute and falsify that same type of proposition by using the authority of the same passages of Scripture will commit the fallacy called "begging the question." For since the true sense of the Scripture will already have been put in doubt by the force of the argument, one cannot take it as clear and secure for the purpose of refuting that same proposition. Rather one needs to take the demonstrations apart and find their fallacies with the aid of other arguments, experiences, and more certain observations. And when the truth of fact and of nature has been found in this way, then, but not before, can we confirm the true sense of Scripture and securely use it for our purposes. Thus again the secure path is to begin with demonstrations, confirming the true and refuting the false.

If as a matter of fact the earth does move, then we cannot change nature so that it does not move. But we can easily eliminate inconsistency with Scripture simply by admitting that we have not penetrated into its true meaning. Thus the secure way to avoid error is to begin with astronomical and natural investigations, and not with Scripture.

I realize that in their explanation of the passages of Scripture pertaining to this issue, all the Fathers agree in interpreting them in the most simple sense and according to the direct meaning of the words; and that therefore it would not be proper, in response to a different point of view, to alter their common interpretation, because that would accuse the Fathers of inadvertence or negligence. I respond by admitting that this is a reasonable and proper concern, but add that we have a most ready excuse for the Fathers. It is that they never explained the Scriptures differently from the direct meaning of the words on this issue because the opinion of the mobility of the earth was totally buried in their day. It was not discussed or written about or defended. Hence no charge of negligence can fall on the Fathers for not reflecting on something which was hidden from all of them. That they did not reflect on this is clear from the fact that in their writings there is not found one word about such an opinion. To the contrary, if anyone says that they did consider it, that would make it much more dangerous to try to condemn it; for after considering it, they not only did not condemn it, but no one even raised a doubt about it.

The defense of the Fathers is, then, quite easy and quick. But on the other hand it would be most difficult, if not impossible, to excuse and defend from a similar charge of inadvertence, the popes, councils, and reformers of the *Index* who for eighty continuous years have failed to notice an opinion and a book which was originally written by order of a pope, which was later printed by order of a cardinal and a bishop, which was dedicated to another pope, which was so unique in regard to this doctrine that it cannot be said to have remain hidden, and which was accepted by the Holy Church, while supposedly its teaching was false and condemned. Thus if the notion of agreeing not to charge our ancestors with negligence should be defended and held in the highest regard, as indeed it should, then beware that in trying to flee from one absurdity, you do not fall into a greater one.

But if someone were still to think that it is improper to abandon the common interpretation of the Fathers, even in the case of natural propositions which they did not discuss and whose opposites have not come under their consideration, then I ask what one ought to do if necessary demonstrations were to conclude that the opposite is a fact in nature. Which of these two rules ought to be altered? That which says that no proposition can be both true and false? Or that which obliges us to take as a "matter of faith" natural propositions learned from the common interpretation of the Fathers? If I am not mistaken, it seems to me to be more secure to modify the second rule, i.e., the one which tries to oblige us to hold as a "matter of faith" a natural proposition which could by conclusive arguments be demonstrated to be false in fact and in nature. Furthermore it should be said that the common interpretation of the Fathers ought to have absolute authority for propositions which they examined and which do not have, and certainly never possibly could have, demonstrations to the contrary. Let me add that it seems to be abundantly clear that the council obliges agreement with the common explanation of the Fathers only "in matters of faith and morals, etc."

Bibliography

Anastase de Saint Paul, P. "Paul-Antoine Foscarini." In *Dictionnaire de théologique catholique*, XII, 53–55. Paris: Letouzey et Ané, 1933.

Ashworth, Jr., William B. "Catholicism and Early Modern Science." In *God and Nature*, edited by D. C. Lindberg and R. L. Numbers, 136–166. Berkeley: University of California Press, 1986.

Bachelet, S. J., Xavier-Marie Le. *Auctarium Bellarminianum: Supplement aux Oeuvres du Cardinal Bellarmine*. Paris: Beauchesne, 1913.

———. "Bellarmin à l'Index." *Études* 108 (1907): 227–246.

———. *Bellarmin avant son cardinalat, 1542–1598: Correspondance et documents*. Paris: Beauchesne, 1911.

———. "Bellarmin et Giordano Bruno." *Gregorianum* 4 (1923): 193–210.

———. *Bellarmin et le Bible Sixto-Clémentine: Étude et documents inédits*. Paris: Beauchesne, 1911.

———. *Prédestination et grâce efficace: Controversies dans le Compagne de Jésus au temps d'Aquaviva (1610–1613)*. 2 vols. Louvain: Museum Lessianum, 1931.

Baldini, Ugo. "Additamenta Galilaeana: I. Galileo, le nuova astronomia e la critica all'Aristotelismo nel dialogo epistolare tra Giuseppe Biancani e i revisori romani della Compagnia de Gesu." *Annali dell'Instituto e Museo di Storia della Scienza di Firènze* 9 (1984): 13–43.

———. "L'astronomia del Cardinale Bellarmino." In *Novità celesti e crisi del sapere*, a cura di P. Galluzzi. Firènze: Giunti Barbèra, 1984, 293–305.

———. "Uno fonte poco utilizzata per la storia intellettuale: Le 'censurae librorum' e 'opinionum' nell'antica Compagnia di Gesu." *Annali dell'Instituto Storico Italo-germanico in Trento* 11 (1985): 19–67.

Baldini, Ugo, and George V. Coyne, S.J. *The Louvain Lectures (Lectiones Lovanienses) of Bellarmine and the Autograph Copy of his 1616 Declaration to Galileo.* Vatican City: Specola Vaticana, 1984.

Bangert, S.J., William A. *A History of the Society of Jesus.* Second edition. St. Louis: Institute of Jesuit Sources, 1986.

Basile, Bruno. "Galileo e il teologo 'copernicano' Paolo Antonio Foscarini." *Rivista di Letterature Italiana* 1 (1983): 63–96.

Bellarmino, S.J., Roberto Cardinal. *Opera omnia.* 6 vols. Neapoli: Apud Josephum Giulano, 1856–62.

———. *Opera oratoria postuma.* 11 vols. Edited by S. Tromp, S.J. Roma: Aedibus Pont. Universitatis Gregorianae, 1946–69.

Berti, Domenico. "Antecedenti al processo galileiano e alla condanna della dottrina copernicana." In *Atti della R. Accademia dei Lincei.* 1881–1882. Serie terza. *Memorie della classe di scienze morali, storiche e filologiche.* Vol. 10, 49–96. Roma: Salvicuci, 1882.

———. *Copernico e le vicende del sistema copernicano in Italia nella seconda metà del secolo XVI et nella prima del XVII.* Roma: G. B. Paravia, 1876.

———. *Giordano Bruno da Nola: sua vita et sua dottrina.* Torino: G. B. Paravia, 1889.

———. *Vita di Giordano Bruno da Nola.* Torino: G. B. Paravia, 1868.

Biancini, Giuseppe. *Aristotelis loca mathematica ex universis ipsius operibus collecta et explicata.* Bononiae, 1615.

———. *Sphaera mundi, seu cosmographia demonstrativa, ac facili methodo tradita.* Bononiae, 1620.

Blackwell, Richard J. "Foscarini's Defense of Copernicanism." In *Nature and Scientific Method,* editied by Daniel O. Dahlstrom, Washington, D.C.: Catholic University of America Press, forthcoming.

Bonansea, Bernardino M. "Campanella's Defense of Galileo." In *Reinterpreting Galileo,* edited by William A. Wallace, 205–239. Washington, D.C.: Catholic University of America Press, 1986.

Bricarelli, S.J., Carlo. "Galileo Galilei e il Cardinale Roberto Bellarmino." *Civiltà Cattolica* (1923) III, 481–497; IV, 118–131, 415–427.

Brodrick, S.J., James. *The Life and Work of Robert Francis Cardinal Bellarmine, S.J.* 2 vols. London: Burns Oates and Washbourne, and New York: P. J. Kenedy, 1928. Revised edition: *Robert Bellarmine, Saint and Scholar.* Westminster, Md.: Newman Press, 1961.

Burke-Gaffney, S.J., M. W. *Kepler and the Jesuits.* Milwaukee: Bruce, 1944.

Campanella, Thomas. *The Defense of Galileo.* Translated by Grant McColley, *Smith College Studies in History* 22, nos. 3–4 (1937): pp. xliv + 93.

Cano, O.P., Melchior. *De locis theologicis.* In *Opera,* vol. I–III. Roma: Ex typographia Forzani et Soc., 1890.

Caroti, Stefano. "Un sostenitore napoletano della mobilità della terra: il padre Paolo Antonio Foscarini." In *Galileo e Napoli,* a cura di F. Lomonaco et M. Torrini, 81–121. Napoli: Guida, 1987.

Certeau, Michel de. "La réforme de l'intérieur au temps d'Aquaviva." In *Le Jésuites: Spiritualité et activités,* 53–69. Paris: Beauchesne, 1974.

Chemnitz, Martin. *Examen Concilii Tridentini.* Hrsg. E. Preuss. Darmstadt: Wissenschaftliche Buchgesellschaft, 1972. English translation by Fred Kramer: *Examination of the Council of Trent.* St. Louis: Concordia, 1971.

Clavius, S.J., Christopher. *Opera mathematica,* 5 vols. Moguntinae, 1611–12.

Congar, O.P. Yves. *La tradition et la vie de l'église.* Paris: Libraire Artheme Fayard, 1963. English translation by A. N. Woodrow. *The Meaning of Tradition.* New York: Hawthorn Books, 1964.

Coyne, G. V., M. Heller, and J. Życiński, eds. *The Galileo Affair: A Meeting of Faith and Science.* Vatican City: Specola Vaticana, 1985.

Decreta, canones, censurae, et praecepta Congregationum Generalium Societatis Jesu. Avenione: Ex typographia Francisci Sequin, 1830.

D'Elia, S.J., Pasquale. *Galileo in China: Relations through the Roman College between Galileo and the Jesuit Scientist-Missionaries*

(1610–1640). Translated by R. Suter and M. Sciascia. Cambridge, Mass.: Harvard University Press, 1960.

Denzinger, H., and A. Schoenmetzer, S.J., eds. *Enchiridion symbolorum, definitionum, et declarationum de rebus fidei et morum.* 32nd edition. Freiburg im Breisgau: Herder, 1963.

Drake, Stillman. *Cause, Experiment, and Science: A Galilean Dialogue Incorporating a New English Translation of Galileo's "Bodies that Stay atop Water or Move in It."* Chicago: University of Chicago Press, 1981.

_____. *The Controversy on the Comets of 1618.* Philadelphia: University of Pennsylvania Press, 1960.

_____. *Discoveries and Opinions of Galileo.* New York: Doubleday, 1957.

_____. *Galileo at Work: His Scientific Biography.* Chicago: University of Chicago Press, 1978.

_____. "The Galileo-Bellarmine Meeting: A Historical Speculation." In L. Geymonat, *Galileo Galilei*, 205–220. New York: McGraw-Hill, 1965.

Epistolae selectae praepositorum generalium ad superiores Societatis. Roma: Typis Polyglottis Vaticanis, 1911.

Espinosa Pólit, Manuel María. *Perfect Obedience: Commentary on the Letter of Obedience of Saint Ignatius of Loyola.* Westminster, Md.: Newman Bookshop, 1947.

Fabris, Rinaldo. *Galileo Galilei e gli orientamenti esegetici del suo tempo.* Vatican City: Pontifical Academy of Sciences, Scripta varia 62. 1986.

Favaro, Antonio. "Serie nona di scampoli galileiana #63: Paolo Antonio Foscarini." *Accademia Patavina di Science, Lettere, ed Arti, Atti e Memorie.* (Padua) 10 (1894): 33–36.

Ferrone, V., and M. Firpo. "From Inquisitors to Microhistorians: A Critique of Pietro Redondi's *Galileo eretico*." *Journal of Modern History* 58 (1986): 485–524.

Finocchiaro, Maurice A., ed. *The Galileo Affair: A Documentary History.* Berkeley: University of California Press, 1989.

_____. "The Methodological Background to Galileo's Trial." In *Reinterpreting Galileo*, edited by W. A. Wallace, 241–272. Washington, D.C.: Catholic University of America Press, 1986.

Fitzpatrick, Edward A. *St. Ignatius and the Ratio Studiorum.* New York: McGraw-Hill, 1933.

Foscarini, Paolo Antonio. *Lettera sopra l'opinione de' Pittagorici e del Copernico . . .* Napoli: Lazzaro Scoriggio, 1615.

Galilei, Galileo. *Le Opere di Galileo Galilei.* Edizione Nazionale, cura et labore A. Favaro. 20 vols. Florence: G. Barbèra, 1890–1909. Reprinted: 1929–39, 1964–66.

———. *Sidereus nuncius, or The Sidereal Messenger.* Translated with an Introduction, Conclusion, and Notes by Albert van Helden. Chicago: University of Chicago Press, 1989.

Galluzzi, P., ed. *Novità celesti e crisi del sapere.* Firènze: Giunti Barbèra, 1984.

Garin, Eugenio. "Alle origini della polemica anticopernicana." In *Colloquia Copernicana,* vol. II. Studia Copernicana 6, 31–42. Wrocław: Ossolineum, 1975.

Geymonat, Ludovico. *Galileo Galilei.* Translated by S. Drake. New York: McGraw-Hill, 1965.

Gieselmann, Josef. "Das Konzil von Trient über das Verhältnis der Heiligen Schrift und der nicht geschrieben Traditionen." In *Die mündliche Überlieferung,* edited by M. Schmaus. Munich: Huebner, 1957. French translation in *Istina* 5 (1958): 197–214.

Gingerich, Owen. "The Censorship of Copernicus' *De revolutionibus.*" *Annali dell'Instituto e Museo di Storia della Scienza di Firènze* 6 (1981) Fasc. 2: 45–61.

———. "The Galileo Affair." *Scientific American* 247, no. 2 (August 1982): 132–143.

———. "The Great Copernicus Chase." *American Scholar* 49 (1979): 81–88.

Grisar, S.J., Hartman. *Galileistudien.* Regensburg: Friedrich Pustet, 1882.

Hooykaas, R. "Rheticus' Lost Treatise on Holy Scripture and the Motion of the Earth." *Journal for the History of Astronomy* 15 (1984): 77–80.

Inchofer, S.J., Melchior. *Tractatus syllepticus.* Roma: Ludovicus Griganus, 1633.

Jedin, Hubert. *Geschichte des Konzils von Trient.* 4 vols. Freiburg im Breisgau: Herder, 1957. English translation by Dom Ernest

Graf, O.S.B. *A History of the Council of Trent*. 2 vols. London: Thomas and Sons, 1961.

Johnson, Francis R. *Astronomical Thought in Renaissance England*. Baltimore: Johns Hopkins Press, 1937.

Kepler, Johannes. *Gesammelte Werke*. Band III. *Astronomia nova*. München: C.H. Beck'sche Verlagsbuchhandlung, 1937.

———. "Introduction," to *Astronomia nova*. Translated by Owen Gingerich. In *The Great Ideas Today 1983*, edited by Mortimer J. Adler and John van Doren, 309–323. Chicago: Encyclopedia Britannica, 1983.

Kircher, S.J., Athanasius. *Iter extaticum coeleste . . .* Herbipoli: Sumptibus Joh. Andr. and Wolffg. Jun. Endterorum Haeredibus. Prostat Norimbergae apud eosdem. 1660.

Kuhn, Thomas S. *The Copernican Revolution*. Cambridge, Mass.: Harvard University Press, 1957.

Langford, James R. "Science, Theology, and Freedom: A New Look at the Galileo Case." In *On Freedom*, edited by Leroy S. Rouner, 108–125. Notre Dame, Ind.: University of Notre Dame Press, 1989.

Langford, Jerome J. [James R.] *Galileo, Science, and the Church*. Ann Arbor, Mich,: University of Michigan Press, 1966.

Lerner, Lawrence S., and Edward A. Gosselin. "Galileo and the Specter of Bruno." *Scientific American* 255, no. 5 (November 1986): 126–133.

Lindberg, D. C., and R. L. Numbers, eds. *God and Nature: Historical Essays on the Encounter between Christianity and Science*. Berkeley: University of California Press. 1986.

Loyola, St. Ignatius. *The Constitutions of the Society of Jesus*. Translated, with an Introduction and Commentary, by George E. Ganss, S.J. St. Louis: Institute of Jesuit Sources, 1970.

McMullin, Ernan. "Bruno and Copernicus." *Isis* 78 (1987): 55–74.

———. ed. *Galileo: Man of Science*. New York: Basic Books, 1967.

———. "Giordano Bruno at Oxford." *Isis* 77 (1986): 85–94.

Mercati, Angelo. *Il sommario del processo di Giordano Bruno con appendice di documenti sull'eresia e l'inquisizione a Modena nel secolo XVI*. Vatican City: Biblioteca Apostolica Vaticana, 1942.

Michel, Paul-Henri. *La cosmologie de Giordano Bruno*. Paris: Hermann, 1962. English translation by R. E. W. Maddison. *The Cosmology of Giordano Bruno*. Paris: Hermann; London: Methuen; Ithaca, N.Y.: Cornell University Press, 1973.

Moran, F.S.C., Gabriel. *Scripture and Tradition: A Survey of Tradition*. New York: Herder and Herder, 1963.

Morpurgo-Tagliabue, Guido. *I processi di Galileo e l'epistemologia*. Milano: Edizione di Comunità, 1963.

Moss, Jean Dietz, "Galileo's Letter to Christina," *Renaissance Quarterly* 36 (1983): 547–576.

Namer, Émile. *Giordano Bruno*. Paris: Seghers, 1966.

Pagano, S. M., ed. *I documenti del processo di Galileo Galilei*. Vatican City: Pontifical Academy of Sciences, 1984.

Pedersen, Olaf. *Galileo and the Council of Trent*. Vatican City: Specola Vaticana, 1983.

Pereyra, Benedictus. *Commentariorum et disputationum in Genesim tomi quatuor*. Roma: Apud Georgium Ferrarium, 1591–95.

―――. *Commentariorum in Danielem prophetam libri sexdicem*. Roma: Apud Georgium Ferrarium, 1587.

Poupard, Paul Cardinal, ed. *Galileo Galilei: 350 ans d'histoire 1633–1983*. Tournai: Desclée International, 1983. English translation by Ian Campbell. *Galileo Galilei: Toward a Resolution of 350 Years of Debate, 1633–1983*. Pittsburgh: Duquesne University Press, 1987.

Redondi, Pietro. *Galileo eretico*. Torino: Giulio Einaudi, 1983. English translation by R. Rosenthal. *Galileo Heretic*. Princeton, N.J.: Princeton University Press, 1987.

Reidl, John O. "Bellarmine and the Dignity of Man." In *Jesuit Thinkers of the Renaissance*, edited by G. Smith, S.J., 193–254. Milwaukee: Marquette University Press, 1939. (Bellarmine Bibliography: 242–254.)

Riccioli, S.J., Giovanni Battista. *Almagestum novum*. Bononiae: Typis Haeredis Victorii Bendatii, 1651.

Rosen, Edward. "Was Copernicus's *Revolutions* Approved of by the Pope?" *Journal of the History of Ideas* 36 (1975): 531–542.

Russo, Françqis. "Galileo and the Theology of His Time." In *Galileo Galilei: Toward a Resolution of 350 Years of Debate, 1633–1983*, edited by Paul Cardinal Poupard, 103–124. Pittsburgh: Duquesne University Press, 1987.

Santillana, Giorgio de. *The Crime of Galileo.* New York: Time Incorporated, 1962.

Scheiner, S.J., Christopher. *Rosa ursina sive sol.* Bracciani: A. Phaeum, 1626–30.

Schroeder, O.P., H. J. *Canons and Decrees of the Council of Trent: Original Text with English Translation.* St. Louis: B. Herder, 1941.

Serarius, Nicolaus. *Josue ab utero ad ipsum usque tumulum.* Maguntiae, 1609–10.

———. *Prolegomena biblica et commentaria in omnes epistulas canonicas.* Magnuntiae, 1612.

Shea, William R. "La Controriforma e l'esegesi biblica di Galileo Galilei." In *Problemi religiosi e filosofia,* edited by A. Babolin, 37–62. Padova: Garagola, 1975.

———. "Galileo and the Church." In *God and Nature,* edited by D. C. Lindberg and R. L. Numbers, 114–135. Berkeley: University of California Press, 1986.

———. "Melchior Inchofer's 'Tractatus Syllepticus': A Consultor of the Holy Office Answers Galileo." In *Novità celesti e crisi del sapere,* edited by P. Galluzzi, 283–292. Firènze: Giunti Barbèra, 1984.

Spampanato, Vincenzo. *Documenti della vita di Giordano Bruno.* Florence: Leo S. Olschki, Editore, 1933.

———. *Vita di Giordano Bruno, con documenti editi e inediti.* Messina: Casa Editrice Principato, 1921.

Stimson, Dorothy, *The Gradual Acceptance of the Copernican Theory of the Universe.* New York: Baker & Taylor, 1917.

Védrine, Hélène. *Censure et pouvois: Trois procès: Savonarole, Bruno, Galilée.* Paris: Mouton, 1976.

Wallace, William A. "Aristotle and Galileo: The Uses of HUPOTHESIS (Suppositio) in Scientific Reasoning." In *Studies in Aristotle,* edited by D. J. O'Meara, 47–77. Washington, D.C.: Catholic University of America Press, 1981.

———. *Galileo and His Sources: The Heritage of the Collegio Romano in Galileo's Science.* Princeton, N.J.: Princeton University Press, 1984.

———. *Galileo's Early Notebooks: The Physical Questions.* Notre Dame, Ind.: University of Notre Dame Press, 1977.

———. *A Prelude to Galileo: Essays on Medieval and Sixteenth-Century Sources of Galileo's Thought*. Dordrecht: Reidel, 1981.

———. Ed. *Reinterpreting Galileo*. Washington, D.C.: Catholic University of America Press, 1986.

Westman, Robert S. "The Copernicans and the Churches." In *God and Nature*, edited by D. C. Lindberg and R. L. Numbers, 76–113. Berkeley: University of California Press, 1986.

Yates, Frances A. *Giordano Bruno and the Hermetic Tradition*. Chicago: University of Chicago Press, 1964.

Zuñiga, Diego de [Didacus à Stunica]. *Commentaria in Job*. Toledo, 1584.

Index